# A
# book
# for

# IELTS

# McCarter, Easton & Ash

# Preface

This is a self-study publication with two audio-cassettes for students preparing for the Academic Module of the International English Language Testing System (IELTS), which is administered by The British Council, the University of Cambridge Local Examinations Syndicate (UCLES) and by IELTS Australia.

The book covers the four modules of the IELTS exam: listening, reading, writing and speaking. Special features of the book are: the reading exercises, the detailed Keys for these exercises, the wide range of exercises to help you prepare for Writing Task 1, and the detailed Key for the Reading Tests.

The publication may also be used as a course book, or as a supplement to a course book.

So that you may repeat the exercises in this book, we would advise you to avoid marking the text.

*Sam McCarter, Julie Easton and Judith Ash*

*1999*

# Acknowledgements

The authors would like to thank the following colleagues and friends for their help and support during the writing and production of this publication:

*Edward Easton, Hilary Finch, Marie Kerrigan, Mohamed Koker, Zoran Momcilovic, Micky Silver, and Roger Townsend.*

The articles in the Reading Tests were specially commissioned for this publication and we would like to thank the following writers for their contributions:

*Dr Susan Beckerleg, Richard Campbell, Dr Thomas Cocke, Hilary Finch, Brita Forsstrom, Mick Garner, Judith Gregory, Professor Mike Riley, Wendy Riley, Maureen Sorrel, Dr Robyn Young.*

We would like to thank the following people for their help in producing the cassettes with this publication:

*Bradley Borum, Madeleine Coburn, Tony Corballis, David Easton, Thomas Hope, Jane Headley, Doug Foot, Geoff Farrer, Hilary Finch, Pippa Kember, Felix Milns, Micky Silver, Roger Townsend, Robert Wakuluk and Douglas Young.*

We would like to thank Michael Scherchen at Boundary Row Studios London for help in recording the cassettes and John Bales at SRL Cassettes London for help in the production of the cassettes.

The authors and publishers are grateful for permission to reproduce the following material:

*Inland energy consumption* (the graph in Exercise 6 in the Writing Section) comes from Key Data (1996), Crown Copyright 1996 and is reproduced by permission of the Controller of HMSO and of the Office of National Statistics.

*Passenger death rates by mode of transport* (the graph in Exercise 17 in the Writing Section) comes from Key Data (1996), Crown Copyright 1996 and is reproduced by permission of the Controller of HMSO and of the Office of National Statistics.

The diagram on making a daily newspaper (Writing Exercise 20) has been reproduced by permission of the Newsprint and Newspaper Industry Environmental Action Group.

A special thanks is due to Val Sweeney for her support and for making this publication possible.

We would also like to say a very special thank you to Drs Gill and Bruce Haddock for their sterling work.

# Contents

**Essay writing for Task 2**

**Writing Tests**

**Section on Speaking**

**Keys**

# About the authors

**Sam McCarter** is a lecturer in academic and medical English at Southwark College, where he organises IELTS courses for overseas doctors and other health personnel, and courses in medical English – including preparation for the OSCE component of the PLAB.

Sam is also the creator and organiser of the Nuffield Self-access Language Project for Overseas Doctors and works as a freelance consultant in medical English specialising in tropical medicine.

**Julie Easton** is a lecturer in academic and medical English at Southwark College, teaching on courses preparing doctors for the IELTS and the OSCE. Julie has considerable experience in both areas.

**Judith Ash** is a former lecturer in academic and medical English at Southwark College. She now writes freelance and is working on distance learning programmes for IELTS.

# About Southwark College

Southwark College has an international reputation as a centre for teaching IELTS and medical English. The College is situated in the centre of London.

Telephone: 0171 815 1600 and Fax: 0171 261 1301.

## Future publications from IntelliGene

IntelliGene will soon be publishing a book on IELTS Reading Tests by Sam McCarter and Judith Ash.

IntelliGene will be publishing a major book on communication skills in medicine by Sam McCarter.

# Listening Module

## Introduction &
## Practice Tests 1-4

# Introduction to the Listening Module

In the IELTS exam, the Listening Test forms the first part of the exam and lasts for about 30 minutes.

In each test, there are four main sections, for which you have to answer a total of approximately 40 questions. Each main section is divided into two and, sometimes, three sub-sections. Before each of these sub-sections, you have time to read the questions and you are advised to write your answers in the question booklet. At the end of each section, you have half a minute to check your answers.

At the end of the full listening test, you have 10 minutes to transfer your answers to the Answer Sheet. Usually, the listening exercises become more difficult as you move from Sections 1 to 4.

**You will hear the test only ONCE.**

The range of question types may include the following:

- multiple choice questions
- short-answer questions
- sentence completion
- summary/notes/flow chart/diagram/table completion
- labelling a diagram which has numbered parts
- matching

| | |
|---|---|
| **Situations** | The first two sections are usually of a social nature. Section 1 usually contains a conversation, e.g. between two people in a shop, and Section 2 a monologue, e.g. a radio broadcast or a talk. Section 3 is usually a conversation in an educational or training context, e.g. a tutorial about a particular subject. In this section, there can be up to four speakers. Section 4 is a monologue, such as a lecture or talk on a subject of general academic interest. |
| | It is important to remember that the test is designed to test your listening comprehension skills. The answers to all of the questions are on the tape. You do not need any knowledge of the topic to be able to answer the questions. |
| **Answer sheet** | After the end of the tape, ten minutes are given for you to transfer your answers to the Answer Sheet. |
| **Hints on listening** | Common problem areas with this part of the IELTS exam include the following: |
| **Misreading instructions** | It is important that you read all the instructions very carefully so that you are clear about what is required for the answer to each of the questions. The instructions are usually clear and easy to follow, and an example is given in some cases. |
| | It is worth pointing out here that candidates often fail to read the instructions carefully or just glance at them. Students rely on the fact that the instructions are exactly the same in the Test as they are in the textbook(s) they have been practising with. |
| **Changing** | Sometimes, the speaker may give a piece of information and then change his or her mind. So always watch out for this. |
| **Anticipation/ prediction** | When you are speaking to people normally in your own language, it is possible to predict what the person you are talking to is going to say. It is easier in this situation to do so, because you are part of the conversation and know the context. When you are just listening, it is just a little harder, because you are not actively involved in developing the context. However, you can do it with just a little extra concentration. |
| **Concentration** | It is important to concentrate from the beginning. Some candidates think that the first section is going to be easy and do not listen carefully enough. They miss a few answers which affects their final score. If you are aiming for a high score, like a 7 or a 7.5 you should be aiming to answer all the questions in the first two sections correctly, as they are the easiest. |
| **Practice** | If you do not have access to many IELTS textbooks to practise, use listening exercises from the other Cambridge exams, e.g. for the First Certificate and the Cambridge Advanced. The listening exercises are not the same but they give you similar practice. Also listen to the radio and watch TV, and if possible speak to people in English. |

# Practice Test 1: Section 1

Complete the Account Details using NO MORE THAN TWO WORDS for each blank space.

**Account Details**

| | |
|---|---|
| **Example:** | |
| *Account holder:* | ____No____ |
| *Discount offered:* | |
| *First year students:* | (1)_____. |
| *Name:* | Nasreen (2)_____ |
| *Address:* | (3)_____ Mansions, Compton Street, London. |
| *Postcode:* | SE (4)_____ |
| *Telephone number:* | 0181 (5)_____ |

Put a tick in the spaces below, if the information is correct. Or fill in the blank with the correct information, if it is wrong. The first one has been done for you as an example.

Example  _____✓_____

Physics in the Age of Technology

A Stern

Out of Stock

7. _____

Experimental Science

£29.50

Simon Blair & Violet Boyd

6. _____

Mathematics in Physics

£27.95

Professor I Lovatt

8. _____

Physics for the first year student

£20

A Laska

## Questions 9 & 10

Circle the appropriate letter.

9.    To collect the books the student must bring
      A     three forms of identification.
      B     two forms of identification.
      C     one form of identification.
      D     two forms of identification and the university confirmation letter.

10.   The books will be kept
      A     in the Chemistry Department in the basement.
      B     in the Physics Department in the basement.
      C     in the Physics Department on the first floor.
      D     in the Maths Department in the basement.

# Practice Test 1: Section 2

### Questions 11–14

Circle the appropriate letter.

11.  There are _____ student counsellors at the university.

> **A**  six        **B**  four        **C**  five        **D**  three

12.  The speaker has come to talk about the _____ .

> **A**  Student Union        **B**  Student Welfare Service
>
> **C**  student health        **D**  Student Accommodation Service

13.  The number of main sites is . . .

> **A**  three        **B**  four        **C**  five        **D**  six

14.  Where on this site is the student counsellor's office?

**A**  Queen's Building

| |
|---|
| 4th |
| 3rd |
| 2nd    Counsellor's Office |
| 1st |
| Ground floor |

**C**  Mason Building

| |
|---|
| 4th |
| 3rd |
| 2nd |
| 1st    Counsellor's Office |
| Ground floor |

**B**  Queen's Building

| |
|---|
| 4th    Counsellor's Office |
| 3rd |
| 2nd |
| 1st |
| Ground floor |

**D**  Queen's Building

| |
|---|
| 4th |
| 3rd |
| 2nd |
| 1st    Counsellor's Office |
| Ground floor |

### Questions 15–20

Complete the notes below using NO MORE THAN THREE WORDS for each answer.

15.  The information leaflet is available almost _____.

16.  The Helpline in the evenings and weekends is dependent on the _____.

17.  The Helpline is staffed at the weekends for _____.

18.  Students contact the Student Welfare Service for a _____.

19.  If the counsellors cannot help you, they will put you in touch with _____.

20.  The Service gives _____ to all volunteers on the Helpline.

# Practice Test 1: Section 3

## Questions 21–23

USE NO MORE THAN THREE WORDS to answer the following questions:

21. On what topic did Jim write his essay?          _____

22. Besides the OECD statistics, what other figures did Jim use?

    _____

23. At the beginning of his essay, what does Jim say the 19th century Luddites and people today are worried about?

    _____

## Questions 24–27

In Jim's essay, there are **3 reasons for people's fears** and **2 reasons why people's fears are unjustified**. In each case below, choose the option which accurately describes the point. The first one is an example.

> *Example:  The first reason for fear:*
> ✓a    *IT affects service and traditional industries*
> b    *Electricity affects service and traditional industries*

24. *The second reason for fear:*
    a    The introduction of IT is more demanding than other technologies
    b    The introduction of IT is happening more quickly than for previous technologies

25. *The third reason for fear:*
    a    IT makes it easier to change jobs
    b    IT makes it easier for employers to move jobs around

26. *The first reason why people's fears are unjustified:*
    a    There has been a continuous rise in people in work and income in rich countries
    b    Technological advance has industrialised rich countries

27. *The second reason why people's fears are unjustified:*
    a    New jobs are not upsetting old ones
    b    New jobs are replacing old ones

## Questions 28–30

Circle the appropriate letter.

28.  *New technology does not always reduce employment,*

    **A**  people do not need to work as hard as before.

    **B**  new products are a necessity.

    **C**  it can create new demand.

    **D**  it can slow down output.

29.  *In his conclusion, Jim says that IT should not destroy job.*

    **A**  there is a balance.

    **B**  the workforce are favourable.

    **C**  the workforce are businessmen.

    **D**  the workforce have a good education and they are skilled.

30.  *The phrase, a favourable business climate, means an environment where*

    **A**  there is not too much in the way of protectionism.

    **B**  there are many restrictions, rules and regulations.

    **C**  minimum wage levels are too high.

    **D**  restrictions on work practices exist.

Listening

## Questions 31–3

Complete

31

# Practice Test 1: Section 4

the notes using NO MORE THAN THREE WORDS for your answer.

The speaker is a specialist in _____.

32. The speaker is giving the _____ of the term.

33. The focus of her talk is the purpose of _____.

34. Good design leads to _____.

35. One facet of the role of design is to make sure that products do the job they are _____.

36. People are persuaded to buy products by _____ and _____.

37. A shopper may buy a personal stereo for its _____ as well as its trendy appearance.

## Questions 38–41

Circle the appropriate letter.

38. The role of the designer is becoming more important, because ...
    A  the progress of technology is slightly faster than it was.
    B  there are possibilities for new ideas.
    C  products break more easily these days.
    D  every model has to be updated more quickly.

39. In the medical field, the designer is engaged in ...
    A  developing a range of new equipment.
    B  old equipment that is developing.
    C  everything related to hospital portering equipment.
    D  advising inventors.

40. Designers can help manufacturers by ...
    A  exporting their designs.
    B  helping to make their products attractive.
    C  making their products appreciated by other manufacturers.
    D  training them to appreciate design.

41. Design is important in life, because ...
    A  existing is more than living.
    B  it is part of our attitude.
    C  it improves the quality of our daily life.
    D  we do not want things that do not look good, even if they do not work.

A book for IELTS

# Practice Test 2: Section 1

## Questions 1–4

Circle the appropriate letter.

> Example: *Angela would like to order*
>
> **A** some chocolates.  **C** some chocolates and some flowers.
> **B** some flowers.    **D** some sweets.

1.  Which picture shows the kind of flowers Angela would like to order?

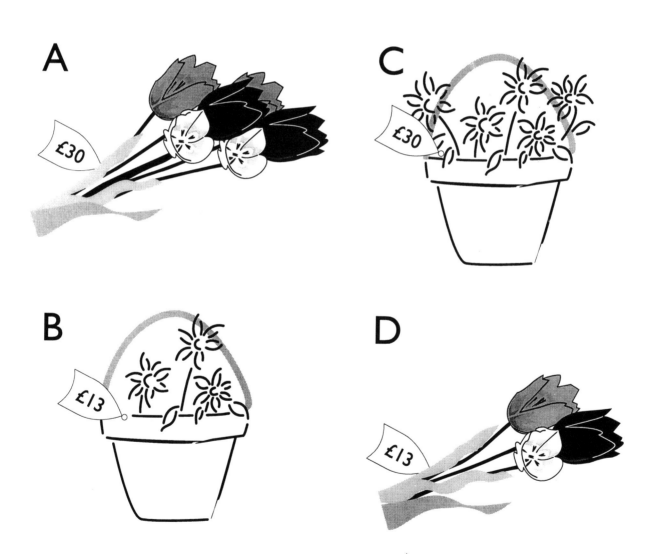

2.    Which box of chocolates does Angela order?

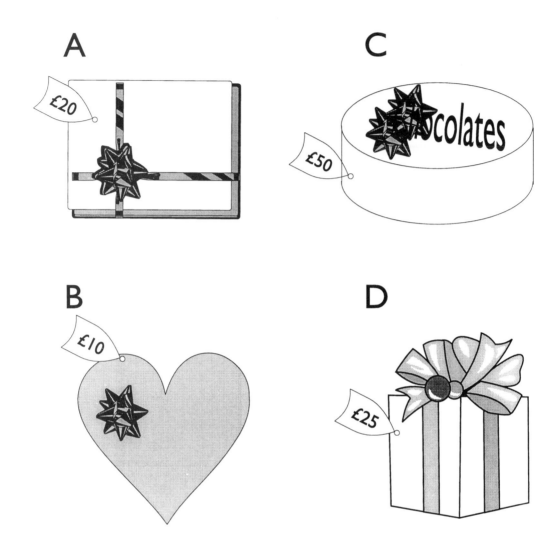

3. *Angela would like to send*
    **A**  a mixture of chocolates, mostly liqueurs.
    **B**  a box of liqueurs.
    **C**  a mixture of chocolates, mostly white chocolates and some liqueurs.
    **D**  a mixture of chocolates, mostly white, but no liqueurs.

4. *The cost of delivering both items is*
    **A**  90 pence
    **B**  £38
    **C**  £19
    **D**  £9

## Questions 5-10

Complete the following Order Form by USING NO MORE THAN THREE WORDS to complete each blank space:

ORDER FORM

Name:       **Angela Love**
Address:    **144a Orchard Heights**
            **Marsh Drive**
            **Edinburgh**

Telephone number:        **O963 371 555**

Credit card number:      ____**N/A**_____

Switch card number:      **569 000 (5)** _____ **884 223 7**

Sendee's name:           **Mrs (6)** _____
Sendee's address:        **27 (7)** _____
                         **Cardiff CA13 8YU**

Message (if any):        **Congratulations on (8)** _____!
                         **Just let me know when you are out on the road. Love Angie**

Any other details:       **Delivery Date: (9)** _____

                         **(10) Deliver between** _____**and** _____ **in the morning.**

# Practice Test 2: Section 2

**Questions 11–13**

Circle the appropriate answer.

11. *Information about the sports facilities can be found on*
    **A** billboards in parts of the campus.
    **B** notice-boards throughout the campus.
    **C** posters in the campus.
    **D** maps all over the campus.

12. *The speaker is*
    **A** showing a map on a screen.
    **B** talking about a map in a leaflet.
    **C** referring to a diagram on a screen.
    **D** talking about a map on the wall.

13. *The university sports complex is*
    **A** in Burse Road.
    **B** on the right of the police station.
    **C** in Thames Street.
    **D** opposite the city library.

**Questions 14–17**

Tick the **four** other facilities below which are mentioned as **future developments** in the university sports complex. One (**C**) has been marked for you as an example. Write your answers in Boxes 14–17 on your answer sheet.

FACILITIES

**A** Two badminton courts _____
**B** Three squash courts _____
**C** A sauna ___✓___ (Example)
**D** A full-sized Olympic swimming pool _____
**E** A dance theatre _____
**F** A bar _____

**G** An ice-skating rink _____
**H** A cafeteria _____
**I** Two courts for tennis _____
**J** A soft-ball court _____
**K** A modern gym _____

**Questions 18–20**

Circle the correct letter.

18. Choose the correct location (**A,B,C**, or **D**) for the sports ground on the map below.

    Sports ground = A, B, C, or D?

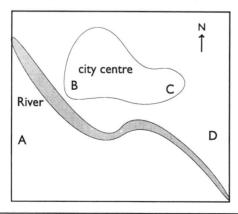

19. The direct bus to the sports field is the
    **A** 553        **C** 43
    **B** 33         **D** 53

20. The last bus at night is
    **A** around half past 12 in the morning.
    **B** at 2.30 a.m.
    **C** at 1.30 a.m.
    **D** at midnight.

# Practice Test 2: Section 3

**Questions 21–26**

USING NO MORE THAN THREE WORDS for each space complete the details about the **FBT Award** below.

**FBT Award**

The FBT Award gives students money to _____21_____.

***Conditions to be met:***

Applicants have to:

be in their _____22_____ year.

be a British or Commonwealth citizen.

be among the _____23_____ in their year in the final exams.

hand in the application by the _____24_____.

be under _____25_____ at the end of their course.

give the names of _____26_____referees.

**Questions 27–30**

Circle the appropriate answer.

27.  *The award Sandra is applying for is*
   A  awarded twice a year.
   B  not as hard to get as the one Derek is after.
   C  not for as much money as the FBT Award.
   D  much harder to obtain than the one Derek is after.

28.  *To apply for the Bisiker Award, students have to*
   A  write a 5,000 word outline of their project and complete a detailed application form.
   B  write a 5,000 word outline of their project and complete a form with their details.
   C  fill in a short application form.
   D  write a 50,000 word outline of their project and fill in a form with their details.

29.  *The lecturer puts great emphasis on*
   A  the need for the summary to be original.
   B  making five copies of the application.
   C  having it read through by someone before submitting it.
   D  studying previous applications.

30.  *The lecturer also lays great emphasis on the fact that*
   A  the Bisiker Award is not much harder to get than the one Derek is after.
   B  the application should, if possible, be typed, neat and bound with a ring binder.
   C  there is no need to type the application.
   D  the application has to be typed, be very neat and bound with a ring binder.

# Practice Test 2: Section 4

**Questions 31–36**

Complete the lecture notes below. Use NO MORE THAN THREE WORDS to complete each space.

---

**Europe goes grey**

refers to the _____31_____ in Europe since the 60s.

---

## Projections

– by 2029 approximately _____32_____ % of the UK population will be over retirement age.

– roughly 23% of the population of _____33_____ will be 65 or over by 2020.

– the number of centenarians in the UK will be increasing by_____34_____ percent per year in the 21st century.

---

Reasons for increased life-span:
- **a**. better diet
- **b**. better housing
- **c**. the _____35_____ of health care

The birth rate in Europe has fallen  as a consequence of:
- **a**. _____36_____
- **b**. education of women
- **c**. more women working

**Questions 37–40**

Circle the correct letter.

37.  *The speaker says that the elderly*
- A  generally need care.
- B  can be both happy and retired.
- C  vary in their situations and needs.
- D  worry about who will care for them.

38.  *Unlike in the past, today families*
- A  don't care about their grandparents.
- B  tend to live in the same area.
- C  don't take care of grandparents.
- D  share the care of the elderly.

39.  *As regards the elderly, financial assistance is needed to*
- A  pay the wages of carers.
- B  help independent old people.
- C  create new medical services.
- D  increase the level of pensions.

40.  *The speaker suggests that in the future*
- A  people should be helped to prepare financially for their old age.
- B  existing houses of the elderly should be adapted.
- C  retirement ages should be increased.
- D  people should respect the elderly more.

# Practice Test 3: Section 1

**Questions 1–7**

Complete the questionnaire below using NO MORE THAN THREE WORDS for each space.

### Questionnaire

*Example*

*Year:_____2nd_____*

*Subjects:*   Chinese and  (1)_____ *Age:*   (2)_____

*Type of accommodation:*  flat off-campus _____            room on-campus _____
*(Please tick)*                    flat on-campus ✓           room off-campus _____

*Name of block (if applicable):*        (3)_____

| **ACTIVITIES** | *Number of times per month student takes part* <br> A = 1–2       B = 3–5       C = 6–8       D = 9–10 <br> *Write A, B, C, or D below* |
|---|---|

**Sports**

| (4)_____ | _____B_____ |
|---|---|
| Basketball_____ | (5)_____ |
| Football_____ | _____C_____ |

**Clubs**

| (6)_____ | _____A_____ |
|---|---|
| Amateur dramatics_____ | (7)_____ |

**Questions 8–10**        Circle the appropriate letter.

8.  How much of
    his income
    does the
    student
    spend on
    socialising?

    A
    B
    C
    D

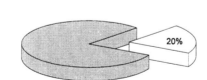

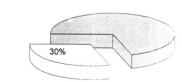

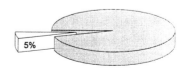

9.    How much of his income does the student spend on accommodation and food?

A

40%

B

50%

C

45%

D

60%

10.    *Apart from books, what does the student spend the rest of his money on?*

    A  small luxuries like chocolate and cakes.
    B  lots of luxuries.
    C  food.
    D  small luxuries.

# Practice Test 3: Section 2

**Questions 11–13**

Complete the notes below about the Hoverplane using **NO MORE THAN THREE WORDS**.

*Hoverplane*

*The hoverplane will be able to travel at a maximum speed of ____11____ per hour.*

*The craft is efficient, because it uses one ____12____ of the normal fuel of a ferry.*

*The larger planned version will be able to carry ____13____ and freight at 300 kilometres an hour.*

**Questions 14–16**

Answer the questions below according to the information you hear about a new computer-based police communication system.

For each blank space use NO MORE THAN THREE WORDS.

**Police Communication System**

14.  What can a radio scanner warn a criminal about?  _____.

15.  With the new police system, what will take the place of most radio traffic?

_____.

16.  What may be transmitted to police cars in future? _____.

**Questions 17–20**

According to the information you hear about chickens and electricity, complete the summary below. Use no more than TWO WORDS to complete each blank space.

## Chickens and Electricity

Dung is a ____17____ of the chicken farm. A British firm has proved that the answer to communities' needs for electric power is profitable. So, at the moment, it has ____18____ stations in Britain, which are powered by dung, and other European countries are showing interest.

In many countries, ____19____ is a headache so the company is solving two problems at one time, namely: burning dung to make much needed fertiliser and producing cheap____20____.

# Practice Test 3: Section 3

**Questions 21–23**

Circle the appropriate answer.

21. *Dave thinks the last tutorial*

   A  was exciting and Sarah disagrees.
   B  was not exciting and Sarah disagrees.
   C  wasn't very interesting, but Sarah does.
   D  was good and Sarah feels she has to agree.

22. *Sarah states that she understood*

   A  a very small part of the tutorial.
   B  all of the tutorial.
   C  most of the tutorial, but parts of it were incomprehensible.
   D  none of the tutorial.

23. *Sarah and Dave have just attended a tutorial on*

   A  study skills for English Literature.
   B  reading in literature.
   C  writing in literature.
   D  general studies.

**Questions 24–27**

Listen and complete the table below with the appropriate numbers.

|                 | Sarah | Dave     | Terry    | Arnold   |
|-----------------|-------|----------|----------|----------|
| Pages per hour  | 25/30 | (24)_____ | 120      | (25)_____ |
| Books per week  | 1     | (26)_____ | (27)_____ | 20       |

**Questions 28–30**

Using **NO MORE THAN THREE WORDS** for each blank space, complete the sentences below.

Terry thinks it is important to develop one's reading speed to _____(28)_____.

Terry felt _____(29)_____ after his first tutorial with Dr Pratt.

When Terry first arrived at university, his reading speed was _____(30)_____ pages per hour.

# Practice Test 3: Section 4

Circle the correct letter.

31.    What four qualities do actresses and actors need to survive?

   **A** fear, determination, persistence and ability to accept a challenge.

   **B** hunger, thirst, persistence and talent.

   **C** hunger, determination, talent and persistence.

   **D** anxiety, doggedness, talent and persistence.

32.    The unemployment rate in the acting profession is

   **A** around 70 percent.

   **B** between 80 and 90 per cent.

   **C** not mentioned in the lecture.

   **D** over 90 per cent.

33.    Actors, on average, work

   **A** 10 weeks per year.

   **B** 11 weeks per year.

   **C** 7 weeks per year.

   **D** 12 weeks per year.

34.    Actresses, on average, work

   **A** 14 weeks per year.

   **B** 17 weeks per year.

   **C** 7 weeks per year.

   **D** 12 weeks per year.

Complete the lecture notes below. Use NO MORE THAN FOUR WORDS to complete each space.

**Finding an agent**   Except in special circumstances, agents have to see actors or actresses in some

kind of _____35_____.

For example, they can send a show-reel with their _____36_____.

**Equity Cards**   Getting work without an Equity Card is _____37_____. The main disadvantage of the new system

is that there are more people going for the _____38_____.

**Photographs**   Photographs are essential and they have to be _____39_____, black and white and the size

of a _____40_____.

# Practice Test 4: Section 1

**Questions 1–5**

Circle the correct answer.

**Example:**
The student ...          A   is Arabic.              C   is studying Hebrew and Arabic.
                         B   is studying Arabic.     D   is studying English and Arabic.

1.   The final destination is
     A   Amman, Jordan.          C   Alexandria, Egypt.
     B   Ankara, Turkey.         D   Athens, Greece.

2.   The student must reach his destination by
     A   12th September.         C   27th September.
     B   31st August.           D   20th September.

3.   The student decides finally to leave on
     A   21st August.           C   20th September.
     B   20th August.           D   27th August.

4.   The student wants to go to Paris by

A

C

B

D

**5.**   The student is afraid of

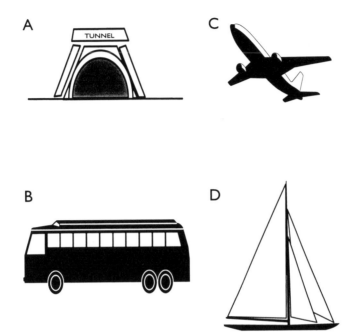

## Questions 6–9

Tick the **four** pieces of information below which give correct details about the rest of the journey.
Then write the answers A–H in Boxes 6–9 on your answer sheet.

A      The student is planning to fly from Paris to Vienna. _____

B      The student is planning to fly to Athens via Budapest from Vienna. _____

C      The student has not sorted out his visa requirements. _____

D      The Vienna leg of the journey will cost £142.80. _____

E      The student will spend three days in Athens. _____

F      The student wants to go from Piraeus to Alexandria by ferry. _____

G      The student wants to fly from Piraeus to Alexandria. _____

H      The student wants to travel to Vienna overnight. _____

## Question 10

Complete the blank space below.

**10.**   The booking reference is _____.

# Practice Test 4: Section 2

**Questions 11–16**

Complete the table below as you listen. Use either A NUMBER or NO MORE THAN THREE WORDS to fill each space.

Number of participants in the survey: 4373

|  | Radio South | Radio Soap | New Wake-up start time | The (15) _____ |
|---|---|---|---|---|
| **Approval rating** | (11)_____% | 17% | 87% | 15% |
| **Disapproval rating** | (12)_____% | 64% | (13)_____% | 25% |
| **Don't knows** | Not mentioned | 19% | Not mentioned | 60% |
| **Listeners' comments** | Excellent | Vulgar and puerile | (14)_____ | (16)_____ |

**Questions 17–20**

Circle the correct answer.

17.   *Regarding the message Voicebox, the number of complaints*

   A   has gone up and down in recent weeks.        C   has remained static.
   B   has gone down.                                                    D   has risen in recent weeks.

18.   *The praise for the music on the Wake-up show has come*

   A   only from Australia.           C   from all over South-east Asia.
   B   only from New Zealand.      D   from all over Asia.

19.   *Regarding English Worldwide, the number of listeners*

   A   has increased ten times.      C   has decreased tenfold.
   B   has remained fairly static.    D   will increase in the future.

20.   *The radio station broadcasts*

   A   14 hours per day.        C   24 hours per day.
   B   19 hours per day.        D   22 hours per day.

# Practice Test 4: Section 3

**Questions 21–25**

Circle the correct letter.

**21.** *Regarding the tutorials, Lorraine ...*

A    finds them very useful.

B    is hesitant about saying what she thinks.

C    states that they are useless.

D    thinks they could be improved.

**22.** *Farilla ...*

A    has two daughters who have been causing her trouble.

B    is a single parent with a daughter in her teens.

C    is an immature student.

D    is a teenager.

**23.** *Farilla feels that ...*

A    her eldest daughter is to blame for the family problems.

B    her youngest daughter is to blame for her family problems.

C    her husband is to blame for her family problems

D    her taking the course is the cause of her family problems.

**24.** *When he was 16, Stevie took on a job ...*

A    because he desperately needed the money.

B    for no real reason.

C    to help his mother out.

D    to help his brother.

**25.** *Dr Goldfinch suggests that Farilla should ...*

A    get her daughters a job.

B    speak to Stevie's mum.

C    give up the course.

D    explain the situation to her daughters.

**Questions 26–30**

Complete the notes below. Use **NO MORE THAN THREE WORDS** to complete each blank space.

---

**Stevie's problem**

Stevie had to have his _____26_____ ready for Friday. However, his computer _____27_____ and, unfortunately, he didn't have a copy on disk, but does have a _____28_____.

He has to get his OHPs ready; submit a _____29_____ to Dr Johnson; and give in the full paper after the seminar. If he doesn't do everything on time, he will lose _____30_____.

---

# Practice Test 4: Section 4

## Questions 31–33

Below is a list of steps (A-I), four of which the speaker took in her career. The first step is A. What are the next three steps? Write your answers in the correct order in Boxes 31–33 on your answer sheet.

### Career steps
**A** took an MA in music.

**B** worked as a proof-reader.

**C** was a freelance features writer.

**D** followed a course in journalism.

**E** entered the editorial field.

**F** became a full-time music critic

**G** a music critic on a national newspaper on a retainer.

**H** became a part-time music critic.

**I** became a sub-editor for an educational publication.

## Questions 34–36

The speaker mentions **four** disadvantages to being a music critic. One has been marked for you. Tick the other **three** disadvantages. Write your answers in Boxes 34–36 on your answer sheet.

### Disadvantages
**A** being pestered by the concert-goers while working ✓

**B** being bothered by enthusiastic accountants

**C** the loneliness

**D** having to deal with people on the telephone

**E** the low pay

**F** being glamorous

**G** meeting uninteresting people

**H** writing reviews of concerts within tight time limits

## Question 37

Circle the correct letter.

37. *As regards travelling, the speaker ...*

    **A**    enjoys it a little.

    **B**    goes abroad ten times a year.

    **C**    visits other European countries at least ten times a year.

    **D**    goes to Iceland regularly.

## Questions 38–40

Using N0 MORE THAN THREE WORDS for each space, complete the banks below.

38. Michael Ignatieff's TV series dealt with the _____ _____.

39. The critic's job is to foster the talent of _____.

40. As people are so unsure of themselves, what a critic says can act as an objective _____.

# Reading Exercises 1-22

# INTRODUCTION

The Reading Test in IELTS lasts for 60 minutes.

There are three reading passages, which may include pictures, graphs, tables or diagrams. The reading passages are of different length, from approximately 500 to 1,000 words. The total for the three passages is between 1,500 and 2,500. Each reading passage has several different types of questions, which may be printed either before or after the passage. Often the texts and the questions become more difficult as you read from Passage 1 to 3.

## Question type

You may have to answer any of the following question types:

- multiple choice questions
- gap-filling exercises
- matching  paragraph headings with paragraphs in the Reading Passage
- matching the two parts of split sentences
- short answers to open questions
- Yes/No/Not Given statements
- the completion of   - sentences
                      - summaries
                      - diagrams
                      - tables
                      - flow charts
                      - notes

## Problems

Candidates have a number of problems with this part of the IELTS exam, which may include the following:

### Misreading instructions

It is important that you read all the instructions very carefully so that you are clear about what is required for the answer to each of the questions. The instructions are usually clear and easy to follow, and, in some cases, there is an example.

Candidates think that the instructions will be exactly the same as the textbook or other material they have been using to prepare for the exam. This may not always be the case, so make sure you read the instructions carefully in the exam itself.

### Timing

Candidates often achieve a lower score than expected in this component of the IELTS exam, because they spend too much time on some sections and do not finish the test. It is very important to attempt to finish the test. You will not have time to read and enjoy the passages; instead, you should learn to work out what the question you are doing requires and find each answer as quickly as possible.

Candidates often find it difficult to leave a question that they cannot answer. This is understandable, but in the IELTS it is disastrous. While you are not answering a difficult question you could be answering two or three, or even more, easier ones. Then you can come back to those you have left blank afterwards.

## Topics

The reading passage topics vary, but are all of an academic nature. Candidates sometimes panic when they are faced with a reading passage on a subject about which they know nothing at all. It is important to remember that the answers to all of the questions are in the text itself. You do not need any specialist knowledge of the topic to be able to answer the questions. The test is designed *to test your reading comprehension skills, not your knowledge of any particular subject.*

## Answer sheets

You must complete the answer sheet within 60 minutes. You will not have extra time to transfer your answers from the question paper to your answer sheet. Candidates often think that, because they have time to transfer their answers in the listening section, the same thing happens in the reading section. It doesn't.

## Hints on reading

Students often ask what is the best way to read for the exam.

Below are some hints about what you can do.

- Read as widely as you can, e.g. newspapers, journals, specialist magazines and so on. If you are preparing for a particular academic subject at university e.g. law, medicine, engineering, you should make sure that you develop the skills of reading with speed outside your subject area.

- As you read, look for patterns in the organisation of the texts. The different types of paragraphs are finite, but their arrangement can make them appear infinite in variety. See **Reading Exercises 5, 12 and 13**.

- When you are reading, try to train yourself to read to understand the meaning of the passage rather than just reading the words. See **Reading Exercises 1–11**.

- As you read, always practise predicting what you are about to read.
  See **Reading Exercises 10 and 11**.

- As you read generally, try to summarise a paragraph by giving it a brief heading. This will then come to you automatically with practice. See **Reading Exercises 12 and 13**.

- Learn to increase your speed while still reading the organisation and meaning of a passage. See **Reading Exercises 14–16**.

- Students often focus on words they do not know. This is dangerous in the exam, as it wastes time. You have to learn *to let go* and look at the overall meaning. See **Reading Exercise 16**.

- Spend a specific period each day reading.

- Don't try to focus on all of the above at one time. Even focusing on one for a short period of time each day is tiring.

---

**Exercise 1**: How to read, or how to read efficiently?

---

When people are taught to read, generally speaking, they learn to read **words**. To read efficiently, however, you also need to read at another level: you need to be able to read *meaning*, **and** *organisation* in a text. As the reading section of the IELTS exam primarily tests your understanding of meaning and your ability to find your way around a text, it is, therefore, not enough just to be capable of reading words alone.

This exercise helps you to begin developing different strategies to read a text fast and efficiently. The exercise looks at the *organisation* in a paragraph. Read the paragraph below **slowly**, and then answer the questions which follow.

> The building, completed in 1785, was erected by the enigmatic Frederick Hervey, Earl of Bristol and Bishop of Derry, in honour of Mrs Mussenden, the Earl's cousin. The Earl Bishop used the folly, which became known as the Mussenden Temple, as a library. Standing dangerously on the edge of a sheer drop into the North Sea, the temple dominates the coastline to the West. The structure's classical simplicity, with its dome and Corinthian columns, is in stark contrast to the haunting Celtic landscape.

1. There are four sentences in the text. Which sentences give you the information below?

   A   The function of the building.

   B   The physical structure of the library.

   C   The location of the building.

   D   The history of the building.

2. None of the phrases in number 1 above can be used as titles for the paragraph. Why?

3. The author wrote the paragraph ...

   A   to describe the Mussenden Temple.

   B   to describe the Celtic landscape.

   C   to express his opinion of the madness of Frederick Hervey.

   D   to describe the function of the library.

4. The writer uses a series of synonyms in the paragraph. Which words are they?

5. What is the purpose of these words?

6. What type of paragraph is it?

   A   Is it argumentative?

   B   Is it a cause and effect paragraph?

   C   Does it express an opinion?

   D   Is it descriptive?

7. Below is a list of titles. Which is the most appropriate title for the paragraph?

   A   The enigmatic Frederick Hervey.

   B   The mystery of the Celtic landscape.

   C   The Mussenden Temple.

   D   The classicism of Frederick Hervey's folly.

8. What is the relationship between the first sentence and the second?

9. What is the relationship between the third sentence and the fourth?

---

**A book for IELTS**

**10.** There is a division in the text. Where does it occur?

**11.** What is the relationship between the two parts of text on either side of the division?

**12.** Look at the following sentence:

> The building, erected by the enigmatic Frederick Hervey, Earl of Bristol and Bishop of Derry,
>
> in honour of Mrs Mussenden, the Earl's cousin, was completed in 1785.

Compare this with the first sentence in the paragraph above.

What has happened to the information in the sentence?

What is the main information in the sentence above?

---

**Exercise 2:** Learning to read *organisation*

---

You can see from the previous exercise that to read a text effectively, you need to be able to *read organisation.* You need, therefore, to learn to see a text in a different way.

In the passage below, there are 105 words. Each of the words has a meaning. These words and meanings are then divided into five sentences. Each sentence has, in turn, a specific meaning, which comes from the sum of the words in the sentence. This meaning is different from the sum of the individual parts, i.e. the words of each sentence. Take the following sentence, for example:

*Museums and art galleries should be free of charge to the general public.*

If you add all the words together (13 words), the total is a proposal or suggestion about the issue of charges for museums or art galleries. You can see that when you put the words together you get something different: meaning at another level. And not just one meaning! The sentence does, in fact, have other meanings, but you will see that later (see **Reading Exercises 5–8**).

Another way of looking at the sentence is that the words *proposal* and *suggestion* are summaries of the sentence. If you then add up the meanings of the sentences in a paragraph, you will have a different level of meaning. In other words, the sum of the meaning of the sentences, can help you work out the title of a paragraph.

Obviously, therefore, it is more economical to be able to read the organisation of the meaning of a paragraph and dip into sentences, where necessary. Individual words then become much less important. This exercise develops further the basic techniques about organisation that you learnt in the previous exercise.

---

Read the statements below and study the paragraph which follows. Decide which statements about the paragraph are **true or false**.

a   the paragraph talks about drivers and their opinions.

b   the paragraph has no focus sentence.

c   the paragraph contains three examples which illustrate drivers' high opinion of themselves.

d   the second sentence is a transition sentence.

e   you could remove the second sentence and put **For example**, at the beginning of sentence 3.

f   the basic organisation in this paragraph is: *problem/solution.*

g   the paragraph needs more text markers like **then, indeed** etc

h   the author wrote the paragraph to show what happens when drivers are arrogant about their driving abilities.

i   a suitable title is: **Driver arrogance and the consequences.**

---

Drivers often have an over-inflated opinion of their own driving abilities and think that most other people on the road fall well below their own high standards. Some even take it upon themselves to show their fellow road users how to drive. Car drivers commonly treat the road as a stage where they show other motorists how skilful they are by out-manoeuvring them. Another frequent sight on the road is an irate man hanging out of the window of his car instructing another driver on the art of road-craft. A similar situation is the football stadium full of referees, yelling instructions at the man in black.

---

**Exercise 3:** More about reading *organisation*

---

This exercise gives you more practice in reading *organisation*. Read the following paragraph as quickly as you can:

For many people, all the frustrations they face in their daily lives are relieved on the battlefields of the road. The cashier in the bank, or at the post-office, is also frequently the object of vented anger. And how often do we read in the newspaper dramatic stories about trolley rage in the supermarket, phone rage, air rage and so on? Admittedly, we do have the tendency to take out our pent-up emotions on others. But, surely, a better way to deal with these situations would be simply learning how to control our feelings.

Now decide which of the statements about the paragraph are true or false:

  a    the first sentence gives the focus or topic of the paragraph.
  b    the purpose of the paragraph is to show how people relieve their frustrations.
  c    the structure of the paragraph is as follows:

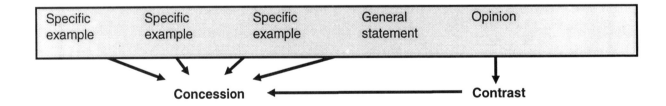

  d    the fourth sentence is a generalisation or general statement, which acts as a summary of the examples in the previous three sentences.
  e    the fifth sentence is judgmental.
  f    this is a **list** or **and** paragraph.

**g**   All of the following are suitable titles for the paragraph:

        (i)     Relieving frustration
        (ii)    The best way to relieve frustration
        (iii)   The best way to deal with emotion in fraught situations
        (iv)   Dealing with frustration

---

**Exercise 4:** A summary of functions

---

You saw in Exercise 2 that it is possible to summarise a sentence in a paragraph by giving it a name. These summaries then help you to read more efficiently as you are learning automatically to summarise sentences, and then larger chunks of text, i.e. paragraphs.

In this exercise, you are going to identify the meaning of sentences and paragraphs.

# Baboons in trees

(i) Let us use a tree as a vehicle for our explanation, where the tree represents the way of thinking. (ii) Some thinkers, content to stick to the mainstream, stay on the trunk of the tree, while others with a bit more daring move out onto the sturdier boughs. (iii) The reckless few, not satisfied with sitting complacently on the branches, have to move out to the flimsier twigs and branches. (iv) These are the radical thinkers, the iconoclasts, the people who do not fit in. (v) However, they are not the dangerous ones. (vi) Beware the truly menacing type of thinker: the predator who sits like a baboon on the stronger branches, waiting for the twigs to thicken and become stronger. (vii) Once the way has been prepared, it is the baboons who move in, taking credit for and stealing the ideas of those who dare.

1.   There are seven sentences in the text above. Below, there is a **List of Functions (A–M).** Decide which function is suitable for each sentence and why. Some of the functions do not describe any of the sentences.

*For example, for Sentence i, the answer is G.*

2.   Which one of the banks of functions (**A–D**) below relates to the text above?

*List of Functions*

| | | | |
|---|---|---|---|
| *A* | *giving another example* | *H* | *a contrast* |
| *B* | *making a proposal* | *I* | *giving an advantage* |
| *C* | *giving a solution* | *J* | *making a criticism* |
| *D* | *stating a consequence* | *K* | *giving a fuller explanation of the* |
| *E* | *drawing a conclusion; a development of* | | *previous example* |
| | *the previous sentence* | *L* | *giving examples; an expansion* |
| *F* | *stating a cause* | | *of the focus sentence* |
| *G* | *a focus or topic sentence/ statement* | *M* | *a warning; an example* |

| A. | A focus sentence | B. | A focus sentence |
|---|---|---|---|
| | Example 1 | | Solution 1 |
| | Example 2 | | Solution 2 |
| | Explanation | | An expansion |
| | Example 3 | | A contrast |
| | A warning | | A warning |
| | Explanation/Conclusion | | Conclusion |

| C. | A focus sentence | D. | A focus sentence |
|---|---|---|---|
| | Consequence 1 | | Cause 1 |
| | Consequence 2 | | Cause 2 |
| | An expansion | | An expansion |
| | A contrast | | A contrast |
| | A warning | | A warning |
| | Conclusion | | Conclusion |

3. What type of paragraph is it?

4. Is the text an **and** paragraph?

5. Which, if any, of the texts in the previous exercises is it similar to?

6. Would it have been better to put a few more markers, e.g. for example, *moreover*, in the paragraph?

7. Where does the writer take the title from and why is it a good title?

---

**Exercise 5:** Recognising paragraph types

---

It is possible after some practice to recognise different types of paragraph. You have already looked at three types, perhaps without realising it, in the previous exercises: *a description, cause and effect, etc.*. This exercise gives you some more specific practice.

If you feel, at this stage, that your reading is slowing down rather than becoming faster, then that is a *good sign*. It means that you are trying to absorb a new mechanism. If necessary, leave the exercises and repeat them again, another time.

Alternatively, use the **Key** to help you complete the parts of the exercises you cannot do. The main thing is that you *learn to acquire the mechanism* rather than just learning words. This applies to all the exercises.

Read **Paragraph 1** below and decide which of following statements about the paragraph are **false**.

a   The author wrote the paragraph to show the effects of too many data on people's ability to work.

b   The paragraph is purely descriptive.

c   The author wrote the paragraph to give examples of the different types of data that people receive.

d   The sentence, **The repercussions are grave**, is not a transition sentence in the paragraph.

e   The text is basically a list paragraph.

f   The writer has organised the paragraph around the principle of **cause and effect.**

g   The sentence, **The repercussions are grave**, acts as a divider between the two parts of the text.

h   The third sentence gives the focus of the paragraph.

i   The last sentence is a conclusion of the information in the first three sentences.

j   Only one of the following titles is suitable: **Overwhelmed by data; The effects of too much information; Increasing amounts of data.**

---

## Paragraph 1

Daily, people are being bombarded with a mountain of facts and figures. At one time, it was possible to cope with the influx of information. Now, office workers find themselves assailed not just by written information, but also by ever increasing volumes of data through the Internet, electronic mail, voice boxes and the answering machine. The repercussions are grave. People feel so overwhelmed that they are unable to work normally, with the upshot being that they feel helpless and find it impossible to extract the information needed from the constant flood of detail.

**Read the paragraph below as quickly as you can.**

## Paragraph 2

The relationship between success and failure is more intricate than people generally realise. Failure is seen as something that should be avoided. It is frowned upon and reviled; so much so, in fact, that we all avoid doing certain things, if we are afraid of failing. Instead, people should be taught the value of failure and how to use it as a stepping stone to success. We buy a classic novel or the latest best-seller and we are not told how many times the author was refused before the book came into print. Likewise, we are not told how many auditions an actor went to before he or she became a star. More emphasis obviously needs to be laid upon the necessity to fail in order to achieve success!

*[handwritten annotation: Complicate]*

**Now answer the following questions about the paragraph, as quickly as you can:**

a   What type of paragraph is it? Is it a cause and effect paragraph? An explanation? A description? Or is it a general/specific paragraph?

b   Is it a paragraph which contains a list of information, i.e. is it an **and** paragraph?

c   Where is the focus of the paragraph?

d   Is it similar to the text in Exercise 1, 2 or 3?

e   Which sentence shows why the writer wrote the paragraph?

f   Which of the questions below does the paragraph answer?

   (i)     **What is failure?**
   (ii)    **What makes people happy?**
   (iii)   **How are failure and success linked?**
   (iv)    **What effect does success have on people?**

g   Which, if any, of the titles below is acceptable?

   (i)     **Failure as a learning process**
   (ii)    **Making society a happier place**
   (iii)   **The need to avoid failure**
   (iv)    **Failure as a route to success**

---

**Exercise 6:** Simultaneous functions

---

This exercise takes the idea in Exercise 5 a step further. Students often do not realise that meaning and organisation also operate at different levels at the same time. In this exercise, you are going to look at this idea. Read the paragraph below and then the **Lists of Functions**. Decide which list of functions best describes each sentence. Two of the lists do not relate to any of the sentences.

If you have to look at the **Key** to help you complete the exercise, then leave it and try to do it another time.

*Example: The answer for Sentence 1 is C. For an explanation look at the **Key**.*

## The teaching of thinking

(1) If you are of the opinion that reading, writing and numeracy are taught badly, then what about the art of thinking? (2) Generally speaking, people are not taught how to think at all. (3) There is a very laisser faire, non-interventionist approach to education that encourages students to discover things for themselves, when they are all crying out for some prescriptive guidance. (4) What appears to have escaped the theorists is the basic concept of the need to learn rules in order to break them. (5) When it comes to thinking, no guidelines are given; students are either just taught facts or left to fend for themselves. (6) If only a little thought were given to teaching young people some mechanisms for thinking: the 'how' rather than the 'what'! (7) Children would then be able to absorb and use knowledge better. (8) For it is not knowledge itself that bestows power, but the ability to process and manipulate knowledge: in other words, being able to think.

**Lists of functions**

A   reformulation of the central problem; making a criticism; stating a reason

B   returning to the focus of the paragraph; stating a specific problem; a criticism; an opinion

C   a topic sentence; an organising sentence; posing a question

D   a conclusion; a general statement

E   describing the present situation; giving background information; stating a general problem; an explanation; a reformulation of the previous sentence

F   a hypothetical result; a certain result; a development

G   a strong recommendation; a conclusion

H   a wish; a regret; a solution; sarcasm; a complaint; a criticism; giving a solution; a proposal

I   an advantage

J   giving a reply describing the present situation; giving background information; a contrast

---

---

**Exercise 7:** Reading control

---

Reading and, at the same time, keeping the understanding of a text under control is difficult, especially if you have to do it in another language. As you read, you have to deal with words and the sum of the words: meaning. Unfortunately, the words often interfere with the meaning, because you cannot climb on top of them to look down at the text from above. If you can overcome this problem, you can read the organisation of a text, and control your interpretation. It will then be possible to follow the meaning without your concentration wandering. This exercise will help you to start doing this.

Read the paragraph below and then read the **Lists of functions** describing each sentence. Some of the functions in each list are not suitable. Decide which ones are **not suitable** and why.

**The first one has been done for you as an example.**

# A case for trolley buses and trams

(1) Not that long ago, trolley buses and trams were being condemned as rather out-moded forms of transport. (2) Yet, now they are being hailed as the answer to the ills afflicting modern transport systems. (3) A vast swathe of South London from Tooting on the Northern Line to Croydon is being linked by a new tram system. (4) Motorists do not like it, because the roads are in the process of being churned up in preparation for the tramlines. (5) When the trams are finally up and running, private car owners say the system will lead to more one-way systems, further hindering freedom of movement and increasing the congestion that they were designed to overcome. (6) These points certainly present a strong argument against the tram system. (7) Nonetheless, provided the system is as efficient and cheap to use as planned, many people feel the service will be a resounding success.

**Lists of functions**

*Example: The items below in bold italics in No.1 are wrong.*

1.  ***stating a disadvantage;*** stating the main argument against; ***stating the focus of the paragraph;*** giving general background information

2.  stating an advantage; stating the main argument for; making a general statement; stating a contrast; stating the focus of the paragraph; making a criticism

3.  giving an example; giving general background information; stating an argument for; making a proposal

4.  stating an argument against; stating a reservation; stating a result; giving a reason against; stating a disadvantage

5.  stating a subjective argument against; giving an opinion; stating a reservation; stating an objective argument against; stating a result or implication

6.  summarising the arguments against; summarising the disadvantages; stating an opinion

7.  restating the focus of the paragraph; a contrast; stating an argument for; stating an opinion; stating a tentative result based on a condition; drawing a conclusion

---

---

**Exercise 8:** Spot the difference

---

When you are reading a text about a particular subject, it is often difficult to see what the difference is between the contents of different paragraphs. There are basically two reasons for this. First of all, it may be difficult to see the difference between the general subject and the focus in each paragraph. The second problem is trying to read a text with concentration and prevent one's mind from wandering from the focus of the paragraph to related ideas in one's head. This can lead to misinterpretation. When we are writing, we often find it difficult to focus on the title we have been asked to write about. A similar problem arises in reading.

In this exercise, you are going to analyse the organisation of two very similar paragraphs. Each has the same general subject and most of the information is the same. However, the paragraphs have different meanings and foci.

Read **Passage 1** below and then from the **Function bank** after the passage decide which functions best describe each sentence in the paragraph. Note that each sentence may have more than one function. You may use some items from the **bank** more than once.

Then read **Passage 2** and compare the organisation of the text at paragraph level. Decide what the similarities and differences are.

*If you need to, read the **Key** to help you do the exercise,
then leave the exercise for a while and come back to it later.*

# Passage 1

(1) The government recently invited the water industry and interested parties to make suggestions about how to save water. (2) Debatable though it is, one of the most common ideas put forward was to meter all homes in the country. (3) Many people feel that installing water meters nationwide would turn out to be expensive. (4) However, the longer the delay in doing so, the greater the cost is likely to be, both in terms of water wasted and money. (5) Metering would, in all probability, be the single most important step, simply because it would make people aware of the amount of water they are using, thereby reducing consumption. (6) To many people, this course of action lets water companies off the hook and transfers responsibility to the consumer. (7) Yet, most are of the opinion that nationwide metering needs to be introduced.

### Function bank

giving a reason; a contrast; stating a probability; an objective conclusion;
a hypothetical implication; stating/describing a suggestion; making a suggestion;
a result; a reservation; a development; a focus sentence; a subjective conclusion;
an organising sentence; a real implication; expressing an opinion; stating a fact.

---

# Passage 2

(1) The government recently invited the water industry and interested parties to state how they thought water could be saved. (2) Controversial though it is, one of the most common recommendations the government should initiate is to meter all homes in the country. (3) Installing water meters nationwide is, no doubt, an expensive proposition. (4) However, the longer the delay in doing so, the greater the cost will be, both in terms of water wasted and money. (5) Metering is the single most important step, simply because it will certainly make people aware of the amount of water they are using, thereby reducing consumption. (6) People may be dismissive of this course of action. (7) Yet, I feel that it ought to be taken.

---

**Exercise 9:** Learning to concentrate

---

One of the greatest problems that you will face as you do the reading texts in IELTS is holding different bits of information in your head at the same time. The reading tests are in booklet form and you have to flick back and forward between the exercise and the text. Often, students forget the information they are looking at as they move between the two. All you have to do is listen to the volume of the rustling of paper as students do a test to see how difficult they find it!

It is, therefore, more economical for you to learn to hold and manipulate information as you read. This is another aspect of controlling a text.

This exercise helps you to do just that. It also helps you:

* to read and to predict the text which follows.

* to predict the direction of a text.

* and to see how a text matches a title.

Read the following three titles:

(i)    Cloning's bright future
(ii)   The unacceptable face of cloning
(iii)  The dangers of cloning

Now look at the reading maze below. At each number, choose the text which develops the meaning of title (i). Then repeat the process for each title.

*For example, the first sentence for (i) is 1C and the second is 2B.*

| A | B | C |
|---|---|---|
| 1. Cloning is such an emotive subject that it is impossible to approach the matter with an open mind. | The few obvious benefits of human cloning apart, there is a downside to the cloning of human beings. | There is no denying that mankind will profit considerably from the cloning of human beings. |

**A**

2. Is it, perhaps, the fact that people are created without parents that horrifies many of us?

3. For example, parents may want to have a child with above average intelligence, who is physically perfect and free from disease.

4. Certain disease traits that may be removed from the human gene pool could some time in the future be necessary in our fight against illness.

5. To those who do not believe in an active God, cloning violates nature.

6. And the agony that most, if not all, childless couples are now forced to endure would be swept away for ever.

7. What will happen to those babies who are not sold? Will they be used for spareparts, or killed?

8. No doubt, such a prospect will horrify some, but it will be a delight to most people.

**B**

> The process gives us the opportunity to maximise certain valued human traits.

Many of us find the process totally unpalatable for several reasons.

By cloning persons with these characteristics, the future infant would be guaranteed to possess them.

Conversely, the very characteristics that are now highly desirable may turn out to be harmful and dangerous for coming generations.

Or is it perhaps the vision of batteries of babies being produced in some factory that arouses our horror?

The thought of human beings produced in such farms like chickens for spare-parts is not that far-fetched.

Thus, the way will be paved for the rather dangerous prospect of a race of perfectly modelled human beings.

**C**

The process is unquestionably a landmark in the development of science, but it is not the panacea to the world's ills, as some scientists would have us believe.

Cloning threatens the very survival of the human species.

The general belief is that an infant who has not been created by human sexual congress is a violation of God's will and will not have a divine soul.

Which parent will want to deny their future off-spring such an inheritance?

Moreover, babies with a sell-by-date may well in future be bought in shops much as pets are today.

There is also the strong possibility that we shall be able to create a race of humans free from all disease and handicap.

Identical twins are clones, but we have not heard of twins being used as an organ bank for their siblings, yet.

---

**Exercise 10:** Predicting organisation 1

---

As you have seen briefly in the previous exercise, once you are familiar with the organisation of a paragraph, it is possible to predict the direction of other paragraphs and texts that you read. This is because there is a limit to the different types of paragraph. If you look at other areas of language, you can see that this happens all the time. How often, in your own language, can you predict what someone is going to say? Sometimes, you can even give the exact words. Predicting when you come to reading is no different.

In this exercise, you are going to try to predict the contents of a paragraph.

*To help you, look at the following information:*

- the paragraph is an example paragraph.

- the fourth sentence contains the focus.

- the first three sentences are general information which make up an introduction.

---

Now read the *first four* sentences of the passage:

- try to predict what you think the function **and** content of the rest of the sentences are, after the focus sentence. Think of common examples.

- write your list on a piece of paper.

- read the text and compare your list with the text.

# Life at a faster pace

I blame the fast forward button on the video recorder. How often have you found yourself reaching for the remote control when you find a programme slow or boring? Frequently? Life has to be lived at a much faster pace nowadays. Microwaves enable meals to be prepared in minutes. Computers allow work to be done at a quicker rate than even a few years ago. So much faster, in fact, that people feel that they will be left behind unless they quicken up. People hurtle along on ever faster forms of transport. Planes carry people across the world in ever shorter times. Trains speed along like rockets through the countryside. We have to do everything and get there much more quickly than ever before. No part of our lives is free from the drive to get things done more quickly.

---

**Exercise 11:** Predicting organisation 2

---

This exercise is the same as the previous one.

In this exercise, you are going to try to predict the contents of a paragraph.

To help you, look at the following information:

- the paragraph is a result paragraph predicting the negative consequences of introducing trams and trolley buses.

- the paragraph in this exercise uses the same information in Exercise 7, but the paragraph takes a different direction. Go back and read the text.

- read the title to help you work out the direction of the passage.

Without reading the passage:

- try to predict what you think the function and contents of the paragraph are.

- write your list on a piece of paper.

- read the text and compare your list with the text.

---

# No to trolley buses and trams!

Trolley buses and trams, rather out-moded forms of transport, are mistakenly being hailed as the answer to the ills afflicting modern transport systems. A vast swathe of South London from Tooting on the Northern Line to Croydon is being churned up to build a new tram system. Motorists obviously don't like it, because the roads are in the process of being ripped up in preparation for the tramlines being laid. When the trams are finally up and running, most people will be against the idea, because the system will lead to more one-way systems, thus hindering their freedom of movement and most certainly increasing the congestion that it was designed to get rid of. Then, when the problems start arising, they will have to start dismantling the whole network again at great inconvenience to the motoring public!

---

**Exercise 12: Focus on paragraph headings**

---

Students find the exercise where they have to give a heading to a paragraph in the IELTS exam particularly difficult. However, you have already had some practice at analysing paragraph headings. Perhaps, you can see that there is a relationship between paragraph structure and the heading of a paragraph. In some cases, this may be overt, i.e. obvious, but, in many instances, it may be covert, i.e. hidden.

Below, there are five independent paragraphs and a **List of headings.** Read the paragraphs as quickly as you can. As you read, try to find the main focus and then the direction of the paragraph. Try also to write a suitable title of your own on a separate piece of paper. Then look at the **List of headings** at the end of the exercise and find the correct heading for each paragraph. Note that some of the alternatives are distracters.

1. **Paragraph heading:** _____

   *The segregation of boys and girls at secondary school level only stores up problems for the future. First of all, such an environment does not provide young people of both sexes with realistic preparation for the society in which they will be expected to function when they become adults. In single sex schools, it is not uncommon for both girls and boys to grow up with misconceptions about the opposite sex; for the former, there is the romantic Mills and Boon hero, and the notion of the alluring goddess for the latter. And, thirdly, young people who are brought up in single sex schools have difficulty functioning socially with members of the opposite sex.*

2. **Paragraph heading:** _____

   *Some people mistakenly believe rather strongly that segregating girls and boys at secondary school level is unnatural. Their argument is that such an environment does not provide young people of both sexes with realistic preparation for the society in which they will be expected to function when they become adults. However, speaking from the point of view of someone who has had to undergo the trials of a non-segregated school, I feel, single sex schools, are much better for girls. It has been demonstrated time and time again that girls at secondary level flourish in surroundings where they are not held back academically by an army of pestering, immature boys.*

---

**A book for IELTS**

## 3. Paragraph heading: _____

*The segregation of boys and girls at secondary school level is not exactly natural, as such an environment does not provide young people of both sexes with realistic preparation for the society in which they will be expected to function when they become adults. In single sex schools, it is not uncommon for both girls and boys to grow up with misconceptions about the opposite sex; for the former, there is the romantic Mills and Boon hero, and the notion of the alluring goddess for the latter. By contrast, in a co-educational setting, there is not the slightest possibility that such illusions will survive.*

## 4. Paragraph heading: _____

*Change causes problems, not least because it upsets people's routine and makes them feel uneasy. A good example is the introduction of technology in the workplace. The Luddite in all of us comes out as we are faced with adapting to the onslaught of technological change at work. In the early 19th century, the Luddites revolted against the introduction of what was new technology in their time by breaking machinery which replaced workers. The pace of change today is much faster, and thereby more unsettling. Thousands of workers in factories have been replaced by computers and robots; now voice recognition programmes threaten to replace secretaries; computerised switchboards receptionists and computer video packages instructors and teachers. What area of life is safe from the advance of machines?*

## 5. Paragraph heading: _____

*Change causes problems, but the belief that it destroys people's jobs and lives is totally unfounded. The Luddite in all of us comes out as we are faced with adapting to the onslaught of technological change at work. In the early 19th century, the Luddites revolted against the introduction of what was new technology in their time by breaking machinery which replaced workers. The pace of change today is much faster, which can be unsettling. However, it is now clear that, far from destroying work, thousands of jobs have been created in factories as the power of technological change is harnessed. Witness the development of 'silicon valleys' throughout the world. The fear that robots and computers will replace people in all areas is clearly a myth.*

---

**List of headings**

| | |
|---|---|
| A | A 19th Century revolt |
| B | No reason to fear technology |
| C | The unsettling effect of change |
| D | Machines v. factory workers |
| E | Various effects of segregation |
| F | The main argument against segregation |
| G | Attacking the Luddites |
| H | Teenagers notions about sex |
| I | A modern copy of the Luddites |
| J | A passionate defence of modernisation |
| K | The need for segregation |
| L | The creation of distorted ideas about sex |
| M | Dysfunctional behaviour in girls |

---

---

**Exercise 13:** Foreground and background information

---

You saw in the previous exercise that working out the heading of a paragraph is basically about organisation. You need to be able to see the thread of information going through the text connecting the information to a heading.

Most people think of analysing the title as a forward-looking exercise. Yet, when a writer is writing he is constantly looking backwards to his plan or guidelines (in this case the title). When you are writing an essay in the IELTS, you need to look back at the title constantly to make sure you are writing the correct essay. If the examiner cannot match your essay to the essay question in the exam, you have a problem. The same applies in the case of paragraph headings.

This exercise gives you more practice with paragraph headings. This time each paragraph has a heading. Read the paragraphs and decide why the heading is correct. Make a photocopy of the texts and underline the words and phrases that give you the theme of the paragraph. If you can, make a rough plan to help you see the layout of each paragraph.

Look at the **Key** for the previous exercise before you attempt this one. The plan will help you see why the writer wrote each paragraph.

Note the paragraphs are not connected to each other. You will also find that several of them are similar to, but not the same as, paragraphs you have already read.

In this exercise, like the last one, if you need to use the **Key** to help you understand the mechanism, feel free to do so. However, try to do the exercise first without any help.

1. **Heading**: *Hooked on change*

   Change causes problems, not least the anxiety it generates among those whose very livelihood is threatened. Yet, there are people who seem to thrive on change, enjoying the constant flow of challenges. There is a bit of the Luddite in all of us when we are faced with adapting to the onslaught of technological developments at work. In the early 19th century, the Luddites revolted against the introduction of what was new technology in their time by breaking machinery which was replacing workers. The pace of change today is much faster, a situation in which certain types of people flourish. To them the constant movement involved in change is like a drug. They become addicted very quickly, harnessing the power of technological advances and creating new opportunities, not just for themselves, but for others as well.

2. **Heading**: *Welcome to new technology*

   Change causes problems, not least because it upsets people's routine and makes them feel uneasy. A good example is the introduction of technology in the workplace. The Luddite in all of us comes out as we are faced with adapting to the onslaught of technological change at work. In the early 19th century, the Luddites revolted against the introduction of new technology. The pace of change today is much faster, and thereby more unsettling. But the belief that it destroys people's jobs and lives is totally unfounded. Thousands of workers in old-fashioned factories may have been replaced by computers and robots; it is now clear, however, that, far from destroying work, many more jobs have been created in factories as the power of technological change is harnessed. Witness the development of 'silicon valleys' throughout the world. The advances in the field of technology should, therefore, be embraced with open arms rather than feared.

3. **Heading**: *The North/South driving divide*

   Another interesting observation is how standards of driving seem to deteriorate markedly as you travel down the country. A much more calm and relaxed manner of driving is noticeable to those visitors to Northern cities like Bradford, Leeds, Manchester and Carlisle. There does not seem to be the same mad rush and lack of respect for other road users that is all too apparent in areas like the

---

South-east and London. It is a strange experience to drive down the M1 from the North and feel the traffic gradually start to speed up, with tailgaters appearing in your rear mirror more regularly and undertaking becoming more commonplace the nearer you approach London. In the two to three hours drive South, the journey changes from a pleasant drive at a respectable pace to a mad aggressive rush as the traffic hurtles towards London. Is this yet another example of the differences between the North and South? If so, it is one Northerners should be proud of.

**4. Heading**: *Peace at the wheel*

Another interesting observation is how much more relaxing it is to travel around in the North. A calm and relaxed manner of driving is noticeable to those visiting cities like Bradford, Leeds, Manchester and Carlisle. There does not seem to be the same mad rush and lack of respect for other road users that is all too apparent in areas like the South-east and London. It is a strange experience to drive up the M1 from the North and feel the traffic gradually slow down, with fewer tailgaters appearing in your rear mirror and undertaking becoming less frequent. The tension at the wheel subsides; and a car journey changes into a very pleasant drive at a respectable pace.

**5. Heading**: *The stupidity of ageism*

Age discrimination is rife among the business community. The folly inherent in this process is nothing less than a criminal act. It does not seem to have dawned on employers that the workplace is changing. The number of people dealing with knowledge compared with manual workers is increasing. In the near future, we may find companies clamouring over each other to attract old people as the demographic make-up of the working population changes. Some companies already have a policy of employing older people in their stores, and they have seen a marked turn-around in sales. Could this possibly have something to do with a thing called experience?

**6. Heading**: *The need for legislation to protect older people*

Age is commonly used as a criterion to prevent people from entering a job and, indeed, to rid an establishment of excess personnel. Young people are seen as being fitter physically and mentally, and as costing less. The experience of older people is overlooked. A dose of ageism is needed here, but ageism where there is discrimination in favour of old people. Some companies already have a policy of employing older people in their stores, and they have seen a marked turn around in sales. So, perhaps there is a case for legislating in favour of old people in the workplace.

---

**Exercise 14**: Increasing your reading speed

---

In **Reading Exercises 1–13**, you looked at reading a passage from the point of organisation and meaning. We have pointed out that this may have slowed your reading down, as learning any new skill does. With practice, however, the mechanisms can help to increase your speed as well as efficiency in reading and examining a text.

You also need, however, to have a range of strategies to help you read quickly. Increasing one's reading speed in one's native language is difficult enough; in a second, or possibly third or fourth, it is even more difficult.

Below is a list of mini-exercises to help you focus on increasing your speed.

   1.   *One way to increase your speed is by learning to pick out the most important words in a sentence which will give you a summary of the meaning. Look at the following sentences:*

      A **recent study** of **top executives shows** that **companies** are **wasting valuable time** and **resources**, because **managers** are being **subjected** to **unacceptable levels** of **stress** by **office politics** and **increased pressure**. This **situation** is **further compounded** by **long hours, infrequent breaks** and **sleeplessness**.

   What is the difference between the words that are highlighted and the ones which are not?

**2.** Read the text in 1 above again and then read the following text:

> A recent **study** of top executives **shows** that **companies** are **wasting** valuable **time** and **resources**, because **managers** are being **subjected** to unacceptable levels of **stress** by **office politics** and increased **pressure**. This **situation** is further **compounded** by **long hours, infrequent breaks** and **sleeplessness.**

What is the difference between the highlighted words this time and the original?

**3.** Read the texts below as quickly as you can and mark the words which act as stepping stones and summarise the text for you.

> **(A)** *Participation in the Euro, the new European currency, hinged on whether the criteria set out in the Maastricht Treaty were adhered to strictly. Several countries would like to have seen some of the qualifying conditions relaxed, but that did not happen, as the banks were against any slackening of monetary control. What remains to be seen is whether the governments concerned can stick to the stringent monetary goals they have set themselves.*

> **(B)** *The swingeing cuts introduced by the government have created quite a fracas, but many people believe that they are necessary for the future health of the country. The main target areas appear to be spending on welfare, defence and the road network.*

> **(C)** *One member of the public, a Gladys C Roach, who took part in the survey, stated that she felt it was dangerous to shop in the department store as it was so full of tempting food. She added that she always had to make sure that she went there to shop only on a full stomach. Otherwise, she would spend a fortune.*

**4.** Understanding the relationship between the parts of sentences will also help you. What is the relationship between the parts within the sentences below?

> *a*    *The underlying rate of inflation has remained the same as last month, under-mining the government's attempts to curb interest rate rises.*

> *b*    *Progress in the talks to settle the dispute has been slow: agreement has only been  reached on one item in the list of differences between the two sides.*

> *c*    *The frost wreaked such havoc among the early blossoms at Farkleberry, that there was much consternation at the big house.*

> *d*    *Although he had created a very innovative and effective programme, it was in danger of being destroyed through ignorance and jealousy.*

> *e*    *He had created such an innovative and effective programme, that it was in danger of being destroyed through ignorance and jealousy.*

**5.** Another way to help you read quickly is to learn to recognise the relationship in meaning between sentences. What is the relationship between the pairs of sentences below?

> *a*    *This shows, say many teachers, that standards of English for many secondary school pupils and university students have declined over recent years. The answer is, obviously, that the teaching of grammar should be made compulsory in secondary school and on relevant teacher training courses.*

> *b*    *This shows, say many teachers, that standards of English for many secondary school pupils and university students have declined over recent years. The answer is, perhaps, to make the teaching of grammar compulsory in secondary school and on relevant teacher training courses.*

> *c*    *This shows, say many teachers, that standards of English for many secondary school pupils and university students have declined over recent years. The danger is, obviously, that the teaching of grammar is made compulsory in secondary school and on relevant teacher training courses.*

> *d*    *The number of ships being repaired in the dockyard has declined  steadily since the end of the 60s. Only five ships were repaired or refitted last year as against 30 in 1968.*

6.  In the text in **5a** above, isolate the two main pieces of information. For the first you may use only five words; for the second you may use only eight.

---

**Exercise 15:** More about speed

---

Exercise 15 contains some more strategies to help you increase your speed.

1.  What is the main information in each of the texts below? Read and decide as quickly as you can.

    a   In a paper to be published in the next issue of the Journal, Farilla Bartlett, the eminent anthropologist, of the University of London, argues that the launch of the anti-smoking campaign will fail miserably.

    b   In detailed studies of the sleep patterns of males, the researchers recorded that the amount of deep sleep declines with age, thus leading to a reduction in the body's rejuvenation process.

    c   Scumbling, the use of dry brush to create a hazy effect on paper surfaces not previously covered with a colour wash, is a simple, but subtle technique.

2.  Understanding the basic layout of a sentence can also help you find your way round a text and hence read more efficiently and quickly. Sentences in English are basically divided between old and new information. Look at the following example:

> **A woman entered a building. Suddenly, she saw a large cat. The animal was eating a mouse. The cat looked at the woman. The woman lifted a stick and walked away from the cat**

You can look at the information as follows:

| **New** | **New** | |
| A woman | entered a building. | |
| **Old** | **New** | |
| [Suddenly], she | saw  a large cat. | |
| **Old** | **New** | |
| The animal | was eating a mouse. | |
| **Old** | **Old** | |
| The cat | looked at the woman. | |
| **Old** | **New** | |
| The woman | lifted a stick | |
| **Old** | **New** | **Old** |
| and [The woman] | walked away from | the cat. |

Notice how the information generally jumps back and forward from **Old** to **New**, except in the first and last part of the text! An economical way of reading text is to train yourself to read only the **New** information as you already know the **Old.**

---

In the texts below, find the **Old** and **New** information.

> **(a)** *A car was driving slowly along a road. It turned into the drive of a large white house. The car stopped just short of the front door, but the driver did not get out.*

> **(b)** *Her first acting break in a major film was doing a voice-over in a spy film. This led to a string of similar jobs doing work on adverts.*

> **(c)** *Mr Maguire made a number of predictions for the future of further education in the UK. His forecasts are seriously flawed. They are much too optimistic to be credible.*

> **(d)** *A woman with a manic grin entered a building. Suddenly, the building collapsed. When the dust settled, she walked into another building. Her grin was now even more hideous.*

> **(e)** *The government's version of events was not believed by anyone. It was seen by most people as a cover-up. The whole affair serves to illustrate the fears people have of politicians' inclination to abuse power.*

3. As you have seen in the reading exercises you have done so far, it is helpful to know how a text is organised. If you are able to see how text is organised in general it will help you to move through the reading passages in IELTS quickly and effectively.

   Look at the organisation of the text below. What is the essential information in the sentence? Can you divide the information into three main blocks? Paraphrase the sentence and begin: **Statistics show ...**

   > **According to the statistics available on homelessness, what drives young people away from home is the threat of violence from those within the household.**

4. It is difficult for all of us to hold several pieces of information in our heads at the same time about a text and extract detail. You can, however, practise doing this. Look at the texts below and answer the questions which follow:

   > *(a) Lacking the natural resilience of her mother, Muriel, Mavis, recently devastatingly rebuffed by her aunt Maureen, fell into a long and agonising period of depression.*

   Who became depressed?

   > *(b) Unlike Mr Richardson and Mrs Frome, the previous directors, the new directors, Mrs Allinson, Mr Frome (no relation to Mrs Frome) and Miss Vincent, decided to terminate the contract that had been signed by the above-mentioned Mr Richardson's father prior to his son and one of his daughters taking over as directors of the company.*

   What is the relationship between Mr Richardson and Mrs Frome?

5.  Look at the following text and complete the sentence which follows:

> **In a tense hour-long Whitehall meeting the day before yesterday, Mrs Cartlebury, sitting with Sir Charles Drew and Charles Drewmore, the chairman and chief executive of Silver, Finch & Finch, respectively, the main auditors employed by the Ombudsman, and Samantha Ali, Head of the Personal Investment Authority, which is overseeing the multi-billion mis-selling review, laid down the rules.**

The rules_____ by Mrs Cartlebury.

---

**Exercise 16:** Words that slow you down

---

Students often complain that they find it difficult to read a text because they do not know certain words. These words do not stop you from understanding a text. What stops you is focusing on individual words and not the overall meaning. There is a saying in English that *the devil is in the detail.* He is there, so do not let him hold you back!

Below is a series of short texts and sentences. Each text contains a blank space where a word which would normally cause difficulty has been left out.

After each text, there is a sentence in a box to complete like the questions you have in the IELTS exam. Do not try to complete the blank spaces in the first text in the exercise, as the original words are rather difficult. The exercise aims to show you how irrelevant individual words can be to your understanding of a text.

*Example*
*Students are often totally _____ when they come across words that they do not know in a text*

Words that _____ frequently confuse students.

The missing words in the box are: they do not know. You do not need to know the missing word.

Now complete the blank spaces **in the boxes** under each **Text** below using no more than four words from the first **Text** in each case.

**1.**  The _____ in the reading passage distracts people so much that they cannot read the text comfortably. Certain words, like waves interfering with a radio transmission, affect students' ability to extract the meaning from a passage, because they are unable to leave the words they do not know alone. They do not realise that it is possible to understand the meaning without knowing every single term.

Certain terminology prevents people from reading a text _____.

**2.**  In writing and reading, _____ is a basic form of connecting a text. Examples of such reference are words like: it, they, synonyms etc.

Referring backwards in written text is an elementary form of _____.

**3.**  _____ in her attempts to modernise the company while trying to satisfy the investors and the financial markets at the same time, she reluctantly decided to _____ her resignation.

She resigned from her post because her endeavours to _____ were opposed.

**4.** It seems that the _____ instruments were thrown into the rubbish pit rather than being taken back for mending.

> The instruments that did not work were thrown into _____.

**5.** _____ institutions soon run into trouble when they find that they cannot pay for the day-to-day administration of their establishments.

> Bodies which do not control their spending _____.

**6.** They thought that the plot that they had _____ was foolproof, but they were soon found out and severely punished.

> Their plot was not _____.

**7.** The style seen here in this church is the _____ of the achievement reached at the height of the Italian Renaissance.

> The church represents the style of _____ at its height.

**8.** The difficulties experienced over the last few weeks have been _____ by the introduction of new measures to combat the rise in crime. The recent rights riots have only served to exacerbate an already difficult situation.

> The new measures to fight the _____ have made the situation worse.

**9.** The situation will easily be rectified by a _____ programme focusing on the most pressing aspects of the problem.

> The programme can focus on the _____ of the problem.

**10.** The distinction between both sides of an argument can often become quite _____ .

> There is a grey area between both _____ .

---

**Exercise 17:** Problems with meaning

---

This exercise is an attempt to illustrate a problem that students have as they try to analyse the reading texts in IELTS, particularly **Yes/ No/ Not Given** exercises. It is a problem that they do not realise exists and which interferes with their analysis of the texts. As you have seen in previous Exercises, particularly **Reading Exercises 5 and 6**, sentences can have several meanings at the same time.

Likewise, there are two basic mechanisms at work as you are analysing a text. Look at the following pair of sentences:

> **A**    Growth will slow down in the near future.
>
> **B**    It is predicted that the pace of growth will decline.

At a glance, the sentences have the same meaning. You see that Sentence B is a paraphrase of Sentence A. Obviously, it does not contain all the information that is in Sentence A. It is not exact enough, because it does not specifically mention a time (in the near future). It is, nevertheless, a paraphrase of Sentence A.

Now look at the same sentences the other way round:

      **B**    It is predicted that the pace of growth will decline.
      **A**    Growth will slow down in the near future.

Sentence A does not paraphrase Sentence B, because it adds additional information to the information in Sentence B! Remember that in the exam you are analysing the text using the sentences in the exercises. *You are not analysing the exercises using the text.* The danger, of course, is that students, consciously or sub-consciously, read also from the reading passage to the exercise, as they look from the statement in the exercise to the information in the text. This, as we have seen, can give you the wrong answer!

Now compare the above pair of sentences with the following:

      **A**    The dog gave chase to the cat.
      **B**    It was the cat that was pursued by the dog.

**A** has the same meaning as **B** and vice versa!

In this exercise, you have pairs of sentences 1–15. Read the sentences as quickly as you can and decide whether the sentences in each pair have exactly the same meaning. You will probably have to do this exercise several times. If necessary, use the **Key** to help you.

1.   **A** *The man sank his teeth into the dog's ear.*
      **B** *It was the dog's ears that were bitten off by the man.*

2.   **A** *Joseph stopped smoking cigarettes.*
      **B** *Joseph stopped to smoke.*

3.   **A** *Mohamed was too optimistic about the future.*
      **B** *Mohamed was not that hopeful about the future.*

4.   **A** *Everyone should take up some form of exercise to help them relax.*
      **B** *It is necessary for everybody to get involved in some form of exercise to help unwind.*

5.   **A** *Various instruments were studied as part of the research.*
      **B** *A variety of instruments were studied during the research.*

6.   **A** *Few people grasp this point at the first attempt.*
      **B** *There are not many who understand this straight-off.*

7.   **A** *It's going to rain soon.*
      **B** *The forecast is for rain.*

8.   **A** *Adapting to change induces a number of unpleasant side effects.*
      **B** *Depression and physical illness are brought on by having to adapt to change, which is never a pleasant or easy experience. Change also induces stress and unhappiness.*

9.   **A** *The final contract did not fully meet the union's demands.*
      **B** *What was approved in the end fell short of what the union had asked for.*

10.   **A** *Parents fear that standards at all levels of education, but especially at secondary school, are falling.*
      **B** *Parents are afraid that not enough attention is being paid to education at primary school level.*

11.   **A** *If only the fire brigade had arrived sooner the building would have been saved.*
      **B** *It is regrettable that the building was destroyed because the fire brigade did not arrive sooner.*

12.   **A** *There is a slim possibility that the accused may not have committed the murder.*
      **B** *It is highly likely that it was the accused who committed the murder.*

13.   **A** *Everyone is aware that the centre has improved significantly.*
      **B** *It is not widely appreciated that the centre has got better.*

14.   **A** *He is only 65.*
      **B** *It is surprising that he is 65 years of age.*

15.   **A** *The stolen vase is priceless.*
      **B** *The value of the vase that was taken is beyond price.*

---

**Exercise 18:** An introduction to 'Yes'

---

This exercise helps you focus on the technique required to answer the **Yes/ No/ Not Given** type of question in the exam. It is more important for you to learn the analytical process in this type of question than to find the correct answer. The exercise has, therefore, been designed in such a way that you need to hold information in your head while you try to find the correct answer. You may need to do the exercise several times.

In the column on the left, you have 14 statements. On the right, there are 17 statements (**a–q**). How many statements on the left can you find that have a statement with the same meaning in the right-hand column?

---

For example, the answer for **Sentence 14** is (**a**).

---

1. All that is necessary to ensure the future viability of the Project has been done.

2. What surprised the government most was the rapidity with which their fortunes were reversed.

3. Why the second report has been hushed up is not entirely clear.

4. Why the previous report was hushed up is patently obvious.

5. The ability to separate emotion from rationality is a rarity.

6. The government's discomfort at their misfortune was not surprising.

7. Intelligence can surely be nurtured and developed in most individuals.

8. Doctors are made not born.

9. The government were attacked for not acting promptly to sort out the situation.

10. As the train departed, the sky was promising a heavy burst of rain.

11. Superstition is far from being rare among educated people.

12. The government should have acted sooner to take the pressure out of the situation.

13. There is nothing new under the sun.

14. He epitomises everyone's idea of the old breed of policeman.

*a.* He is a perfect example of what people now think of as the old-fashioned type of police officer.

*b.* It looked as if there was going to be a downpour, when the train set off.

*c.* The government was discomfited by the reversal of their fortunes.

*d.* Not all of us find it difficult to separate our emotion from our reason.

*e.* The reason for burying the second report is completely unknown.

*f.* The speed with which matters deteriorated took the government aback.

*g.* The motives behind the suppression of the second report are not 100% clear.

*h.* Doctors are born not made.

*i.* Learned people are more often than not superstitious.

*j.* No stone was left unturned to protect the future Project.

*k.* Criticism was levelled at the government for not acting more quickly to resolve the matter.

*l.* The reason for hushing up the previous report is generally unknown.

*m.* Everything has been done to make sure the Project will survive.

*n.* The overwhelming majority of people are incapable of keeping emotion apart from their rational side.

*o.* The qualities necessary to be a physician are not inherited, but taught.

*p.* It was raining as the train left.

*q.* Everything seems the same.

---

---

**Exercise 19:** An introduction to 'No'

---

This exercise helps you focus on the technique required to answer **No** in the **Yes/ No/ Not Given** type of question in the exam. As in the previous exercise, it is more important for you to learn the analytical process in this type of question than to find the correct answer. The exercise has, therefore, been designed in such a way that you need to hold information in your head while you try to find the correct answer. You may need to do the exercise several times.

In the column on the left, you have 9 texts. On the right, there are some words and phrases (**a-t**) are suitable parts of the text on the left with these words and phrases so that they disagree with or contradict the original texts. Some statements may be changed in more than one way. One cannot be changed.

One sentence has been done for you as an example. Try not to mark the text so that you can repeat the exercise.

| | |
|---|---|
| 1. The company made a *healthy* profit from the sale of its publishing arm. <br> *[ Answer = j]* | **a**    *duplicity* |
| | **b**    *unbelievably pessimistic* |
| | **c**    *atypical* |
| 2. Fertile fields flecked with blood-red poppies sped past the carriage window. | **d**    *police* |
| | **e**    *not sanguine enough* |
| 3. Re-negotiating the new treaty has been hampered by the fact that several of the governments involved are facing general elections at the present time. | **f**    *As he lay dying,* |
| | **g**    *deplorable* |
| 4. The behaviour of the policeman was commendable in all respects. | **h**    *advertising* |
| | **i**    *slightly covered* |
| 5. His honesty is typical of the new breed of politician. | **j**    *small* |
| 6. His predictions for the future of the welfare state in many European countries are seriously flawed. They are too optimistic to be credible. | **k**    *felt unbelievably optimistic* |
| | **l**    *crawled slowly by* |
| | **m**    *hindered* |
| 7. The story is obviously apocryphal. Nonetheless, it serves to illustrate the fears people have surrounding the problem. | **n**    *integrity* |
| | **o**    *true* |
| 8. In the very middle of his life, he found himself in the dark wood of despair. | **p**    *big loss* |
| | **q**    *have just won a plebiscite* |
| 9. Travelling with a purpose is better than travel for travel's sake. | **r**    *pessimistic* |
| | **s**    *leg* |
| | **t**    *old* |

---

---

**Exercise 20:** Meaning in a text

---

This exercise gives you some more practice with paraphrase at sentence level. Read through the passage below, which has 9 sentences. Then read the texts (**A–Q**), which follow, and replace each sentence below with one of the texts (**A-Q**) with the same meaning. There are more texts in the **list** than you can use.

(1) What is the difference between knowledge and experience? (2) Knowledge is basically information that is stored in the brain. (3) The process for this is one way - from an outside source like a book or the TV to the brain. (4) Experience is something altogether different. (5) It is a process whereby stored knowledge of any kind is moved around the brain. (6) Take learning to drive a car. (7) We can read all there is to know about driving, but until we start connecting and using the different pieces of knowledge we have acquired, the information is useless. (8) So, to make the information we have in our brains useful, we need to be able to manipulate it. (9) The examples are endless.

**List of texts**

- **A**   Information is basically knowledge we have learned or acquired.
- **B**   The difference between knowledge and experience.
- **C**   A good example here is learning to drive a car.
- **D**   Knowledge is not that different from experience.
- **E**   People need to be capable of applying the knowledge they have for it to be of any benefit.
- **F**   The number of examples is limited.
- **G**   Is there a difference between knowledge and experience?
- **H**   Experience is a very different animal.
- **I**   Experience entails moving different pieces of knowledge in the brain.
- **J**   Knowledge is not the same as experience.
- **K**   In this process, information in the brain is moved around, e.g. learning to drive.
- **L**   A basic definition of knowledge is information or facts that we have learned or acquired.
- **M**   Knowledge is an external resource.
- **N**   If we learn a lot of information about driving, but do not use it, the data are then useless.
- **O**   Knowledge is different from experience in that the former is a static, passive entity, whereas experience requires knowledge to be activated.
- **P**   People acquire knowledge from sources outside, not inside themselves.
- **Q**   This can be exemplified time and time again.

---

---

**Exercise 21:** 'Yes', 'No', or 'Not Given' 1

---

This exercise and the next one focus on the tricky question of deciding whether a statement in relation to a text is **Yes/ No/ Not Given**.

In the exercise below, each text is followed by three statements. For each alternative, write:

| Yes | if the statement agrees with the information in the text |
|-----|---------------------------------------------------------|
| No | if the statement contradicts the information in the text |
| Not Given | if it is impossible to say whether the statement agrees with or contradicts the information in the text |

1. *Many lecturers find their jobs very rewarding.*
   - a Many lecturers are well paid.
   - b All lecturers get something positive from their work.
   - c The majority of lecturers get satisfaction from their work.

2. *Computers are gaining in popularity, despite their cost.*
   - a Computers are getting cheaper.
   - b Computers are expensive.
   - c Computers used to be more popular than they are now.

3. *As a result of increasing affluence, an ever larger number of families now have two cars.*
   - a Most families nowadays have two cars.
   - b People are getting richer.
   - c Cars are becoming more expensive.

4. *Educational standards in schools have, in general, been gradually improving.*
   - a Schools have been getting better.
   - b The education in schools has not been improving.
   - c Educational standards are not as unsatisfactory as they used to be.

5. *In families, the traditional roles of men and women are often reversed if the man becomes unemployed.*
   - a Unemployment can affect the way that families operate.
   - b In families where the woman has a job, men and women usually have traditional roles.
   - c Unemployment does not affect the role of a man in the family.

6. *Although the hazards of boxing have been well publicised, the government has yet to introduce a total ban on the sport.*
   - a The government does not want to ban boxing.
   - b The hazards of boxing are not very well-known.
   - c A ban on boxing has not been introduced yet.

7. *There is as much money to be made from the sale of umbrellas on rainy days, as there is from cold drinks when the temperature rises.*
   - a Cold drinks sell well when it gets warmer.
   - b When it rains, older people buy umbrellas.
   - c The author is a shopkeeper.

8. *While it has been acknowledged for many years that an increasing number of animals are bound to become extinct, it is only recently that the problem has been addressed by politicians.*
   - a Recently people have been writing to our politicians about animals becoming extinct.
   - b We have known for a long time that more species of animals will disappear.
   - c Politicians have been fighting animal extinction for many years.

---

9. *Most people would be amazed if they realised how many different types of insect life exist in their very own garden.*

      a   The majority of gardeners are not surprised at the range of insect life in their garden.
      b   It is impossible to count the different types of insect life in a garden.
      c   There are more types of insect life in the average garden than most people think.

10. *In the busy modern world we live in, it is very easy to take for granted many of the things our forebears had to struggle to achieve: adequately heated housing and sufficient food on the table, to name but two.*

      a   In the past, not all houses were heated.
      b   Our lives are better than those of people in the past.
      c   Two things today are better than they used to be.

---

**Exercise 22:** 'Yes', 'No', or 'Not Given' 2

---

This exercise gives you further practice with deciding whether a statement is **Yes/ No/ Not Given**, but this time in longer texts.

In the exercise below, each text is followed by three statements.

For each alternative write:

| Yes | if the statement agrees with the information in the text |
| --- | --- |
| No | if the statement contradicts the information in the text |
| Not Given | if it is impossible to say whether the statement agrees with or contradicts the information in the text |

Read the text as quickly as you can, and then try to answer the statements without looking at the text again. If you find this too difficult, then read the text again.

1. *Good health is something that people assume is a right to which everybody should be entitled. However, the means of maintaining good health are not always at the disposal of every citizen, this particularly being the case in societies where a two-tier health service is in operation. The unfortunate consequence here is that the financially disadvantaged also tend to become disadvantaged in terms of the standard of health care they receive.*

      **a**   In some societies, the health care an individual receives depends on how wealthy you are.
      **b**   Poor people tend to have more health problems.
      **c**   Nearly everybody believes good health is a basic human right.

2. *For students in full-time education one of the major worries is how to make ends meet. Studying and, therefore, receiving no income, they need to obtain financial support from somewhere. The first option is, for those who are eligible, a government grant; although this may have to be paid back at a later date. Reliance on parental support or a bank loan are also possible avenues open to some, but not all, students. It is important, however, to match the financial arrangements carefully to the individual concerned.*

      **a**   Part-time students are not as anxious about money as full-time students.
      **b**   The author thinks that financial support from parents is easily available for most students.
      **c**   Full-time students have little money, because they do not work.

3. *The myriad of new sporting activities which have recently sprung up means that any individual who is considering taking up a different form of exercise is very much spoilt for choice. From scuba diving to skateboarding, and from abseiling to snow boarding, the young and fit throw themselves with enthusiasm into these new sporting pursuits. Caution, however, is to be advised for the hitherto unsporty individual,*

---

*who risks serious injury if physically unprepared for, or incapable of coping with, the physical challenges many such activities involve.*

   a   The writer thinks the sporting activities mentioned should be attempted only by young people.
   b   Many new sports are physically demanding.
   c   Recently there have not been many new sporting activities.

4.  *In any inner-city area, there are certain to be problems associated with a great number of people living in close proximity to each other. Whilst it may be possible for people in such communities to exist perfectly amicably, it is more common for there to be a certain amount of tension and animosity brooding beneath the surface. Flare-ups that result in injury, and even violent death, are not uncommon occurrences, as frequent newspaper reports bear witness.*

   a   People in inner-city, high-rise flats live in a permanent state of tension.
   b   Densely populated inner city areas are breeding grounds for all kinds of dubious activities.
   c   In inner city areas, tension has led to violent gun battles.

5.  *The taking of exams is a ritual that all students encounter throughout their academic career, whether it be at school level or at a higher academic level, for example, at college or university. Many theories and methods have been propounded as to the best way to ensure exam success, but all students need to be reminded that a consistent approach to studying is certainly not inconsequential in achieving exam success.*

   a   Exam success is a consequence of a consistent approach to studying.
   b   Passing exams is a problem only for pupils at school.
   c   Several hypotheses have been put forward about the best way to pass exams.

# Reading

# Test 1

You should spend about 20 minutes on **Questions 1–15**, which are based on **Passage 1** below.

# A rose by any other name would smell as sweet

In the past few years, the trend has been away from hybrid tea and floribunda roses towards shrub and species roses. While this change has, in part, been driven by recent fashions in garden design coupled with adroit marketing, there is no doubt that shrub and species roses offer a number of cultural advantages. Of course, there are aesthetic considerations too: some growers preferring the wide colour range and high-centred blooms of the hybrid teas, while others choose shrub roses, because they integrate more easily into an overall garden design. This is largely a question of taste and lies beyond the scope of the present article.

Before examining the cultural advantages of shrub roses, mention should be made of their diversity and antiquity. There are three distinct races of rose, which can be traced back to the Middle Ages: the gallicas, the albas, and the damasks. Gallica roses were first recorded in the 13th century, and probably the most famous of all, *Gallica officinalis*, is among the flowers depicted on the famous Ghent Altarpiece, painted by the Flemish artist Jan Van Eyck in the 14th century. Another gallica, *Rosa mundi*, with its characteristic red and white petals has been cultivated for at least six centuries. Albas too have a long history. *Alba × semiplena* is the world's oldest 'working' rose and is still grown in the Kazanluk region of Bulgaria for its highly scented petals, which are harvested each June to make the perfume, attar of roses. Damasks, as the name implies, were thought to have come from Damascus. Their origin is more obscure, but they are certainly related to wild roses still growing in parts of the Middle East and Iran. There are in cultivation more recently introduced varieties of roses too, such as Bourbons, hybrid musks, and hybrid perpetuals as well as rugosas, which originate in the Far East.

As a result of this genetic diversity, shrub roses have two major cultural advantages for the horticulturalist, and the amateur gardener: resistance to disease and tolerance of a wide variety of climate and soil types. Many shrub roses show resistance to fungal diseases such as black spot and rust, to which hybrid teas are highly susceptible. Rugosas are particularly disease-free. In poor soil conditions, shrub roses, having deep vigorous root systems, are more tolerant of drought and do not suffer to the same extent from nutrient deficiency diseases. For the horticulturalist, this means that less time and money need be spent on applying fertilisers or spraying for disease. Similarly, there are some shrub roses which will grow well in shady or windy conditions, or even against a north-facing wall. Large specimen shrubs may be found growing happily in the most unpromising situations.

However, there are other practical issues to consider. Where space is at a premium, it is important to remember that the majority of shrub roses, which do not require regular hard pruning in order to encourage them to flower, will eventually grow into large bushes up to two metres high, with a spread of two to three metres. For small gardens, hybrid teas, rarely growing more than one metre tall, are more practical. The size and density of shrub roses can, however, be an advantage where a large permanent bush is required. Some varieties are sufficiently dense as to be suitable for hedging.

Another factor is length of flowering period. Many shrub roses have a short, but spectacular flowering season. The famous old rose *Cuisse de Nymphe*, for example, is covered in succulent pink blossom for about a month in midsummer, but does not bloom again. There are, however, other varieties, which are repeat or perpetual flowering, including *Madame Isaac Pereire*, probably the most intensely fragrant rose of all. Moreover, there are a number of varieties with attractive ferny foliage and graceful, arching habit. This contrasts with the upright stance and coarse leathery leaves of hybrid teas. Species roses also produce bright red fruits (hips) in September–October, and their leaves often acquire attractive autumn tints.

All these factors need to be taken into consideration when choosing a rose for a particular site. Shrub roses are long-lived, easy to propagate, and require less pruning and maintenance than a hybrid tea. A detailed catalogue of varieties will give details of colour, flowering period, size, preferences of soil and aspect, optimum planting times, and general cultural requirements.

## QUESTIONS 1– 6

Use **NO MORE THAN THREE WORDS** from the passage to complete each blank in the diagram below.

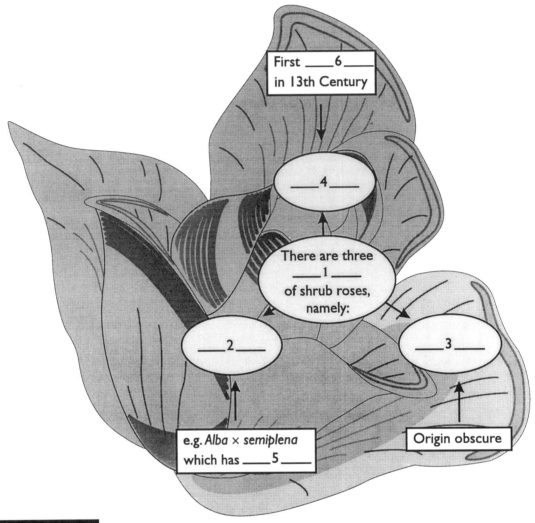

First _____6_____ in 13th Century

_____4_____

There are three _____1_____ of shrub roses, namely:

_____2_____

_____3_____

e.g. *Alba* × *semiplena* which has _____5_____

Origin obscure

## QUESTIONS 7–13

Complete the text below, which is a summary of paragraphs 3, 4 and 5. Choose your answers from the **Word List** below the summary and write them in **Boxes 7–13** on your answer sheet.

There are more words or phrases than spaces, so you will not be able to use them all. You may use each word or phrase only once.

**Factors governing the choice of rose**

Example:     The _____ (Example) _____ of shrub roses can be an advantage when a
             large permanent bush is required.

Answer:      size

There are different types of shrub roses, some of which are able to resist disease and others which suit diverse climates and soils, features that are of _____(7)_____ to both horticulturalists and gardeners, as, in the long run, such adaptability saves both time and money. The _size_(8)_also_ is another factor that needs to be taken into account when choosing a rose. _most_(9)_benefit_ shrub roses _____(10)_____ without having to be cut back regularly. In fact, they can _____(11)_____ grow to a height of nearly two metres and up to three metres _____(l2)_____. So for small gardens hybrid teas are more practical, because they rarely grow more than one metre tall. The length of the flowering season also _____(13)_____ the choice of rose, as does the shape of the plant.

### Word List

| | | |
|---|---|---|
| gives | across | spread |
| most | beneficial | spacing |
| majority | slowly | over |
| in the end | also | circumference |
| area available | dictates | blossom |
| benefit | always | advantage |
| | | size |

## QUESTIONS 14 & 15

Choose the appropriate letters **A–D** and write them in **Boxes 14 & 15** on your answer sheet.

**14.**    Which of the statements below is true about *Madame Isaac Pereire*?

    **A**    It is one of the most fragrant roses of all roses.

    **B**    It is impossible to say whether the writer is talking about shrub roses or all roses when he says it is probably the most intensely fragrant rose of all.

    **C**    It is probably the most intensely fragrant shrub rose.

    **D**    It flowers only once per year.

**15.**    The flowering season of shrub roses ...

    **A**    is short but spectacular.

    **B**    is repetitive.

    **C**    is perpetual.

    **D**    varies.

You should spend about 20 minutes on **Questions 16–29**, which are based on **Passage 2** below.

# Road rage all the rage!

To many people the term 'Road Rage' describes a relatively modern concept of drivers 'getting worked up due to some incident whilst on the road and resorting to physical violence or damage to property'. Most people would say that this has only really become a problem in the last five years or so. It has certainly attracted great media interest in recent times, but it has, in fact, been part of motoring for quite some time now.

A psychologist, employed by the Royal Automobile Club (RAC), defines 'Road Rage', thus: 'unchecked behaviour designed to cause harm to another road user; behaviour which is not normally in the behavioural repertoire of the person. 'Road Rage' is an altering of an individual's personality whilst driving caused by a process of dehumanisation. This dehumanisation is caused by road use frustrations and an artificial sense of insulation, protection and empowerment provided by the car. This leads the person to behave in a way designed to cause harm or endanger other road users'.

Most motorists can remember an occasion at some time in their motoring career when an impatient, or short-tempered, driver has 'cut them or someone else up' with an aggressive display of driving, forcing the victim to take evasive action to avoid a collision. At the time, they probably thought: what a dreadful piece of driving; and mentally clapped themselves on the back for being such controlled, calm drivers. Media attention, focused on particularly gruesome incidents, has bestowed a certain notoriety on this sort of driving. As a professional driver in inner London and a motorcycle instructor, I have witnessed such driving all too often over the years.

The 1996 Lex Report on motoring, published by Lex Service PLC, the UK's leading vehicle retailing and leasing group, provides us with some startling statistics. In the last 12 months, there have been: 1.8 million instances of people who have been forced to pull over or off the road; 800,000 instances of people being physically threatened; 500,000 people in their cars being deliberately driven into; 250,000 people attacked by other drivers; and 250,000 people having their cars deliberately damaged by another driver. A survey also carried out by Lex confirms that up to 80% of motorists have been the victims of 'Road Rage' and that driver confrontation is on the increase.

The RAC has also much to say on the topic. One of their surveys reveals that as many as 90% of motorists have suffered at the hands of seriously anti-social drivers and that the effects upon them have in many cases been wholly disproportionate to the level of threat or actual violence inflicted.

The examples are both chilling and legion: a driver had his nose bitten off following a row with another motorist; a 78 year-old man was killed after being punched by a man half his age; an RAC patrolman, flagged down on the motorway by a motorist, was violently assaulted and verbally abused by the motorist. The list goes on and on ...

The 1991 Road Traffic Act takes a very dim view indeed of dangerous and careless driving and, as with assaults, provides stiff

**A book for IELTS**

custodial sentences for those guilty of such crimes. To date, however, there is no such offence in the statute books known as 'Road Rage'. There can be assaults or criminal damage, followed or preceded by dangerous driving, but no offence that incorporates both – a change in the law which the public are clamouring for in the face of increasing anarchy on the roads.

Conversely, the Association of Chief Police Officers denies that 'Road Rage' exists; or, indeed, that there is a trend. There have been suggestions from the same quarter that 'media interest and reporting are, in fact, creating the problem by causing unnecessary anxiety in the minds of the motoring public in a direct analogy with fear of crime'.

Most of us probably imagine violence on the road to be an entirely male preserve, as men are naturally more competitive and aggressive, especially when it comes to driving. Melanie Flowers of Oxford Brookes University, however, has the following to say: 'Women can be more aggressive in cars than they ever would be when they are walking along the street. In fact, you could even argue that smaller or weaker people, who might be victims when they are out of their cars, often feel they can even things up a bit when they are behind the wheel. When you are driving you're judged by your car rather than your physical attributes. It makes some women feel stronger than they really are'.

An interesting study, but how often do you see women fighting at the roadside or kicking in body panels?

If all this is a general reflection of the driver of the 90s, then the professionals have an uphill struggle. But they are tackling the problem head on. The RAC and Auto Express, a motoring journal, have joined forces in a Campaign Against Rage (CAR). They aim to promote driver courtesy, offer advice on avoiding 'Road Rage', and even Rage Rehabilitation for violent offenders in an attempt to avoid re-offence.

The courts are looking at stiffer penalties. And the RAC is suggesting that sign-posting be improved to try and stop city drivers losing their way, a constant source of annoyance and aggression, and they have also proposed the introduction of variable message signs that can help improve driver behaviour. Some police traffic control cars are now equipped with these message signs on the roof or rear of their vehicles.

And the future? The Autoclass survey, published in 1997, shows that parents are creating the next generation of road-ragers. The research among 10–16 year-olds found that 62 per cent of fathers and 55 per cent of mothers get angry while driving.

One thing is a certainty: the Road Rage phenomenon is not going to disappear overnight, even after stiffer sentencing or improved driver training.

## QUESTIONS 16 & 17

Using the information in the passage, complete the table below. Write your answers in **Boxes 16 & 17** on your answer sheet.

| **Percentage of motorists affected by Road Rage** |
| --- |
| The Lex Report – up to _____**16**_____ % |
| RAC Survey – up to _____**17**_____ % |

## QUESTIONS 24–27

Do the statements agree with the information in **Reading Passage 2**? In Boxes **18–23**, write:

| | |
|---|---|
| **Yes** | if the statement agrees with the information in the passage |
| **No** | if the statement contradicts the information in the passage |
| **Not Given** | if there is no information about the statement in the passage |

> **Example :** The Lex Report was published in 1997.
> **Answer:** No

18. Road Rage is not in itself a violation of the law.

19. According to a psychologist employed by the RAC, cars give their drivers an unreal feeling of being safe.

20. Motorcycling is an exciting, but safe mode of transport.

21. The Lex Report states that the incidence of conflicts between drivers is rising rapidly.

22. The survey on Road Rage carried out by the RAC is very thorough.

23. According to the writer, Road Rage is a relatively modern phenomenon.

## QUESTIONS 24–27

Using **NO MORE THAN THREE WORDS** from the passage, complete the sentences below.

24. Professionals face an _____ in their fight against Road Rage.

25. _____ are being considered by the law courts.

26. Violent behaviour by motorists is, in all probability, considered by many to be exclusively a _____.

27. The Association of Chief Police Officers attributes the problem of Road Rage to media _____.

## QUESTIONS 28 & 29

Choose the appropriate letters **A–D** and write them in **Boxes 27 & 28** on your answer sheet.

28. Melanie Flowers of Oxford Brookes University states that ...

   A   cars make women stronger.

   B   cars frequently make women more combative than usual.

   C   cars sometimes make women less meek than they would be on the street.

   D   small women feel as meek in cars as they do outside.

29. The writer's view of the eradication of 'Road Rage' can be summarised as follows:

   A   optimistic.

   B   pessimistic.

   C   depressed.

   D   too pessimistic.

You should spend about 20 minutes on **Questions 30-40**, which are based on **Passage 3** below.

# 900 YEARS: THE RESTORATIONS OF WESTMINSTER ABBEY

**A.** The exhibition in the summer of 1995 illustrated how Westminster Abbey has been transformed over the past nine centuries. Both its structure and its contents have been changed and changed about, but the identity of the building has never been lost. This process of change deserves chronicling as a subject in its own right, not as an apologetic footnote explaining why certain original features have been modified. For those of the Gothic Revival, such as William Morris, even by the 1890s the exterior of the Abbey had been 'damaged so vitally... that we have nothing left us but a mere outline, a ghost'. The 'ghost' has proved remarkably robust, the latest century of its history encompassing both aerial attack and painstaking restoration. This is a story worth telling.

**B.** Restoration, according to the meaning we give it today as a self-conscious process of repair and reinstatement of earlier features, only came to the Abbey at the end of the seventeenth century, with the campaign of comprehensive repair devised and carried out by Christopher Wren and his successors. This programme of work, covering the entire building both inside and out and setting out deliberately to respect the style of the original structure, was exceptional for its date, not only in England but anywhere in Europe.

**C.** Restoration can also be used in a wider sense to cover a process of renovation whereby the original fabric is replaced to a different design and in a different style, but respecting the meaning and ethos of the building. A famous example was the replacement by Bramante of the Early Christian basilica of St Peter's in Rome with his Renaissance design, not regarded then as an act of vandalism, but as a restatement of the significance of the building for a new age. The continuing vitality of an institution can be said to be expressed better by refashioning its buildings in a fresh style, rather than by patching up the old. It is in this way that the replacement of Edward the Confessor's Romanesque abbey church (11th century) by Henry III (13th century) in the up-to-date Gothic style can be considered as a work of restoration, not as a new building.

**D.** The meaning of restoration at Westminster can be vividly illustrated by an unexpected example: the history of the effigy of Queen Elizabeth I. This figure was dismissed for years as a second-rate eighteenth-century copy of the original. Indeed, the exterior of the Abbey has been regarded in a similar way. However, in the effigy as in the building, not only is the eighteenth-century interpretation of the earlier period important in its own right, but the early fabric turns out to remain at the heart. The effigy acquired a new head and new clothes in 1760, not through insensitive vandalism, but to show off Elizabeth's central role in the Abbey's history more effectively, just as Wren and Nicholas Hawksmoor had refaced the fabric of the building a few decades before. To try to strip away the contribution of later generations in order to reveal some mythical prime original is a profound misunderstanding of Westminster's rich complexity.

**E.** The relationship between the historical overview depicted in the exhibition and the restoration work in progress seen in the adjacent Mason's Yard was vital to the exhibition. The two parts gave meaning to each other: the historical context gave validity to the current works, showing how this process of organic renewal has been present at the Abbey from the start, while the display of work in progress brought vividly to life the physical reality of the works exhibited.

## QUESTIONS 30–33

Choose one phrase (i–x) from the **List of phrases** to complete each key point below. Write the appropriate letters (i–x) in **Boxes 30–33** on your answer sheet.

The information in the completed sentences should be an accurate summary of the points made by the writer.

NB. There are more phrases (i–x) than sentences, so you will not need to use them all. You may use each phrase once only.

30.   The effigy of Queen Elizabeth I was  ...

31.   The Renaissance design for St Peter's was  ...

32.   A comprehensive assessment of the past was  ...

33.   A narrow, modern meaning of restoration states that it is  ...

---

### List of Phrases

| | |
|---|---|
| i | regarded as an act of vandalism. |
| ii | completely restored in 1760. |
| iii | retaining the original design. |
| iv | at the time considered appropriate. |
| v | a method of repairing and reintroducing characteristics from earlier times. |
| vi | a poor replica of the original. |
| vii | as important as the work exhibits in the Mason's yard. |
| viii | the validity of the current works. |
| ix | respecting the original structure and ethos of a building. |
| x | for a long time considered a poor replica of the original. |

---

## QUESTIONS 34–36

Choose the appropriate letter **A–D** and write them in **Boxes 34–36** on your answer sheet.

34.   At the end of the seventeenth century the Abbey was  ...

    **A**   thoroughly repaired.

    **B**   conscientiously repaired.

    **C**   designed by Sir Christopher Wren.

    **D**   unusual for buildings of the time.

35.   Which of the following has the Abbey retained through centuries of change?

    **A**   structure and contents.

    **B**   original features.

    **C**   identity.

    **D**   outline.

---

**36.** The writer believes that it is better ...

    **A**    to remove the work of later generations to expose the original features of a building.

    **B**    not to remove the work of later generations to expose the original features of a building.

    **C**    to reveal the mythical original architecture of a building.

    **D**    to enhance the rich complexity of a building.

## QUESTIONS 37–40

Reading Passage 3 has 5 paragraphs (**A–E**). Choose the most suitable heading for each paragraph from the **List of Headings** below. Write the appropriate numbers (**i–xi**) in **Boxes 37–40** on your answer sheet.

One of the headings has been done for you as an example.

NB. There are more headings than paragraphs, so you will not use all of them.

    **37.**    **Paragraph A**

    **38.**    **Paragraph B**

    **39.**    **Paragraph C**

    **40.**    **Paragraph D**

Example: **Paragraph E**

Answer: **vii**

| | **List of Headings** |
|---|---|
| **i** | Bramante's artistic and architectural skills |
| **ii** | A royal example |
| **iii** | Restoration in Europe |
| **iv** | The importance of recording change |
| **v** | An extensive and unusual scheme |
| **vi** | Keeping the meaning |
| **vii** | History alongside progress |
| **viii** | Hawksmoor's effect on the Abbey |
| **ix** | Wren and Hawksmoor at the Abbey |
| **x** | A summer exhibition |
| **xi** | An organic renewal |

# Reading

## Test 2

You should spend about 20 minutes on **Questions 1–14**, which are based on **Passage 1** below.

# Translation: from the sublime to the ridiculous?

According to the *Oxford Dictionary*, 'to translate' is 'to express the sense in or into another language'. But what is 'the sense' really? Translating a piece of writing is not just a question of picking up the foreign language dictionary and substituting one set of words for another. Although it represents the substitution of a set of words from one lexicon for those from another, it is ultimately a form of communication, concerned, as Peter Newmark says, with transmitting culture and truth. For this reason, a translation should only be attempted after the translator has carefully studied the whole text, and asked herself a number of questions.

Firstly, it is important that she considers the purpose of the said text. Insofar as all writing is a form of communication, does this particular text aim – user instructions for a household appliance, for example – simply to transmit information to a would-be user? Or does it strive – an advertisement or hotel brochure or any other piece of publicity material – to arouse interest so that the reader will want to buy the product, or stay in the hotel? Or is its purpose – like that of a piece of literature, or a film – to stimulate the imagination, to inspire and to entertain – as well as, perhaps, to instruct?

Once she has ascertained the purpose of the text, the translator needs to consider who the readers of the translated text will be. The readers of the translation will, of necessity, comprise a different group from the readers of the original – but they are likely to share certain characteristics. If the original text was aimed at a wide audience – the 'man in the street' anxious to get to grips with his new coffee-maker, for example – then the reader of the translated text is likely to fall into the same category and have the same expectations. But perhaps the original was aimed at a more discrete and well-defined group, perhaps by its style and content it has defined its readership.

Will the reader of the translation be someone with a good knowledge of the culture from which the original has sprung, or will he be someone with a very sparse knowledge of it? It has been said that everything is translatable 'on condition that the two languages belong to cultures that have reached a comparable degree of development'; how up-to-date will he be with the requisite technical knowledge? Balancing the expectations of the potential readers with those of the writer is, in this way, part of the tightrope which the translator treads; it will dictate, for example, the extent to which annotations and footnotes will be needed in the translation, and the way in which culturally-specific references and items of specialist vocabulary are (or are not) translated.

The *style and register* of the translated text should, for reasons of integrity and coherence, mirror that of the original. It would be misleading if the translator of a text written in a discursive and amusing style were to render it ponderous in translation; just as it would be wrong for a translator to over-simplify what was originally an erudite piece of prose. However, this is not to ignore the fact that there might well be instances in which a text – awkwardly written in the original – could be made more accessible by the translator. It is a question of judgement.

The style in which something is written often represents a large part of what the writer is trying to convey, and this is particularly likely to be the case with a work of literature, such as a poem or novel: it is not only what the writer is saying, but how she says it which is important. Allusions, deliberate ambiguity, humour, parody, and language which contains alliteration and assonance, are likely to be features of such a text, and to represent problems which the translator needs to solve appropriately. To that extent, translating is rather like doing a jigsaw puzzle. Other kinds of writing – a piece of advertising, for example – may well contain subliminal messages to which the translator will need to be alert – as to any kind of 'sub-text'.

Much translation is, by default, given to those with an inadequate grasp of either the source or target language – and often of both. It is frequently overlooked that the successful translator needs an excellent knowledge of the source language and a perfect mastery of the target language in its technical and colloquial aspects. The target language, for the best results, should be her mother-tongue but, as Peter Newmark says, many translators who translate out of their own language 'contribute greatly to many people's hilarity in the process.' So, for example, it once happened that 'la sagesse normande' became, in English, 'Norman wisdom'.

## QUESTIONS 1–3

Complete the sentences below with information from the reading passage. You may use **NO MORE THAN THREE WORDS** for each answer.

1.  Translating a text is more than merely _____ for others.

2.  Each text whether informative, stimulating or instructive has _____ that the translator needs to take into account.

3.  The reader of the translation may have only a _____ knowledge of the culture from which the original comes.

## QUESTIONS 4–6

Choose the appropriate letters **A–D** and write them in **Boxes 4–6** on your answer sheet.

4.  Anything can be translated, provided that ...

    **A**   the two languages are equally developed.

    **B**   the two languages have similar levels of cultural development.

    **C**   the translator is up-to-date.

    **D**   the translator has the same expectations as the reader.

5.  According to the writer, it is sometimes possible to make a translation ...

    **A**   clearer than the original.

    **B**   overly simple.

    **C**   humorous.

    **D**   ponderous.

6.  When translating a literary text, which one of the following is important for the translator?

    **A**   The way in which a writer says something as much as the content.

    **B**   Subliminal messages.

    **C**   Allusions.

    **D**   Jigsaw puzzles in texts.

## QUESTIONS 7–10

The writer mentions a number of **Judgements** that need to be made by the translator. Which **Four** of the **Judgements** below are mentioned? Write your answers **(A–H)** in **Boxes 7–10** on your answer sheet.

7.    _____

8.    _____

9.    _____

10.   _____

---

**List of Judgements**

A    Weighing up why a writer says what she says.

B    Determining the importance of poetry.

C    Making a decision as to how far to stick to the original.

D    Judging who the target audience of a translation will be.

E    Whether translating is best done from the mother tongue.

F    Deciding how many explanations, footnotes and comments on vocabulary to include.

G    Deciding on which information to use from dictionaries.

H    Whether to oversimplify a text.

---

## QUESTIONS 11–14

Answer the questions below using information from the passage. You may use **NO MORE THAN THREE WORDS** from the passage for each answer. Write your answers in **Boxes 11–14** on your answer sheet.

11.   Translation is a form of communication; what does it, in essence, transmit?

12.   What do readers of a translation and readers of the original text often share?

13.   Which aspects of the translated text should reflect the original?

14.   What, according to the text, should a translator look at carefully before trying to do a translation?

You should spend about 20 minutes on **QUESTIONS 15–29,** which are based on **Passage 2** below.

# A buzz in the world of chemistry

A.  For the past few years, one of the buzz terms in the pharmaceutical, agrochemical and biotechnology industries has been 'combinatorial chemistry'. Surf the net and find thousands of references to it. Read any of the general science weeklies, such as *Nature* or *New Scientist*, and every few issues, another worthy author is going to save the 21st century from everything nasty with this miraculous technology. Some of the more specialist journals have even devoted whole issues to reviewing combinatorial chemistry.

B.  These reviews all have the same format. First, there is a section from the Research and Development Director of a major chemical company, a person who has not worked at the bench for years, if not decades. This is filled with business-speak; the jargon keeps the shareholders happy and makes them proud to own a bit of something at the forefront of science. Section two is from a director of a venture capital funded synthetic chemistry company located on a green field site, probably in a portacabin, or, perhaps, in a new business park, rent free for the first five years from the local authority of a small town no one has heard of. He discusses the molecular modelling packages that they are using to build 'virtual' libraries containing millions of compounds. The third section is by someone who, in fact, practises combinatorial chemistry and who has developed automated systems to do the syntheses and to assay the products. They can probably synthesise a few thousand compounds per week.

C.  We know that organic chemistry is the chemistry of carbon, biochemistry the chemistry of life and physical chemistry the application of physics to chemical behaviour. What then is combinatorial chemistry?

D.  Combinatorial chemistry is a branch of synthetic organic chemistry. We all remember mathematics classes at school just before the end of term when we were given silly sums to do: How many ways can five differently coloured beads be arranged on a string? (120). Maths teachers call these permutation and combination problems; hence, combinatorial chemistry.

E.  After the development of solid phase peptide synthesis in the 1960s by Merrifield, soon synthetic peptide chemists were also doing permutation and combination sums. There are 20 naturally occurring amino acids, the building blocks of peptides and proteins, the workhorse molecules of life. How many ways can these be arranged, or chemically bonded, to synthesise novel peptides which might be put to any number of uses in the pharmacy? If we take just one molecule of each of the 20 amino acids and join them together to form a peptide, we find that we can arrange these in 20! or $2.432902008177 \times 10^{18}$ ways. Nature knows no such restraint; it can use multiple copies of each amino acid, and so can synthesise $20^{20}$ or $1.048576 \times 10^{26}$ twenty amino acid peptides. Proteins contain hundreds of amino acids. The numbers of possible sequences are truly innumerable!

F.  They become even more so when one considers the other polymeric molecules of life: the lipids, carbohydrates and nucleic acids.

G.  Classically trained synthetic chemists strive for purity. One remembers twelve years ago a chemist synthesising a 20 residue peptide. He went off to the lab, was ever so busy, producing a different high performance liquid chromatography (HPLC) trace every few days to show his biologist customers how the reactions were progressing. A few months after the request was placed, the biologists were given a few milligrams of their desired peptide and half a rain forest worth of HPLC printout!

H.  That was fine when only one product was sought. Now the demand is for thousands of products to satisfy the automated high-through-put screening systems employed by the major pharmaceutical companies. How can this be achieved?

I.  Let us consider solid phase synthesis strategies. In these, the compound of interest is synthesised on a solid support, a resin bead. These beads are typically 100 microns in diameter and made from cross-linked polyvinyl benzene or polyethylene glycol polymers.

J.  Using the Tea-bag method, developed by Houghten in the 1980s, typically about 100 mg of the 100 micron beads are put into polypropylene mesh sacs which have a 75 micron mesh size. These are thermally sealed closed and the synthesis takes place on the resin beads within the sac. During the synthesis reaction cycles, the sacs are transferred from reagent pot to pot in sequence, and at the end of the synthesis, the product is cleaved off the bead, characterised and purified as need be. Using this strategy, one needs to use a separate sac for each compound to be synthesised and automated systems have now been developed for multiple sac manipulation.

K.  The sensitivity of compound analytical techniques has developed apace with the technology, and whereas, in the 1980s, one required several millimoles of product to characterise, now this can be done with femtomoles or in some cases attomoles ($10^{-18}$ moles)! Therefore, one need only recover product from 1 bead, about 2–3 picomoles. Automated systems are now being developed to synthesise on single magnetic beads using only 2–3 nanolitres of reagent per cycle. When the 'classical' Tea-bag strategy was developed, 100 millilitres per cycle were considered to be a phenomenal solvent cost-cutting exercise.

L.    The development of high-through-put automated screening has demanded from synthetic chemistry large arrays or libraries of compounds to satisfy the investment made in installing these systems. Will combinatorial chemistry be able to meet this demand? Are the syntheses well enough developed to meet this? Peptide and oligonucleotide solid phase strategies have been well developed over the past 30 years. Will solution methods and other novel chemistries be able to keep apace? Can 'virtual' chemicals be used to remedy 'real' problems? After all, we are living in a real world.

## QUESTIONS 15–20

Complete the text below, which is a summary of paragraphs **A–E**. Choose your answers from the **Word List** and write them in **Boxes 15–20** on your answer sheet.

> Example:    **There is a wealth of_____ (Example) _____ to combinatorial chemistry on the Internet.**
> Answer:    **references**

There are more words than spaces, so you will not be able to use them all. You may use each word only once.

**How Combinatorial Chemistry began**

Combinatorial chemistry as an _____15_____ of synthetic organic chemistry has been very much _____16_____ in recent years, _____17_____ in a plethora of articles written by experts in the field. Moreover, all the reviews in specialist publications _____18_____ the same formula. But what about the origin of combinatorial chemistry? It comes from permutation and combination problems in mathematics. _____19_____ solid phase peptide synthesis was developed, synthetic peptide chemists started doing similar calculations as well. The 20 naturally occurring amino acids provided them with _____20_____ possibilities.

### Word List

| | | |
|---|---|---|
| known | in vogue | appearing |
| limitless | in the air | once |
| offspring | until | doubled |
| usually follow | offshoot | limited |
| as | follow religiously | references |

## QUESTIONS 21–25

Look at **paragraphs I and J** which describe the **Tea-bag method.** Using the information in the passage, complete the flow chart below. Write your answers in **Boxes 21– 25** on your answer sheet. Use **NO MORE THAN THREE WORDS** for each answer.

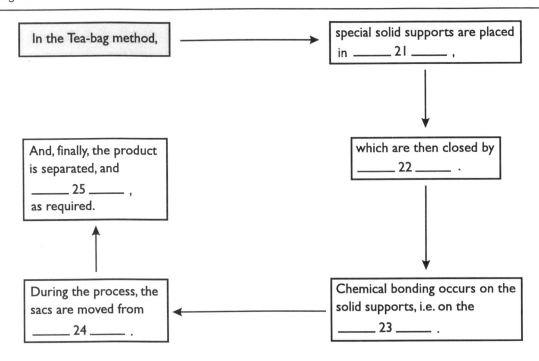

In the Tea-bag method, → special solid supports are placed in _____ 21 _____ ,

which are then closed by _____ 22 _____ .

Chemical bonding occurs on the solid supports, i.e. on the _____ 23 _____ .

During the process, the sacs are moved from _____ 24 _____ .

And, finally, the product is separated, and _____ 25 _____ , as required.

## QUESTIONS 26–28

Below is a list of the regular types of contributor to combinatorial chemistry reviews. Which **three** contributors are described by the writer? Write your answers **A–F** in the order they occur in the text in **Boxes 26–28** on the answer sheet.

A    A director of a technology business park.

B    Someone who is from a major company and involved directly in research.

C    Someone who is involved in the new technology of combinatorial chemistry.

D    An amateur chemist who synthesises thousands of compounds per week.

E    The director of a small, obscurely located and investment funded operation.

F    An out-of-practice director of some major chemical enterprise.

## QUESTION 29

Choose the appropriate letter (**A–D**) and write it in **Box 29** on your answer sheet.

29.    Physical chemistry ...

A    deals with the way physics is applied to chemical behaviour.

B    is closely connected with organic chemistry.

C    deals with the way chemistry is applied to physical behaviour.

D    led to the development of combinatorial chemistry.

You should spend about 20 minutes on **Questions 30–41**, which are based on **Passage 3** below.

# Ice and Fire

The poet W.H. Auden once wrote: 'To me Iceland is sacred soil. Its memory is a constant background to what I am doing. It is a permanent part of my existence. I could say that Iceland is the sun colouring the mountains without being anywhere in sight, even sunk beyond the horizon ...'. The extraordinary and lasting effect that this small island of 270,000 inhabitants invariably has on its visitors is as enigmatic as the land itself. Those once intoxicated by it are likely to become addicts for life; those who recoil in horror at the bleak lava fields, which surround its airport, may never return.

Iceland is as distant in topographical character, modes of life and attitudes from its Nordic neighbours on the Scandinavian mainland as it is geographically. Isolated far north-west in the North Atlantic, its real neighbours are Greenland and the Arctic ice-cap. Far from the forested mountains of Norway or the flat lakes of Finland, its geologically young landscape is constantly being carved by the activity of ice and fire. Volcanoes, glaciers and 700 years of Danish colonial rule have impoverished the land, but enriched the human spirit.

In its cultural history, Iceland has enjoyed no heritage of court patronage, no interfertilisation with the European Renaissance, Baroque or Enlightenment. Yet, from the first murmurings of national affirmation in the latter half of the nineteenth century to full independence in 1944, cultural activity has sprung up like the geysers which shoot high from the country's geothermal energy sources just under the earth's crust.

Reykjavik can now boast as many as 60 musical events per month; it has two lively theatres, an opera company and a flourishing and internationally respected film industry. Much Icelandic art articulates the sense of danger felt in living in a country with at least 30 live volcanoes: when one erupted under a glacier in the autumn of 1996, the subsequent flooding swept away roads and bridges to the tune of six million pounds. And, despite a sophisticated system of damage limitation, maverick avalanches can destroy entire settlements.

Stubbornness, a superiority complex which can, in moments of crisis or loss of confidence, quietly veer towards its opposite, and a laconically oblique view of life characterises the typical Icelander, if such a creature exists. A determination to protect and develop a language basically unchanged since the time of the Sagas has led Iceland to coin its own new words for telephone, television, radio and computer. When gas pipes are laid, the homes of elves and trolls are respectfully by-passed.

One such detour is there for those who have eyes to see on the main route from the airport to Reykjavik city centre. Nobody, though, should feel intimidated. Regular buses connect all towns and settlements around the country's main ring-road: the central wilderness, stunning in its landscape of black volcanic desert and brown glacial moraines, can be traversed only for a few weeks in the summer, when the snow has melted but floods have abated. Few rivers there have bridges.

Four-wheel-drive vehicles, careful research, a good radio, and a sense of humour are essential travelling companions – unless, like the first travellers to Iceland, including William Morris and W.H. Auden, a convoy of sturdy Icelandic horses is preferred. And, as the old saying goes: 'If you get lost in an Icelandic forest, just stand up.'

## QUESTION 30

Choose the appropriate letter **A–D** and write it in **Box 30** on your answer sheet.

30.  Which of the following is true concerning transport on Iceland?

    A    All the settlements and towns in Iceland are linked by four-wheel-drive vehicles.
    B    Sturdy Icelandic horses are needed to get round all parts of Iceland.
    C    All the settlements and towns on the main ring-road are linked by a bus service.
    D    A fleet of coaches serves the entire island.

## QUESTIONS 31–36

Do the statements below agree with the information given by the writer in **Reading Passage 3**?

In **boxes 31-36**, write:

    **Yes**          if the statement agrees with the information in the passage
    **No**           if the statement contradicts the information in the passage
    **Not Given**    if no information is given about the statement in the passage

31.  The natural features of Iceland are in a state of continual transformation.
32.  Iceland is a Danish colony.
33.  Iceland is not dissimilar, from the topographical point of view, to Scandinavian countries on the continent.
34.  Some people are horrified by the starkness of the landscape around the airport.
35.  The majority of people who visit Iceland are intoxicated by it for life.
36.  The author is intoxicated by Iceland.

## QUESTIONS 37–39

Answer the questions below using **NO MORE THAN FOUR WORDS** from the passage.

37.  What is the state of the Icelandic movie business?
38.  To what is the growth of cultural activity in recent decades compared?
39.  What does much Icelandic art reflect about life in Iceland?

## QUESTIONS 40 & 41

Complete the sentences below. You may use **NO MORE THAN THREE WORDS** taken directly from the passage, or based on the information in the passage.

40.  Avalanches can destroy entire settlements, although a system has been set up to _____.
41.  Icelanders are intent on _____ their language.

# Reading

# Test 3

You should spend about 20 minutes on **Questions 1–15**, which are based on **Passage 1** below.

# THE ALEXANDER TECHNIQUE AND DISABILITY

A.  The Alexander Technique is a method of psychophysical re-education developed by F. Matthias Alexander more than a century ago, initially as a result of trying to solve a vocal problem. It is a technique for the elimination of ingrained habits of 'misuse' that interfere with the healthy and harmonious functioning of ourselves as a whole, often the underlying cause of many conditions, such as back pain, neck and shoulder tension, fatigue, breathing disorders and other stress-related illnesses.

B.  Our natural reflex mechanisms for balance and posture are largely dependent on the co-ordination of the head, neck and back. The Technique addresses the causes of 'misuse' and lack of poise that may be interfering with this relationship. When these mechanisms are allowed to work in harmony, 'good use' spontaneously returns, resulting in easier breathing, freer, lighter movement and a greater ability to control our reactions and our movements. In other words, the Technique enables us to 'use' ourselves better, and, in that sense, is concerned with helping anybody – the so called 'able bodied' as well as disabled people to overcome their disabilities. Hence, the Alexander teacher's approach when working with the disabled is, in essence, the same as with any pupil of the Technique.

C.  For example, if we take a violinist with a 'misuse' problem of the upper limbs causing technical limitations to his or her playing, the Alexander teacher will work on improving the pupil's overall 'use' by encouraging the inhibition of the habitual muscular tension pattern that interferes with the co-ordination of the head/neck/back relationship in order to enable him/her to play with more ease. Similarly, when working with a pupil who has lost mobility in the left arm from a stroke, the teacher will first of all address the head/neck/back relationship, and the inhibition of extraneous tension that prevents maximum use of the affected limb. In this way, it is possible to enable the stroke patient to retrain mobility of the paralysed part of the body.

D.  The approach and what results can be expected vary greatly depending on the disability. For the stroke patient, especially if lessons are commenced early after the stroke, the Alexander Technique can play an important role in rehabilitation and mobility retraining. With a blind person, the work is likely to focus instead more directly on eliminating tension habits that have developed to compensate for the loss of sight, e.g. insecurity leading to stiff and overcautious walking, balancing difficulties and poor head poise.

E.  Working with the disabled pupil, the Alexander teacher can offer help with everyday activities, things that the average person takes for granted, such as the ability to brush one's teeth, shave, tie one's shoelaces or cut a slice of bread. By looking at compensatory tension patterns, the teacher can, in many instances, help the disabled person find a new means whereby they can perform these everyday tasks.

F.  In this respect, the lessons may extend to include the disabled person's carer, for example the person who regularly has to help someone in and out of a wheelchair. Using the Alexander Technique, the carer learns not only to lift and give support in the most efficient way to avoid damaging his/her own back, but, as the two learn together, they also become better skilled at working out strategies enabling the disabled person to become more independent.

G.  There are, of course, several factors which have to be taken into consideration when working with disabled pupils. They may suffer intense pain and discomfort, loss of Kinaesthetic awareness (sometimes with total loss of sensitivity in parts of the body), severe lack of co-ordination, loss of mobility, memory loss, blindness, deafness, and speech impairment. The effect this has on the person's emotional and psychological state also has to be taken into account. Some disabled pupils may need longer lessons, because of the time required to move them from the wheelchair, take off casts, slings and other movement aids, etc. Others may only be able to concentrate for short periods of time and, therefore, require shorter lessons more frequently. It often requires a certain amount of inventiveness on the part of the Alexander teacher, both as far as practical arrangements and the approach to teaching are concerned, a challenge that, in most cases, is greatly rewarded by the positive results.

## QUESTIONS 1–5

**Reading Passage 1** has seven paragraphs **(A–G)**.

Choose the most suitable heading from the **List of Headings** below. Write the appropriate numbers **(i–xii)** in **Boxes 1–5** on your answer sheet. Paragraphs **C** and **G** have been done for you.

| | List of Headings |
|---|---|
| i | Co-ordination – important for all |
| ii | Tension and daily routine |
| iii | Brushing one's teeth and slicing bread |
| iv | Fitting the technique to the disability |
| v | Challenges for the Alexander teacher |
| vi | Musical solutions |
| vii | Potential drawbacks |
| viii | Helping the disabled through their helpers |
| ix | Pain problems |
| x | Better body 'use' for all |
| xi | Retraining limbs |
| xii | Breaking bad habits |

1. Paragraph A
2. Paragraph B
   **Paragraph C**    **Answer: (xi)**
3. Paragraph D
4. Paragraph E
5. Paragraph F
   **Paragraph G**    **Answer: (v)**

## QUESTIONS 6–14

Complete the summary below using information from the passage. You may **use no more than two words** from the passage for each blank. Write your answers in **Boxes 6–14** on your answer sheet.

Example:    Alexander Matthias _____ (Example) _____ the technique named after him
            more than a hundred years ago.
Answer:     developed.

With the Alexander Technique, people are _____6_____ in a psychophysical way. The Technique works on the body's _____7_____ so that they all operate _____8_____. As a result, bad habits are _____9_____ and the individual is able to live a healthy life. Alexander's technique can help any of us to _____10_____ ourselves better. As regards _____11_____ person, the expected results and exact method used vary, according to the _____12_____ of the individual, e.g. shorter and more regular sessions in the case of clients who find it difficult to concentrate. With disabled clients, in fact, a number of _____13_____ have to be considered, and for the teacher, who often needs to be very inventive, this is _____14_____.

## QUESTION 15

Does the statement below agree with the information given in **Reading Passage 1**?

> **Yes**        if the statement agrees with the information in the text
> **No**         if the statement contradicts the information in the text
> **Not Given**  if there is no information about the statement in the text

15. The success rate of the Alexander Technique in working with stroke victims is high.

You should spend about 20 minutes on **Questions 16–28,** which are based on **Passage 2** below.

# Science, Technology and the third Millennium: Change, Progress, Fear & Complacency

The 20th Century is drawing to a close, merging rapidly and imperceptibly with its successor – the first 100 years of the Third Millennium. It will deliver an awesome inheritance: a world propelled by science and technology; a world where incredible and accelerating discovery will create changes beyond the scope of our wildest speculations; a world where science and technology have placed *What Is Possible* beyond *What We Can Imagine.*

History may well dub the 1900s *The Century of Change* – the era when science and technology forged a permanent partnership and unleashed the first products of their unique alliance on a largely illiterate, earthbound civilisation. The Industrial Revolution provided the impetus for action and cast the die for the future; two world wars, fought only a generation apart and before 1950, accelerated the process. Life changed quickly and irreversibly – like a moth shedding its cocoon.

Within one life span, top-hatted physicians, gas lamps and horse-drawn transport gave way to transplant surgery, laser beams and space travel. The speed of change and the volume of knowledge defied measurement. Early attempts to do so reflected growing concerns about possible adverse effects on established social values and systems. One widely circulated document estimated that mankind's total knowledge doubled first between the years 1 AD and 1900; again by 1950; and again by 1960. After that, even the best would-be assessors gave up, many of them becoming management consultants. The new profession flourished as modern business faced rampant stress caused by inexorable change, and cut-throat competition in the global marketplace. *Change* and *Progress* became popular themes for training workshops.

Change is often presented as progress. To act on this misconception (as too frequently happens!) is to court disaster. Progress implies change with benefit. It reflects action taken only after management has considered relevant past experiences, current priorities and future objectives. Change for change's sake may reflect the response of a novice manager, or of one more senior who wishes to impress an advisory committee. Technology can convincingly disguise poor drafting styles or a proposal's lack of substance, but its healing influence does not extend to the application of a plan itself. Delays, increased costs, confusion and low staff morale often follow change without benefit. Sadly, solutions offered to such problems are inevitably, further change!

The age of push-button miracles has not eradicated boredom. In the 1960s, the world held its breath as live television and radio transmitted the first lunar landing. Many in the worldwide audience viewed and listened from the comfort of their homes. Technology had deftly demonstrated passive participation and predicted couch potatoes. Local cinemas and sports grounds would close. As the astronauts bounced across the ghostly moonscape and joked with each other and Earth, they demolished a primeval barrier: science fiction became fact. And *anything imaginable* became *possible* – perhaps worse, *inevitable.* For many participants, the mystery and magic of fantasy vanished forever – like a child's perception of Christmas. Technology had become commonplace, its wonders explicable and predictable.

The second moon expedition raised little public excitement. It was, after all, a repeat performance, sure of success. In the 1970s and 80s, repeated success itself bred complacency. But ...! Nearly 30 years later, a space shuttle exploded during the launch and the crew perished. Their deaths provoked intense, but short-term, shock. Commentators soon reflected a popular view: that such accidents, although unfortunate, were also inevitable. The astronauts had known and had accepted the risks; NASA could be proud of its record and rest on its laurels – until the next catastrophe.

Today, as we face a new Millennium, technology and science are simultaneously feared, admired and taken for granted. Enthusiasts and critics alike, increasingly depend on them. In education, for example, computer-based programmes are replacing textbooks, blackboards and tutors; the Internet bridges time and distance and provides access to specialist resources. Factors such as the need for skilled and costly support services are rarely discussed. The principles of learning are established: the way they may be best used in different settings and the results evaluated will vary with client needs. But, no matter how good, no one method can satisfy all the needs of any one client. Books, theatre and technology go well together.

The Third Millennium will open the door to a future filled with a kaleidoscope of scientific and technical wizardry. We have, without resistance, grown very dependent on such attractions. Few of us differentiate between simple and complex uses of technology. The former used routinely (e.g. simple mental arithmetic) may deskill us and increase our dependency - without our being aware of any danger. Artificial intelligence, human cloning and the unimaginable are no longer science fiction.

The time has come to reassess our relationship with science and technology to review the first 100 years and plan ahead. We must reaffirm our roles as creators and directors of that future and help realise its human potential. Without such effort, we may find ourselves victims of our inherent intelligence, curiosity and imagination – and a rather curious complacency.

## QUESTIONS 16–19

Using **NO MORE THAN THREE WORDS** from the text, answer the following questions:

16.  *According to the author, who or what became partners in the 1900s?*

17.  *Something about the speed of change and the volume of knowledge was elusive. What was it?*

18.  *What was the main contributory factor to the growth of the management consultancy profession, as world markets changed?*

19.  *What does progress have that change does not?*

## QUESTIONS 20–23

Choose the most appropriate letters **A–D** and write them in **Boxes 20–23** on your answer sheet.

20.  Progress can be seen as action taken after consideration of ...

   **A**  company priorities for the future.
   **B**  the past, the present and the future.
   **C**  mistakes made in the past.
   **D**  experiences and objectives.

21.  Some types of manager ...

   **A**  are always changing things.
   **B**  make changes for no apparent reason.
   **C**  try to increase staff morale.
   **D**  try to impress their colleagues.

22.  When the first lunar landing happened, ...

   **A**  many people were watching it at home.
   **B**  fact became fiction.
   **C**  a lot of people thought it was a joke.
   **D**  science fiction became like Christmas.

23.  The space shuttle explosion showed that ...

   **A**  nothing is exciting anymore.
   **B**  TV can show shocking things as well as exciting ones.
   **C**  accidents are bound to happen.
   **D**  the astronauts were to blame.

## QUESTIONS 24–28

The text mentions a number of current and future developments. State whether the developments in Questions **24–28** below are:

| | |
|---|---|
| **C** | current, as mentioned in the text. |
| **F** | future, as mentioned in the text. |
| **NG** | not mentioned as current or future in the text. |

24.  machines taking the place of teachers.

25.  a life filled with a variety of magical gadgetry.

26.  recognition of the need for expensive, yet necessary support services.

27.  an adaptation of learning principles to fit different situations.

28.  a re-evaluation of our relationship with the world of science.

You should spend about 20 minutes on **Questions 29–42,** which are based on **Passage 3** below.

# A note on the national minimum wage debate

A.   Much of the literature on the minimum wage has as its main theme the question of whether or not the introduction of a national minimum wage reduces employment. The empirical evidence on this point comes mainly from America and is contradictory and inconclusive. This does not, however, prevent the political debate from using the economic evidence. Advocates from both sides do so, with some rhetorical force, despite its contentious nature.

B.   The proposition that jobs might be destroyed by higher wages follows directly from neo-classical economic theory. However, the empirical studies display findings that are rather milder than theory would expect. A review of such studies by Card and Krueger (1995) concluded that minimum wages had no effect on employment; this despite the evidence of Neumark and Wascher (1992) that the negative effect comes through strongly when teenagers are isolated in the sample. This notion was supported by a later study which showed that teenagers were more likely to be enticed away from education by the higher wages ensuing from statutory minimum wage legislation (Neumark and Wascher 1995).

C.   Critics of neutral and slightly positive evidence claim that studies cannot, by definition, take account of companies driven out of business by minimum wages. Whilst this is true, a more substantial criticism of the literature would be the dearth of studies based on local labour markets and on those of specific industries. Such studies as exist show a clearer picture – which could be summarised as demonstrating a small negative effect on jobs, but, more importantly, showing the strategic processes which managers use to cope with an imposed rise in the price of labour. Certain types of service industry, for example, can show positive employment effects (Alpert 1986).

D.   The irony here is that the best evidence is furthest away from the political debate, which, by its very nature, uses a national perspective. Unfortunately, the contentious nature of the evidential base, which is so unhelpful to the jobs argument, permeates into other areas. For example, if the jobs argument is unresolved, then those arguments surrounding the saving to be made on the payment of social benefits to low paid workers hardly get off the ground, because, if jobs are destroyed, unemployment benefit costs rise and offset the savings on income support. Critics of the minimum wage would, of course, argue that it only benefits people who have a job and, therefore, does nothing for unemployment. Advocates, on the other hand, would contend that income support benefits are a wasteful subsidy to 'bad' employers who are, in effect, gaining a competitive advantage over 'more responsible' employers. In this argument, the minimum wage would encourage better market functioning and more competitive conditions than the subsidies that prop-up bad employers. They would go even further and point to continental Europe, where minimum wage statutes abound, to suggest that minimum wages are an incentive to develop training. Exactly why this should be so escapes British management, who appear to need a better translation of the text of this argument. However, one point that is well understood is that a national minimum wage could cause a run of differential-maintaining pay claims. The fact that the beneficiaries of a minimum wage usually lack bargaining power (Lucas 1995) and that they are unlikely to be a 'reference group' for any sector of organised labour, takes the edge off this argument.

E.   The EEC has recently tossed a new coin into the ring: the notion of maximum working hours per week. So far this has not touched the minimum wage debate, but the connection is inevitable. A new set of arguments about overtime and shorter hours is about to break through. Whether the poor can best be helped by a minimum wage, or a maximum working week, is a matter for empirical evidence. Whatever the evidence is, it will not stop the political debate from maintaining a national perspective. This is a pity, because an increment for the poor does not go on luxury items and foreign holidays. It is spent on the home and on small scale leisure activities in the local market. Furthermore, if adjustments in taxation to help small business through a sudden rise in labour costs are contemplated, they are best executed through local rather than national government. To paraphrase an American political slogan: it's the 'local' economy stupid.

## QUESTIONS 29–32

Use the information in the text to match the authors **(A–D)** with the **Findings (29–32)** below. Write the appropriate letters **(A–D)** in **Boxes 29–32** on your answer sheet.

> **A** Neumark & Wascher
> **B** Alpert
> **C** Lucas
> **D** Card & Krueger

**Findings**

29. The economic influence of those who would benefit most from a minimum wage is not great enough to affect wage differentials.

30. A minimum wage does not influence the number of people who find employment.

31. The beneficial effects of a minimum wage have been observed in some service industries.

32. A minimum wage appears not to have a positive impact as regards teenagers.

## QUESTIONS 33–39

The diagram below summarises some of the main points on the minimum wage provided in paragraphs **B–D**. Complete the diagram with information from the passage. You may use **NO MORE THAN THREE WORDS** to fill each blank space. Write your answers in **Boxes 33–39** on your answer sheet.

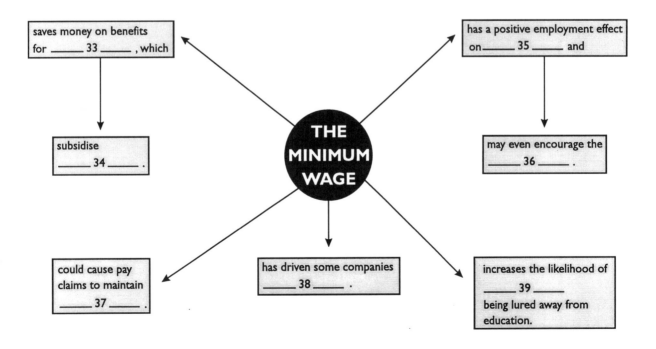

## QUESTIONS 40–42

Choose the appropriate letters **A–D** and write them in **Boxes 40–42** on your answer sheet.

40.     Critics of the minimum wage argue that ...

        ***A***     *it makes services more expensive.*
        ***B***     *it only helps those already in work.*
        ***C***     *it causes inflation.*
        ***D***     *it affects exports.*


41.     According to the writer, the fiscal counterbalance to increased costs should be ...

        ***A***     *at national level.*
        ***B***     *through Income Tax.*
        ***C***     *through VAT.*
        ***D***     *at local level.*


42.     There is a lack of studies based ...

        ***A***     *on international industries.*
        ***B***     *on the national economy.*
        ***C***     *on local labour markets.*
        ***D***     *on specific locations.*

# Reading

## Test 4

You should spend about 20 minutes on **Questions 1–14**, which are based on **Passage 1** below.

# HOW THE PAULI EXCLUSION PRINCIPLE REGULATES THE EVOLUTION OF STARS

All stars (like plants and animals) evolve, with each one following the same general pattern of evolution. Their journey along the evolutionary path, and ultimate fate at stellar death, is determined by their initial mass, which is measured in multiples of the solar mass of our own Sun.

Perturbations of nebulous interstellar clouds in space result in gravitational interaction, with the consequent contraction of gaseous matter to create protostars, which are much larger than the stars they will finally become. As the temperature increases, the gas becomes completely ionised to form plasma and gravitational contraction of the core then takes place. The onset of hydrogen-burning happens at a core temperature of several million degrees, and converts hydrogen to helium through nuclear fusion. The greater part of a star's evolutionary lifetime is spent hydrogen-burning and, during this period, it is said to be on the Main Sequence. The end of hydrogen-burning is marked by the evolution of a star into a red giant, when it is said to leave the Main Sequence. Burning ceases completely in the core, which undergoes gravitational contraction to maintain mechanical equilibrium.

Now, the Pauli Exclusion Principle states that 'no two identical particles can occupy the same quantum state' (Kaufmann, 1994): that is, loosely, they cannot have the same spatial location and momentum. This principle is important in determining the ultimate fate of stars. Consider low Main Sequence mass stars (that is, stars of less than three solar masses) which have passed through the hydrogen-burning phase to helium-burning. Such bodies require extreme compression of the core to raise their temperature sufficiently for the onset of helium-burning. Increasing density of electrons occurs, so that they are squashed into close proximity with each other, until a limit is reached when they resist any further compression. This phenomenon is called degeneracy, and is a manifestation of the Pauli Exclusion Principle. Resistance to further compression results in degenerate-electron pressure which supports the core, preventing its contraction. However, this pressure is independent of temperature, and remains constant while the temperature continues to increase. Helium ignition takes place and the thermonuclear reaction proceeds at an increasing rate until a helium-flash occurs. The temperature is so great that degeneracy cannot be maintained: the core suddenly expands with a corresponding decrease in temperature that abruptly ends the helium-flash. This cycle may be repeated until all the core helium is converted to carbon.

More massive stars do not undergo a helium-flash. Moreover, their cores are sufficiently massive for further element-burning to occur, until they, too, reach a limit imposed by degeneracy. That is, as the product of each phase of element-burning is always nuclei of greater mass, it requires even greater compression of the core remnant in order to raise the temperature sufficiently high enough to initiate the next phase. Such compression can only occur until the degenerate condition is achieved.

Stellar death comes about when the core cannot carry out further element-burning, because of its degenerate nature. Stars of Main Sequence mass less than seven solar masses become white dwarfs. The stability of a white dwarf is only maintained if its final (post-Main Sequence) mass does not exceed the Chandrasekhar Limit of 1.4 solar masses. Degenerate-electron pressure supports the core against collapse, thereby conforming to the Principle.

Neutron stars are the stellar corpses of stars whose Main Sequence mass is between seven and twenty solar masses. Before death, these stars have undergone some further element-burning and the final core mass exceeds the Chandrasekhar Limit. This is too great for degenerate-electron pressure to prevent collapse of the core: electrons and protons are crushed together to form neutrons and neutrinos. Gravitational collapse continues until degeneracy equilibrium is achieved once more. It is degenerate-neutron pressure that halts the collapse, and, thereby, upholds the Principle.

The most massive stars have completed burning to obtain an iron core, and have a Main Sequence mass exceeding twenty solar masses. This is so great that degenerate-neutron pressure cannot support it, and rapid collapse ensues. Since density is inversely proportional to volume and the mass is vast, then, as the volume dwindles, the density tends to infinity and a Black Hole is formed.

Black Holes are a violation of Pauli's Exclusion Principle. If the Principle did not regulate the evolution of stars, nothing would prevent the inexorable collapse of an interstellar cloud from its initial disturbance into a massive Black Hole.

## QUESTIONS 1–7

**The flow chart below summarises Paragraph 2**. Complete the chart with information from the passage and write your answers in **Boxes 1–7** on your answer sheet.

You may use **NO MORE THAN THREE WORDS** to complete each space.

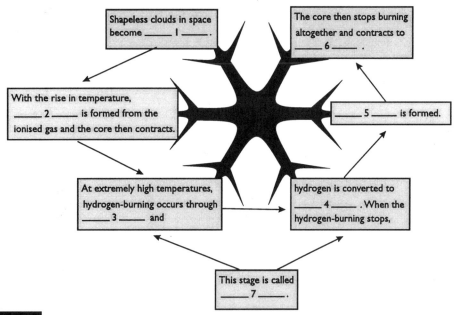

Shapeless clouds in space become _____ 1 _____ .

The core then stops burning altogether and contracts to _____ 6 _____ .

With the rise in temperature, _____ 2 _____ is formed from the ionised gas and the core then contracts.

_____ 5 _____ is formed.

At extremely high temperatures, hydrogen-burning occurs through _____ 3 _____ and

hydrogen is converted to _____ 4 _____ . When the hydrogen-burning stops,

This stage is called _____ 7 _____ .

## QUESTIONS 8–11

Choose the appropriate letters **A–D** and write them in **Boxes 8–11** on your answer sheet.

8. What can be said about degeneracy?

   A  *It violates the Pauli Exclusion Principle.*
   B  *It is not dependent upon temperature.*
   C  *It is the point where the core of a star withstands further compression.*
   D  *It happens to most, but not all stars.*

9. According to the Pauli Exclusion Principle, ...

   A  *no two stars are the same.*
   B  *low mass stars do not degenerate.*
   C  *it is not possible for two identical particles to be in the same space at the same time.*
   D  *when a star is compressed, the temperature and the pressure rise.*

10. Which of the following is true of the largest stars, but not of smaller ones?

   A  *Compression of their core is halted by degeneracy.*
   B  *Their core becomes iron.*
   C  *Their fate is stellar death.*
   D  *They undergo a helium flash.*

11. What affects the development of all stars?

   A  *Their stellar death.*
   B  *Their evolutionary path.*
   C  *Their mass when they are first formed.*
   D  *Their size when compared to our own Sun.*

## QUESTIONS 12–14

Use information from the passage to complete the table below. Use **No More Than Two Words** for each space.

| Stars with main sequence mass of | turn into |
|---|---|
| Less than 7 | _____ 12 _____ |
| Between 7–20 | _____ 13 _____ |
| 20+ | _____ 14 _____ |

You should spend about 20 minutes on **Questions 15 - 28**, which are based on **Passage 2**

# ENVY WITHOUT REASON?

A    Do you come from a culture which places emphasis on the emotion of envy? Without a doubt, envy is something that we all feel at some time in our lives. The *Concise Oxford Dictionary* lists envy as 'resentful or admiring contemplation of more fortunate person'. Instead of sharing in the joy of a new job, car or party dress, a friend either pretends she or he has not noticed the fantastic new BMW or says 'Mercedes are better'. But does it matter? In many parts of the world, the personal satisfaction felt by those who prosper is tinged with concerns about the ill-will which success provokes in friends, and even family members. Envy becomes something to be feared, for it may have the power to cause harm.

B    The Swahili people of Coastal East Africa take envy very seriously. They frequently feel the need to hide or minimise personal success. Hence, boasting can be a dangerous pastime. Envy emanates from neighbours, friends and family. After all, a stranger does not care if you have managed to replace your thatched roof with corrugated iron. But those Swahili who have struggled to build houses which are a little better than their neighbours often paint on the front of their houses the slogan, *hasidi hana sababu*: this means 'envy without reason'. The slogan seems to be a forlorn attempt to remind neighbours and any envious passers-by that the apparent good fortune indicated by a superior house has been earned. The message is that there is no reason for envy, and that those harbouring ill-will should control their feelings. The successful are pleading to be allowed to succeed.

C    In Swahili culture, and many others, envy emanates from the eye of the beholder. The Evil Eye, as a source of harm to those who fall under its gaze, is reported throughout much of the world. Indeed, according to Brian Spooner, an expert on the various ways used to keep envy at bay, the idea of the Evil Eye is so widespread that it can be regarded as a universal phenomenon. In the parts of Europe that border the Mediterranean, in the Middle East and North Africa, the wearing of pendants depicting one large eye is a popular way of repelling envy.

D    Ideas about the Evil Eye moved from the Mediterranean to the New World of America. Atwood Gaines has traced the origin of beliefs about the Evil Eye as a cause of sickness from Spain to Mexico, Haiti and Puerto Rica. The illnesses caused by the Evil Eye are given specific names such as *susto*. In such cases, the Evil Eye is suspected after an illness or misfortune has already occurred.

E    Marcia Inhorn has written about the Evil Eye in Egypt. There, women may attribute infertility and other health problems to the envy of neighbours or friends. But in the Middle East, as elsewhere, envy can occur in many settings. Hence, at the end of an important meeting to discuss a research study, the head of the project noticed that her best silk suit had white marks on both the jacket and skirt. It was ruined. She worked out that after the sumptuous lunch, which had preceded the meeting, the table had been cleaned with bleach. She had then brushed against the table. Nobody else's clothes were damaged. Her Palestinian colleague suggested that envy, harboured by an unknown acquaintance, had ruined her suit. The grounds for envy were either her beautiful clothes or her powerful position within the research team.

F    Some social scientists argue that envy is widespread in societies where resources are scarce and one person's gain is considered another's loss. The reasoning behind this theory of envy is that, when people are poor and in competition with each other, they believe that there is not enough good food, good fortune or good jobs to go around. G M Foster studied peasant society in Latin America and propounded 'the image of limited good'. According to his theory, when somebody from a family or village prospers, they use up part of a stock of limited good and reduce the chances of the success of others. Foster sees the 'image of limited good' as operating in peasant societies where people know and compete with each other in adverse economic conditions. However, the theory may hold good for many other social and economic contexts. Take scholarships, for example. There are only so many to go round. If your best friend gets the scholarship, your chances of getting one too may be greatly reduced.

G    Western psychoanalysts have also studied envy. Melanie Klein sees envy as an emotion felt by the breastfeeding infant towards its mother's breast. Although the infant feels love and gratitude towards its mother, it also wants the goodness of the milk for itself. Some of these scholars, unlike everyday speakers of English, are careful to distinguish between envy and jealousy. Swahili people make the same distinction. Jealousy is a triangular relationship. For example, two friends spend all their free time together until one takes a lover. The neglected friend grows jealous of the affection lavished on the new lover. When there is jealousy, three people are involved. Envy, on the other hand, is more straightforward: one person envies another's achievement, quality or possession. While most English people do not take envy seriously, it remains a matter of concern to people worldwide. It makes ambition and the pursuit of success more difficult, and some would say, dangerous. Many seek ways to avoid falling victim to envy. How do you deal with it?

## QUESTIONS 15–20

Reading Passage 2 below has seven paragraphs (A–G).

Choose the most suitable heading for each paragraph from the List of Headings below. Write the appropriate numbers (i–xv) in Boxes 15–20 on your answer sheet.

Paragraph D has been done for you as an example.

Please note that you may use each heading only once.

|         |             |             |
|---------|-------------|-------------|
| 15.     | Paragraph A |             |
| 16.     | Paragraph B |             |
| 17.     | Paragraph C |             |
| Example | Paragraph D | Answer: viii|
| 18.     | Paragraph E |             |
| 19.     | Paragraph F |             |
| 20.     | Paragraph G |             |

### List of Headings

| | |
|---|---|
| i | Breastfeeding and envy |
| ii | A victim of envy |
| iii | A global remedy for envy |
| iv | What is envy? |
| v | The Evil Eye in Europe |
| vi | Sharing success |
| vii | No grounds for envy |
| viii | Envy and illness |
| ix | Envy where resources are limited |
| x | The Swahili in Africa |
| xi | The work of social scientists |
| xii | Envy in relation to other emotions |
| xiii | A dictionary definition of envy |
| xiv | A universal phenomenon |
| xv | Envy in poor societies |

## QUESTIONS 21–24

Use the information in the text to match the people listed (21–24) with the **Concepts (i–vii)**.

Write the appropriate letter in **Boxes 21–24** on your answer sheet. Note that there are more concepts than names, so you will not use all of them.

**21.** Brian Spooner
**22.** GM Foster
**23.** Melanie Klein
**24.** Atwood Gaines

## CONCEPTS

| | |
|---|---|
| i | the idea that there is only so much good to go round in any one community |
| ii | that there is a relationship between the Evil Eye and illness |
| iii | the theory that the Evil Eye influences infertility |
| iv | keeping envy at bay |
| v | the concept of the Evil Eye being a universal phenomenon |
| vi | the distinction between jealousy and envy |
| vii | that babies envy their mothers' milk |

## QUESTIONS 25–28

Complete the following sentences with information from the passage. Use **NO MORE THAN THREE WORDS** to fill each blank space.

**25.** _____ people in society are often the victims of envy.

**26.** The Evil Eye is a _____ to those who come within its range.

**27.** Among the Swahili, boasting is a _____.

**28.** The Swahili on the East African coast often feel they have to conceal or _____.

You should spend about 20 minutes on **Questions 29–42**, which are based on **Passage 3** below.

# Have you a tea-room?

We have all walked through modern office blocks where the workers are busily tapping away at keyboards. They have their mugs of tea, or coffee, as they work. Some have a packet of something to nibble in the drawer; but how do they manage to make one packet of chocolate digestives last one whole week? There is an area by the wall somewhere with a water geyser perpetually on the boil, and a stack of mugs. There is a palpable air of activity. Productivity must be booming, one thinks. But is it?

How many of these people work late of their own volition, want to obtain a result before going home, and will beaver away happily until well after dark to achieve it? Damned few! Yes! It may seem wonderful to have a constant flow of liquid refreshment at the desk, not to need a tea, or coffee, break – because the whole working day *is* a tea break. Yet, who wants the tea when the ambience, all too often, is that of a concentration camp?

Why not escape from the desk with a cup of tea from time to time? Perhaps, take your break in a comfortable chair, talk about last night's football results or discuss work, seek or offer advice, arrange a game of squash, play bridge. Or, network and enjoy some refreshment at the same time!

What will the Boss say, however? If he has any sense, he will also come and join you. Perhaps, he supports another team? You can discuss the merits of the players and show him how competently you can present a case. He will realise that the tea-room is an ideal place for informal meetings with his staff, where any number of day-to-day problems can be sorted out over a cup of tea, and where anyone who needs a tender warning about something can be quietly given it without the march to *The Office*. If, as a consequence, the communication process improves, the boss may even dispense with a layer of middle management 'twixt you and himself. He will then no longer need to have expensive *Off-site Meetings*, where his middle managers experience *Free Expression*. He can spend some of the savings on light refreshments for his staff to enjoy!

If you, or a colleague, have a problem with some aspect of work, share it with everyone in the tea-room. One of your colleagues will, doubtless, have had similar difficulties in the past and will have discovered a ridiculously simple solution. To your surprise, you will find he is more than happy to share his experience and answers with you over a cup of tea. Both of you will then go back to your desks with added commitment and make a positive contribution to the work of the group.

Every team has its 'specialists'. They are normal people in their everyday lives, but there are those special situations where they seem to excel all the time. It may be that they format new documentation with consummate ease. Maybe, they can bake excellent butter sponge cakes decorated as fax machines ... . The true specialist can train anyone to fulfil his role.

Who will be trained? Keen, eager, people: the raw recruits. Released from the inhibitions of the office environment in the relaxed atmosphere of a tea-room, they have the confidence to ask dumb questions. This is, in fact, the best place to find solutions to problems; and conduct training. In the tea-room, old-hands, freed temporarily from the modern technologies they often do not fully understand, will invariably offer advice. These people, who know all about the way things happen and what the final product should look like, will give free information communicated with an honest confidence. Why have lots of knowledge, if you cannot share it effectively with others? The Boss should observe the information flow between these people.

Situations like these occur in tea-rooms worldwide every day. These are all natural human interactions. There is much that can be said for the idea of fixed tea times during the working day away from one's precise place of work. Suggesting this will make Asset Managers cringe. This room is only being used 4 hours a day!

But let us say we allow staff to enjoy staggered breaks. The morning coffee is between 10.00 and 11.00. Lunch is sometime between 12.00 and 2.00. Afternoon tea is between 3.00 and 4.00. The tea-room can then be used by time-conscious executives to have their meetings. And, since the room is required for refreshment, these meetings must never over-run, unless they are scheduled after afternoon tea ... . Who wants to work late anyway?

## QUESTIONS 29–33

Reading Passage 3 describes a number of **Implications** for the working environment provided certain **Conditions** are met. Match each **Condition (29–33)** in **List A** with its **Implication (A–I)** in **List B**.

There are more **Implications** in **List B** than you will need, so you will not use all of them.

| List A: Conditions | List B: Implications |
|---|---|
| 29. Provided people share and solve problems together, | A the tendency for meetings to over-run is avoided. |
| | B the employer will recognise the positive contribution to team-work. |
| 30. If the atmosphere in the tea-room is totally relaxed, | C they will work harder as part of a team. |
| | D a layer of management will perhaps be removed. |
| | E some executives will be able to work later. |
| 31. Should bosses relax with their employees, | F more experienced staff will have an opportunity to train the more inexperienced staff. |
| | G they will see tea-rooms as an informal opportunity to meet staff and solve problems. |
| 32. When tea-rooms are used as a multi-purpose venue, | H there will be more off-site meetings for middle managers. |
| 33. If communication between boss and staff is improved, | I the boss will see how information is exchanged between staff members. |

## QUESTIONS 34–38

Do the following statements agree with the views of the writer in **Reading Passage 3**?

In **Boxes 34–38** write:

| | |
|---|---|
| **Yes** | if the statement agrees with the views of the writer |
| **No** | if the statement contradicts the views of the writer |
| **Not Given** | if it is impossible to say what the writer thinks about this |

34. A variety of snacks should be provided in tea-rooms.
35. It is surprising that office workers make a packet of chocolate digestives last for a week.
36. The writer suggests workers could, at times, change the setting for their tea breaks.
37. Specialists excel in their everyday lives.
38. Tea-rooms are the best places to ask facile questions.

## QUESTIONS 39–42

Using **NO MORE THAN TWO WORDS** from the passage, answer the questions below. Write your answers in **Boxes 39–42** on your answer sheet.

39. How many people voluntarily work late?
40. On what can the money saved by avoiding off-site meetings be spent?
41. What would Asset Managers do if the tea-room were used only 4 hours per day?
42. What do older and experienced people not always understand?

# Section on Writing

# Introduction to the Section on Writing

The writing section in the IELTS contains two tasks. Writing Task 1 usually contains a diagram of some sort, such as: a graph, a pie chart, a bar chart, a table or a combination of two or more of these items; a diagram of a process; a map; or some other kind of diagram. You have to write at least 150 words and you are advised to spend 20 minutes on this task. There is only one question, so you do not have a choice.

In Writing Task 2, you are asked to write an essay on an academic topic, about which no specialised knowledge is required. The length of the essay should be at least 250 words. Again, there is no choice.

This section of the book contains 20 practice exercises for Writing Task 1, 4 exercises for Task 2 with 3 Writing Tests. The exercises all have a **Key** and for the tasks in the Tests there are model answers. Exercises 1--10 and Exercise 20 in the Section on Reading will also help you prepare for Writing Task 2. You may also want to look at *'a book on writing'* by Sam McCarter, published by IntelliGene, 1997.

## Hints for Writing Task 1

You should train yourself to spend only 20 minutes on this task and to write the minimum number of words you are asked to produce.

The language is academic and formal, so you need to avoid using informal language.

Many candidates are not very familiar with doing this kind of task. Quite often the difficulty they face lies in interpreting the diagram or data given. There are many publications with statistical data in diagrammatic form in libraries. Even if you do not write a description, you should study some of them and look for patterns of organisation.

It is important that you learn to recognise what 150 words look like in your own hand-writing and that you write at least the minimum number of words that are set. We would also advise you not to write too many words, whether practising at home or in the exam.

## Hints for Writing Task 2

*Questions to ask yourself*

In the examination itself, you will not have time to rewrite your essay. You should, therefore, learn to write in such a way that you can avoid re-writing.

This does not mean, however, that you should not re-read carefully and correct what you have written. As you prepare for the exam, you should re-read and correct each of your essays immediately after you have written them so that by the time you take the IELTS this will be a natural thing to do.

Again, it is important that you learn to recognise what 250 words look like in your own hand-writing and that you write at least the minimum number of words that are set. We would also advise you not to write too many words, whether practising at home or in the exam.

Candidates often want to learn examples of essays that have occurred in the exam. This causes several problems. First, the exam questions are quite long and, while it is possible to have an idea of the general subject, it is often quite difficult to find out the exact focus of the essay question. Students frequently memorise essays they have practised and reproduce them in the examination, not realising that the essay they are writing does not have the same focus as the one on the exam paper. So beware!

More seriously, when you write down something from memory the number of mistakes can increase. Try writing out one of the model essays in the Key for the Tests and see how many mistakes you make!

Below are some questions, you should ask yourself, both while you are writing the essay, and also while you are re-reading and checking.

**Essay title**

1.  Have I accurately identified the general subject and the focus in the title?

2.  Am I clear about the organising word(s) in the essay title, i.e. do I understand exactly what I am being asked to write about?

**Organisation**

3.  Is the structure of my essay clear: are there clear paragraph divisions?

4.  As regards the introduction, have I connected it with the title of the essay?

5.  Have each of my paragraphs got a clear topic sentence, and does each one deal with one main point?

6.  Is my conclusion short and concise, and does it more or less repeat what I have written in my introduction?

**Content**

7.  Have I kept to the main theme of the essay? Or, have I made a mistake and strayed from the focus by including points and examples that are not relevant?

8.  Have I made my points clearly?

9.  Have I helped the reader to understand the points I am making by giving clear examples, wherever possible?

10. Am I completing the task I have been set?

11. Is my essay going to be the right length i.e. more than 250 words?

**Grammar**

12. Is the structure of my sentences clear throughout, or are some of my sentences too long and over-complicated, making my essay difficult to read?

13. Have I used appropriate and precise vocabulary?

14. Have I checked carefully to make sure that I have avoided making 'my' mistakes , i.e. language errors which I usually make in grammar, syntax and spelling.

Ask yourself the questions above each time you write an essay, while you are preparing for IELTS. Then, by the time you take the exam, you should be better prepared.

# Graphs and Diagrams for Task 1

**Exercise 1**: Looking for patterns

Many students have difficulty describing information or data in the form of charts, graphs, diagrams etc. There are many reasons for this, but, perhaps, the main reason is that students have not been taught how to interpret diagrams. They then cannot see the organisation and the underlying patterns, which means that, when they describe a chart etc, they do not have a framework within which they can write. Their description turns out to be nothing more than a list, or is just chaotic. This exercise helps you to recognise the organisation of charts etc, and so give you a framework within which to write.

Before you do the exercise, look at the following example:

The bar chart below shows the results of a survey which asked people what they thought the main causes of crime were. Study the chart and look for patterns to help you organise the information.

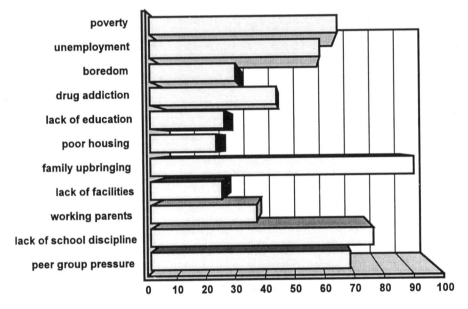

You can organise the above data into three main categories, as follows:

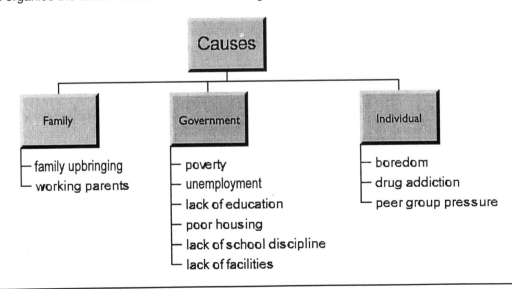

Within this framework, it is then easier to describe and analyse. Your description can move from general points to specific examples. For instance, according to the bar chart, people attribute crime to six causes within the control of the Government. You can, therefore, compare this with the Family or the Individual. You can then move deeper into the bar chart by giving specific examples from within the categories. You can also compare examples within categories, or even across categories, thus moving from general to particular and from particular to particular.

Another possible way to organise the data is:

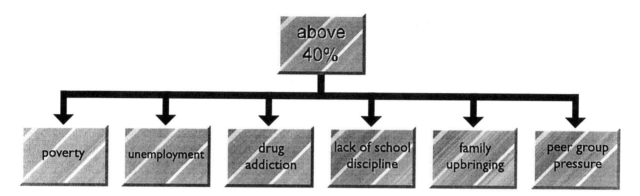

You can then describe and analyse the data within the top band and then within the bottom band. You can see that this approach is more simplistic than the framework above.

Now look at the diagrams and charts in this exercise. Remember that you are looking only for patterns and ways to organise the data. You may find more than one way to do this. If you find the exercise difficult, look at the Key and use it to help you understand how to organise data. Repeat the exercise several times so that you can learn to recognise the mechanism.

The chart (Figure 1) below shows the results of a survey on the leisure activities in which a group of adults in their early 20s participate.

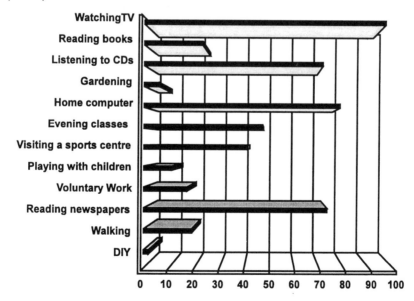

Figure 1 Results of a survey on the leisure activities in which a group of adults in their early 20s participate.

The chart (Figure 2) below shows the same leisure activities as for Figure 1 above for a group of people in their mid to late 60s.

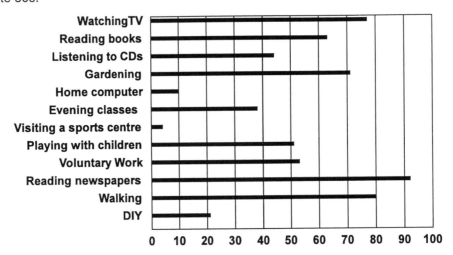

*Figure 2* *The same leisure activities as for Figure 1 above for a group of people in their mid to late 60s.*

Now look for patterns between Figures 1 and 2.

The chart (Figure 3) below shows the sporting activities, in which a sample of inner-city teenagers participated.

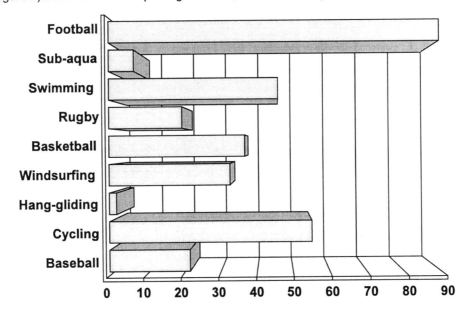

*Figure 3* *The sporting activities, in which a sample of inner-city teenagers participated.*

The graph (Figure 4) below shows the share price of three high-tech companies over a three-year period from their launch.

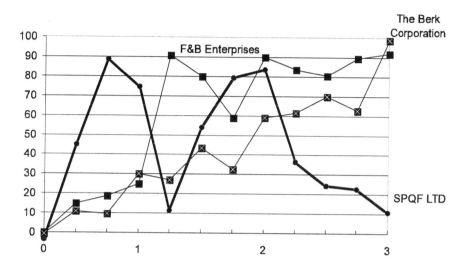

*Figure 4* *The share price of three high-tech companies over a three-year period from their launch.*

The graph (Figure 5) below shows the estimated consumption of four sources of protein in grammes per person per week in a control group over a 35-year period.

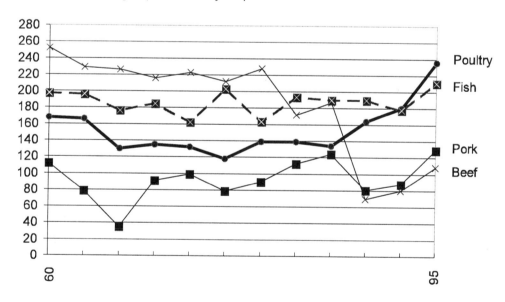

*Figure 5* *The estimated consumption of four sources of protein in grammes per person per week in a control group over a 35-year period.*

**Exercise 2**: Language for graphs

This exercise focuses on the language for describing graphs. Match the texts below with the graphs on the next page. Each graph may have more than one suitable description.

1. *The price did not change over the period.*

2. *There was a steep fall in 1994 followed by a gradual improvement in the subsequent years.*

3. *The price rose and fell over the period, but the trend was definitely upwards.*

4. *The price collapsed in 1994.*

5. *The price plunged dramatically in 1994, but then it regained its previous level, before soaring to a new peak.*

6. *The price plummeted in 1994.*

7. *In spite of the sharp fluctuations in the price, the trend was obviously upwards.*

8. *In 1994, the price fell steeply.*

9. *The price remained static, before experiencing a period of erratic behaviour.*

10. *The price fluctuated slightly over the period.*

11. *The price remained stable.*

12. *The price plunged in 1994.*

13. *Having remained stable for several years apart from a plunge in 1994, the price leaped to a new peak at the end of l997.*

14. *The price dipped slightly several times before sinking to a new low at the end of 1997.*

15. *The price remained the same for a brief period and then fluctuated wildly.*

16. *The price was steady over the period.*

17. *The price was erratic.*

18. *The price was fairly steady over the period.*

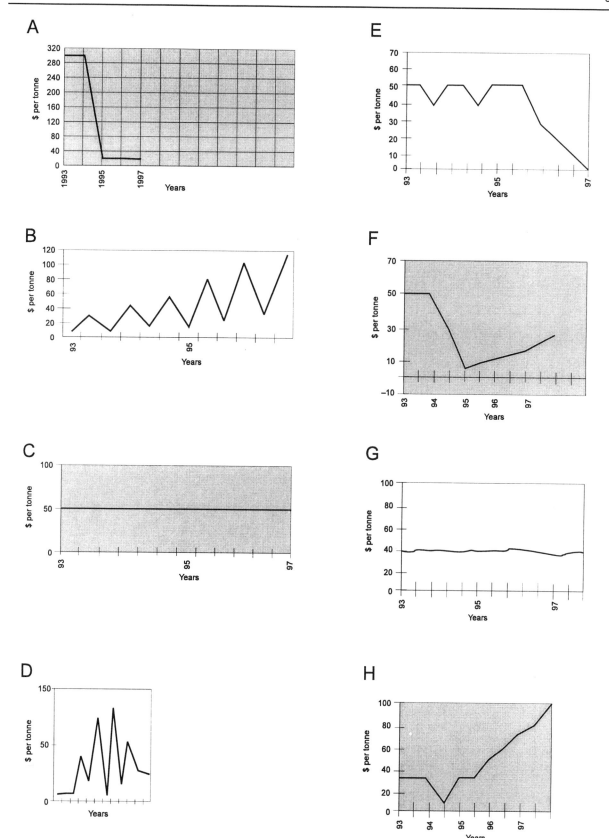

**Exercise 2** *Match the graphs above with the texts on the previous page.*
*Each graph may have more than one suitable description.*

---

**Exercise 3**: Which chart?

Read the text below and look at the charts and graphs (A-D) which follow. Decide which chart interprets the text exactly. Then decide how you have to change the other charts to make them reflect the text exactly.

*The average number of people attending the museum yearly stood at just under 700,000 at the beginning of 1985. Over the subsequent years, attendances saw a modest rise, followed by a period of volatility. During 1989, the museum suffered a steep decline in the number of visitors as a result of the introduction of voluntary charges. The recovery, fitful at first, lasted through to the beginning of 1993, by which time the number of people attending had climbed to a new peak of 750,000. In the first half of 1993, the attendance at the museum went into free fall, nose-diving to approximately 300,000 visitors after charging was introduced. Over the next two years and a half, the number of people coming to the museum fluctuated wildly; the trend, however, was obviously upwards.*

# A

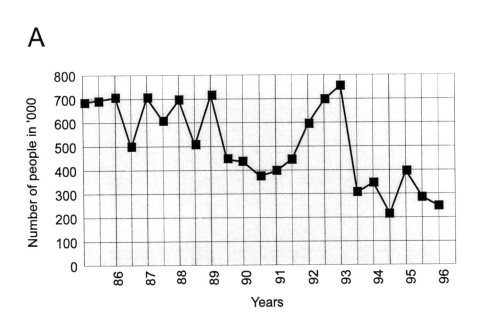

---

B

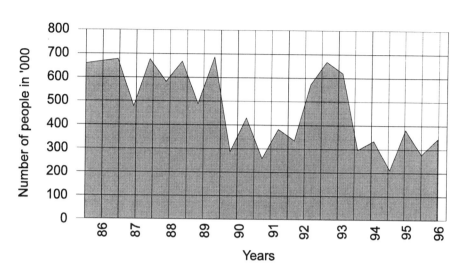

C

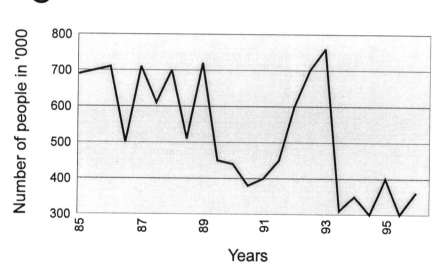

D

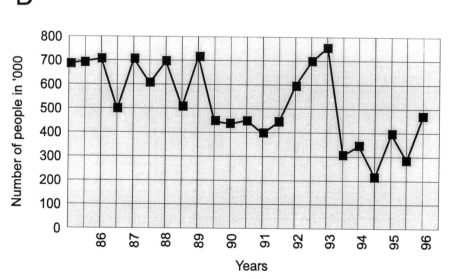

**Exercise 4:** A maze in graph form

In this exercise, you are going to look at the organisation of a graph in another way. Read the text below and then look at the graph which follows. On the graph, there are various lines, which form a jumbled maze. Find your way through the maze using the text as a guide. Where do you end up at the end of the period: Point A, B, C or D?

The share price of FF International Ltd soared spectacularly to more than nine times its value in the first year of the period, before plunging again in the following year losing more than half its previous gain. The share price then recovered, rising once again fairly steeply in the next twelve months, adding roughly a third to its value, only to fall back by more than the same amount in the next year. Over the next year, the price jumped to just under a hundred points short of its 1960 peak. Then, for the space of a year, the share value remained stable, but, in the subsequent three years, the share price experienced a sharp decline, increasing in speed at the end of the fall, to below its value at the beginning of the period. The next movement in the share price was markedly upwards, but then it fell back again to end at just over four times its value at the beginning of the 60s.

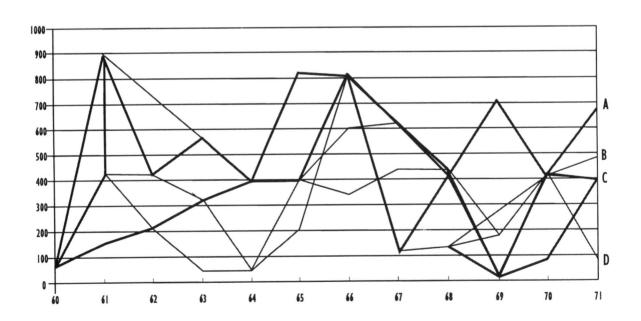

A book for **IELTS**

---

**Exercise 5:** Draw your own graph

---

The bar chart below shows the average number of monthly flights in '000s out of a regional airport called Cranby. Read the text which follows the chart and plot the line graph for the number of flights out of the second airport called Tinbury.

It is better to make a photocopy of the page and to write on the photocopy so that you can repeat the exercise

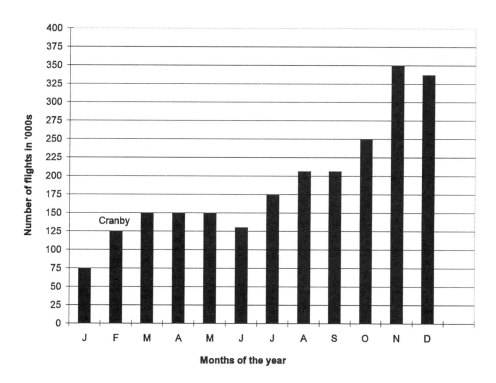

*In January, the number of flights from Cranby airport was exactly half that of those from Tinbury. In the following month, both airports saw a rise of about 50,000 flights, but in March, while flights from Cranby continued to increase, to 150,000, those from Tinbury dropped back to the January level. Flights from Cranby stayed at the March level for the following two months, but, in April, the number leaving Tinbury climbed to 175,000, remaining at this level for the subsequent month. The number of flights from both airports decreased in June, although the reduction was more dramatic in Tinbury than Cranby, by 50,000 and 20,000 respectively. Both cities experienced a rise in the number of flights leaving their airports in July, reaching a common level of 175,000. This increase continued in August, both airports having just over 200,000 outbound flights.*

*However, in September, while the number of flights out of Tinbury continued to climb, to 25,000 more than the February peak, those from Cranby remained at the same number as for the previous month. October saw an increase in the number of flights from Cranby, to 250,000, but a steep drop in those from Tinbury, to the June level. During the last two months of the year, the number of take-offs from both airports went up and then fell. From Cranby, a dramatic rise in November to 350,000 was followed by a slight decline in the subsequent month; while from Tinbury the increase in the number of flights was more marked in November, climbing to a new peak of 375,000, but December then saw the number of flights tumble to 75,000.*

---

---

**Exercise 6:** Graph comprehension

---

Learning to look at a graph so that you can extract information which is relevant to a particular question means that you have to develop the skill to do so.

Before you look at the graph in this exercise read the questions below carefully.

1. *Look at the graph very quickly. Which feature stands out the most?*

2. *What other main characteristics of the graph can you see?*

3. *Is it possible to group the different types of fuel? If so, how?*

4. *Which line represents coal and which represents natural gas? How do you know?*

5. *If you are asked to describe the graph, is it important to put in reasons for the changes in the amount of energy consumed?*

6. *Which tenses are you most likely to use in describing the graph?*

7. *As regards petroleum, you can mention that over the period consumption fluctuated, but ended the period at approximately the same level. What else can you say?*

8. *In writing you should always try to avoid repetition. Are there any synonyms you can use for: consumption, rise, fall?*

Now cover the questions above and study the graph below which shows Inland Energy Consumption in the UK in million tonnes of oil/coal equivalents from 1992 to 1995. After you have done this, look at the graph again and answer the questions.

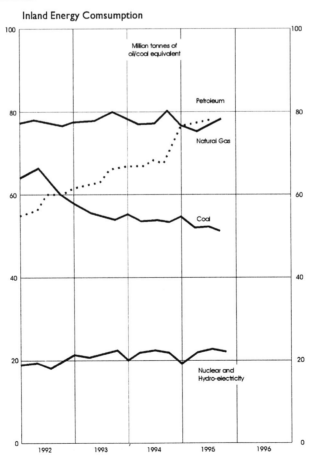

Inland Energy Comsumption

---

**A book for IELTS**

**Exercise 7:** Improving a text

Once students have written a text, it is often difficult for them to recognise the mistakes. The text below is an answer written for the graph in the previous exercise.

Read the text as quickly as you can and see how many mistakes you can find.

1. The graph shows the energy consumption from fossil and non-fossil fuels in UK in million tonnes of oil/coal equivalent from 1992 to l995.

2. A striking feature of the graph is the rise in the use of natural gas. Gas consumption was steadily upwards, overtook coal towards the end of 1992 and finally outstriping petroleum in 1995 to become, for a period, the second most popular energy source.

3. This rise was coincided with a drop in the use of coal during the period 1992 to 1995. At the beginning of 1992, coal consumtion stood at 65 million tonnes or so. In the first quater of 1992, there was a breif, steady climb and, from then until the beginning of the third quarter in 1995, the trend was markedly down. The fall down, first, was quite steep. From the end of 1993, consumption was steady with two miner peeks at the end of 1993 and 1994, which were corresponded with two troughs in the use of nuclear and hydro-electricity. Then from the beginning of 1995 coal consumption resumed its fall.

4. As it can be seen, petroleum was the main source of energy throughout the period with little or no changes in the consumed amount. The use of non-fossil sources of energy, i.e. nuclear and hydroelectricity, over the period was increased gradually with no dramatic rises or falls.

5. Despite the variations, the overall amount of energy consumed during the period shown on the graph was a little changed at the end of 1995.

---

| **Exercise 8:** The language of comparison and contrast |
| --- |

Look at the sentences and texts below. You can see that they are all related to comparing and contrasting.

Now look at the graphs on the next page. Decide which graphs are being compared or contrasted in each of the texts and sentences.

For example, the answer to the first one is F and C.

1. *The number of seats filled at the Bartlett theatre was steady over the period, but at the Ritz attendance was very irregular.*

2. *The trend in attendance at the Ritz was erratic, but nevertheless upwards, while that for the Bartlett enjoyed a steady rise before stabilising at around the 120 mark.*

3. *While attendances at the Ritz rose steadily throughout the year, at the Bartlett they shot up initially before plunging steeply and then remaining stable for the rest of the year.*

4. *Whereas the attendances at the Ritz dipped slightly at the end of March/beginning of April and again in August/September, those at the Bartlett rose during the corresponding periods.*

5. *The numbers attending the Bartlett declined through the year, while, on the contrary, attendance at the Ritz climbed at an even pace.*

6. *Attendances at the Ritz saw a steady rise, whereas the Bartlett's fluctuated wildly.*

7. *Audiences at the Ritz, not very stable for the first part of the year, shot up dramatically. The Bartlett, on the other hand, went through a rather volatile period in the first half of the year, before settling down to a more stable period.*

8. *The number of theatre-goers at the Ritz was fairly steady in the first half of the year, but numbers, plunging in the middle of the year, gradually petered out. The Bartlett, however, experienced a steep rise in attendance in the first half of the year, before falling again.*

9. *The total number of theatre-goers attending the Bartlett fell off during the first part of the year before making a steady recovery. By contrast, the Ritz attendance figures showed a rise followed by a steep drop.*

10. *The attendance rate at the Bartlett went up and down considerably throughout the year with the Ritz, by contrast, enjoying a period of stable, though modest, attendance.*

---

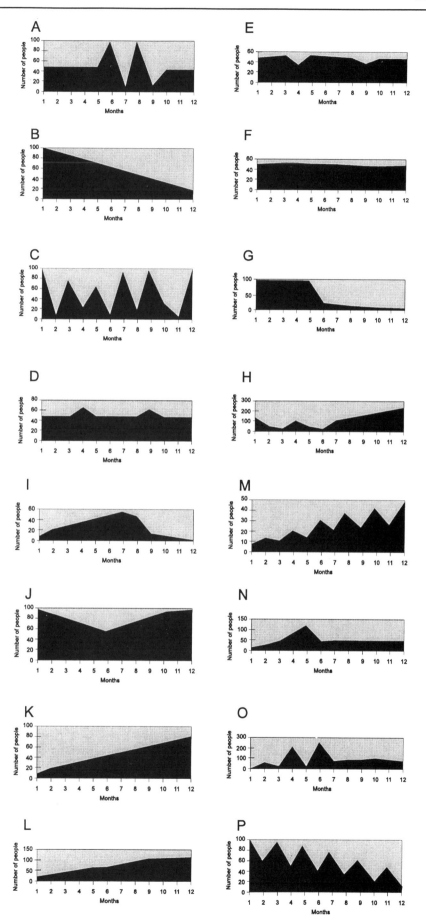

> **Exercise 9:** Graphs and charts combined

The diagram below shows the number of shoppers who visited a new shopping complex in its first year of operation and the estimated number of shoppers over the same period. Below the diagram, there are two charts, which show the sales at the centre in the first and last quarters of the year.

On the opposite page, there is a list of words and phrases and a model answer. All of the items in the list fit into the model, but some of them are more sophisticated than the alternative. Find the appropriate words and phrases to fill each blank and then decide which is the best answer.

For example, the answer for number **1** is **e** or **m**, of which **m** is the better answer.

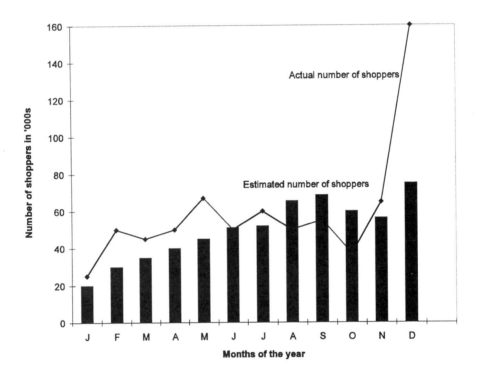

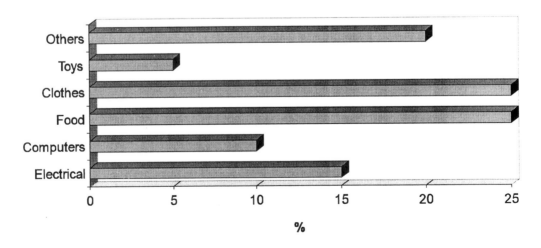

### Sales in percentage terms for first quarter

# Sales in percentage terms for the last quarter

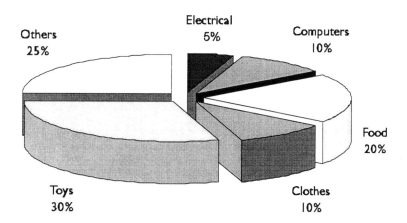

## List of words and phrases

a   in November the number of shoppers increased again

b   fell by a large amount

c   those

d   experienced a hefty fall

e   in the chart

f   outstripping projections by a wide margin

g   outperforming the figures predicted

h   declined further

i   being

j   November saw a noticeable turnaround

k   before they went up

l   forecast for the period

m   as can be seen from the chart

n   which were predicted for the period

o   which is twice as much as the estimated figures

p   they were

q   reveal a marked shift

r   double the estimate for the period

s   before picking up

t   proved

u   hitting a peak

v   were

w   show that there was a change

x   went down

y   during which time they did better  than the figures predicted

z   doing better than expected.

## MODEL ANSWER

_____1_____, in the first two months after the opening of the new shopping complex, the number of shoppers reached nearly 50,000, _____2_____. During March, however, the number of shoppers dropped slightly, _____3_____ during April and May, once again _____4_____. The summer months _____5___ not only rather erratic with the shopper numbers at the end of August _____6_____no higher than _____7_____ at the end of February, and also falling well below the numbers _____8_____.

During September and October, the number of actual shoppers _____9_____, but _____10_____ with the volume of shoppers rising dramatically, _____11_____. December saw this spectacular rise continue with the number of people shopping at the centre for the year _____12_____ of nearly 160,000 visitors per month.

The sales figures _____13_____ in spending patterns at the complex over the year with greater expenditure on Toys, Computers and Other items at the expense of Food and Clothes. For example, Toy sales soared from 5% to over 30%, while at the same time Clothes sales _____14_____.

---

**Exercise 10:** It is predicted that ...

---

This exercise looks at talking about the future. Study the charts below, which show changing trends in leisure in Europe for certain industries.

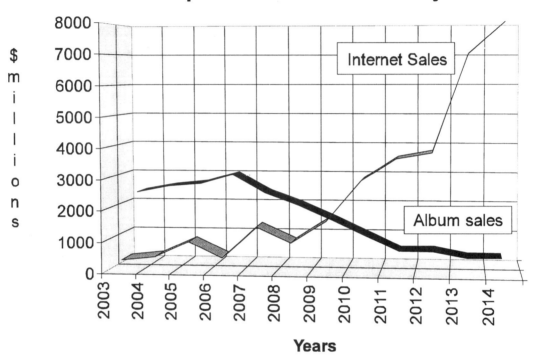

## European Entertainment Industry

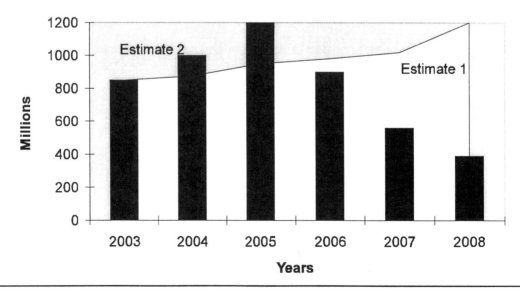

## Forecasts for European cinema attendances

---

Now look at the model below.

It is predicted that European Internet music sales will increase dramatically over the period covered by the graph. Rising fitfully at first, the sales will then leap in two stages to reach a high of $3900 million in 2012, before **rocketing to** a new peak of $8000 million at the end of 2014. Album sales, on the other hand, initially climbing until the end of 2006, are then set to drop steadily throughout the next five years, before bottoming out to end the period considerably below the $1000 million mark.

As regards attendances at European cinemas, there are two diverging forecasts. The first estimate is for numbers to rise steadily between the year 2003 and 2008, increasing from just below 900 million people to 1200 million with the largest rise in numbers going to cinemas expected to be in the year 2008. By contrast, the second forecast paints a different picture. The projection for the first three years of the period shows a rise, but after that cinema attendances are forecast to fall to below 400 million people.

Using the words and phrases below replace parts of the text above. Which version do you prefer? Note that the items below **are in the order that you should replace them**. Number six has been done for you as an example.

1. The prediction is that
2. will go up a lot
3. which the graph covers
4. They will rise erratically
5. and will then rise
6. **going up**
7. which will climb at first
8. before they bottom out and end
9. a lot below $1000 million

10. With European cinema attendances
11. and increase
12. and the biggest jump in cinema visitors is projected
13. But, the second forecast is different.
14. will fall

---

**Exercise 11:** More comparison and contrast

---

This exercise gives you more practice with comparing and contrasting. This time, however, you are going to look at two bar charts and a pie chart.

Study the two bar charts below, which show the average number of books borrowed from a local library per month in each category for the years 1996 and 1997. The pie chart then shows the percentage of books devoted to each category in the library

Look at the first two charts and find patterns in the data. Then compare the data with the information in the pie chart. Make a list of the patterns you find on a separate piece of paper.

### Borrowings per area 1996

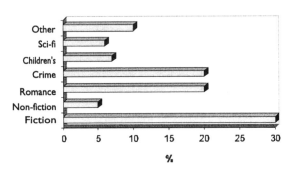

### Borrowings per area 1997

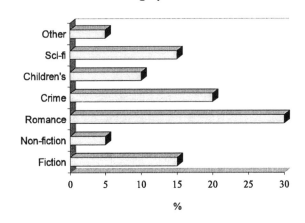

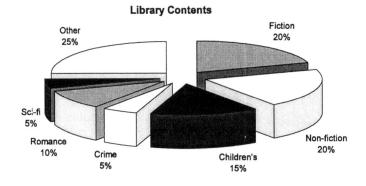

---

**A book for IELTS**

Now look at the text below and insert the following words and phrases in the most appropriate place:

1. in no way
2. For example,
3. In the third category come
4. whereas
5. as another example
6. By contrast,
7. A comparison
8. the latter
9. fall into three categories

10. , however,
11. whereas
12. On the one hand,
13. **the former**
14. by varying degrees

One of the phrases (No. 13) has already been inserted for you.

*of the borrowings for 1996 and 1997 shows that they, those for fiction and the 'other' category fell, **the former** by 50% from 30% of borrowings to 15%, and again by 50% from ten per cent to five per cent.*

*, children's books, romance and sci-fi all rose. Children's increased by several percentage points, books taken out from the romance section rose by 50% between the two years. The number of books borrowed by those reading science-fiction, went up threefold.*

*non-fiction and crime, neither of which saw any rise.*

*The contents of the library are reflected by the books that are taken out in either of the years. ,sci-fi books make up five per cent of the books in the library, while in both years borrowings exceed this amount, by three times as we have seen in 1997. Take non-fiction. Lendings in both years stand at five per cent, 20 per cent of the books fall into this category.*

---

**Exercise 12:** More complex terms

---

This exercise gives you more practice with comparing data. Study the charts below. The bar chart shows the results of a survey of the reading habits of first year female and male university students at a university in the UK. The pie charts show the amount of time male and female students spend on various activities.

### Reading habits of first year university students

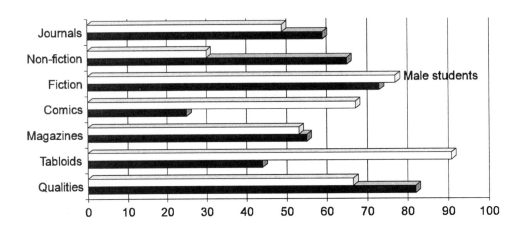

### Female students

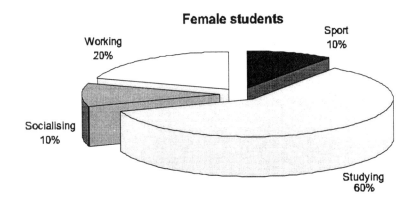

### Male Students

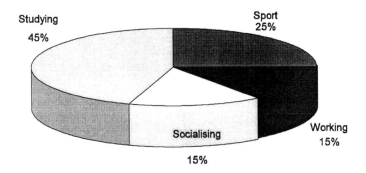

---

A book for **IELTS**

Now read the following text:

_____1_____ the bar chart shows how many first year male and female university students read _____2_____.

_____3_____ the female students appear to read more quality newspapers than _____4_____ by a margin of roughly 20%, male first year students _____5_____ read more tabloids _____6_____. When it comes to non-fiction, the same pattern is repeated; only this time the difference is _____7_____ approximately 65% of female students reading non-fiction _____8_____ 25% of the males.

The _____9_____ for comics. While over 60% of males read comics, only 25% of female students claim to do so. _____10_____, however, male students are ahead of females _____11_____, roughly 78% for the former and 75% for the latter. As regards magazines, _____12_____ both sexes are almost equal.

_____13_____ from the pie charts, a number of differences between the two groups _____14_____. Although female students work more (20% of their time rather than 15% for males, they _____15_____ 15% more of their time to studying. Females also spend less time socialising and much less than men on sport, allowing them more time for studying.

To complete the above text, add the most appropriate phrases to the blank spaces. Note that there are more blanks than words and phrases, so you also have to decide which blank spaces to leave empty!

    **a** pattern is reversed
    **b** devote
    **c** by a narrow margin
    **d** a range of publications
    **e** where fiction is concerned
    **f** their male counterparts
    **g** more pronounced with
    **h** as opposed to
    **i** can be seen
    **j** whereas

---

**Exercise 13:** Some common language mistakes

---

This exercise contains a range of mistakes, e.g. spelling and grammar, that students often make in the language that they use to write about graphs. Some of the sentences have more than one mistake. Can you find them?

1. There was a sharp decrease of the number of people attending the theatre over the period.

2. The increase of the incidence in petty crime has continued in spite of the measures introduced.

3. The charts indicate that the price of the various types of cars fell down considerably.

4. It was predicted that industrial production in Western countries level out, while that in the so-called Tiger economies will rise in the early '90s.

5. The price of computers has drammatically reduced over the period.

6. As regarding noise pollution, a pretty big rise in number of complaints was recorded for 1997.

7. As it can be seen, the rate of increase slowed over the last five years of the period.

8. At 1974, it's output began to stage a gradual recovery.

9. Between February and May, the income was fairly eratic.

10. It is estimated that the number of cars on the road plunge when road prizing is introduced.

11. Sales hit a peek in late summer and then felled back in the consequent months.

12. There was, acording to the graph, no significant changes to sales from 1973 to 1976.

13. The rate of inflation drooped slowly, but surely, in the early '80s.

14. The main charactristic of the bar chart is the large drop in male students applying.

15. The birth rate raised quite slowly over the period.

---

**Exercise 14:** How many correct sentences are there?

---

And now more mistakes! On the left, you have uncompleted texts, some of which are correct and some wrong. In the right-hand column, you again have some texts which are correct and some which are wrong. Match the correct texts in each column to form complete sentences. If you think that the text in the first column is wrong, it cannot then be completed. One of the sentences has been completed for you. In some cases, there may be more than one combination.

e.g. **(9 + e) = Expenditure has climbed considerably over the period.**

1  The graph shows that there was ...

2  The small decline of the use of ...

3  As the chart shows that ...

4  From the informations shown in the charts, ...

5  The graph shows the number of passengers ...

6  The incidence of 'telephone rage' ...

7  Between 1780 and 1850, a large number ...

8  The fluctuations in the consumption of alcohol ...

9  Expenditure ...

10  There was a mild rise ...

11  In case of Liberia, ...

12  The pound ...

13  The incidence of TB ...

14  The rise in cheese production ...

15  A similar rise can be ...

16  The Bartlett's shares of the UK bicycle market ...

17  From the data given,

18  In the case of the UK, ...

a  using trains, buses and the metro rose 7%, 8% and 4%, respectively.

b  a sudden rise in applications to take the course.

c  corresponding peaks in people using public transport.

d  was slight.

e  has climbed considerably over the period.

f  numeracy rates slipped back in the late 1970s.

g  plant equipment will ease off.

h  crept up at an even pace.

i  depend on many factors.

j  on education fell quite severely.

k  trains, buses and the metro rose 7%, 8% and 4%, respectfully.

l  soared slightly against the dollar.

m  we can see the main reason was a desire to meet new friends.

n  rose steeply between 1990 and 1997.

o  is dependent on a number of factors.

p  recovered slightly against the dollar.

q  in education was decreased.

---

**Exercise 15:** Questionnaire 1

---

This exercise focuses on a number of specific language points relating to graphs. Answer the questions as far as you can, and use the Key where necessary.

1.  Look at the list of words and phrases below. Which is the odd one out? And why?

    *decline, fall, drop, go down, decrease, fall down, plunge*

2.  Read the following sentence:

    *Over recent years, the price of white goods **has fallen** considerably.*

    Which of the words or phrases below can replace **has fallen**? There is more than one answer.
    *has reduced, has slowed down, has declined, has dropped, has been reduced,
    has deteriorated, has been dropped, has subsided, has lessened, has gone down,
    has decreased*
    Give reasons for your answer.

3.  Which of the sentences below is correct and why?

    *The number of people in full-time work dipped rather dramatically.*
    *The number of people in full-time work dipped slightly.*
    *The number of people in full-time work dipped rather slightly.*

4.  One major problem that students face in writing is using words that go together.
    In other words, they often use words which do not collocate. For example, you cannot say:

    *The space between the rich and the poor widened considerably.*

    **Space** is obviously the wrong word. The correct word is **gap**.

    Look at the following sentences and decide which word or phrase is not suitable and correct it:
    *(a) The dropping death rate ended the decade at an all time low.*
    *(b) The rising cost of life continued until the end of the decade.*
    *(c) The chart shows a large plummet in the amount of money invested in
    education over recent years.*
    *(d) There has been a deterioration in the percentage of the population in work.*
    *(e) There was a diminution in the price of telephoning internationally.*
    *(f) The downward tendency in traditional skills halted abruptly at the end of the year.*

5.  Look at the following sentence:

    *While the number of tourists visiting the site saw a significant increase, the amount of
    money which they spent on souvenirs fell.*

    What other ways can you use to express comparison here instead of using while?

6.  What other phrases and words do you know with the same meaning as **fluctuate**?

---

7.  *The birth rate did not change over the period.*

    Can you rewrite the sentence and begin: **There was ...**

    What other expressions do you know to express stability?


8.  Which two words and phrases below are the odd ones out?

    *plunge, plummet, deteriorate, take a nose dive, nosedive, decline, collapse,*
    *dive, fall headlong*


9.  One of the main problems that students have in describing graphs etc. is that they have
    difficulty using synonyms. What other words or phrases can you think of to replace the
    underlined words in the texts below?

    *The incidence of teenage crime has levelled off in many parts of the country over recent years.*
    *Nevertheless, we should not become complacent about the situation, as **the incidence of***
    ***teenage crime** is historically high.*


10. When you want to refer to a particular item on a graph you can use an expression like:

    ***As regards** the trend for Sierra Leone, the increase is more marked.*

    What other words or expressions like this do you know?


11. Look at the sentence below. What other words and expressions do you know which can
    replace the word **shows**?

    *The graph shows the percentage of the population of the UK who support the*
    *idea of a single currency.*

---

**Exercise 16:** Questionnaire 2

---

This exercise contains a number of questions about the language you need to describe graphs.

   1.   What other ways can you express sequence in the sentence below instead of just using the word 'next'? You may rewrite part of the sentence if you wish.

   *Next, the information is collated and sent out electronically to other agents.*

   2.   In the sentence below, what do you think is the best word to fill the blank?

   *The main _____ of this graph is the inverse relationship between the decrease in the consumption of beer and the rise in that of wine.*

   3.   In the sentence below there are two pieces of information: the approval rating of the new currency rose and it rose 35%. Can you combine the two pieces of information in another way? Which way is better?

   *The number of companies who registered approval of the new currency rose and the ratings rose by more than 35%.*

   4.   Rewrite the following sentence using the words **followed by:**

   *Mobile telephone sales rocketed in the first three months and then there was a steady decline for the rest of the year.*

   5.   Are both these sentences wrong?

   *The amount of money invested in the infrastructure was increased slowly.*
   *Cinema attendances were increased in the period.*

   6.   Is there anything wrong with the sentence below?

   *A glance at the graph shows that the trend was stable with no significant fall and rise.*

   7.   Look at the following words:

   *predict, forecast, estimate, prophesy, project, anticipate*

   Which is the odd one out?

   8.   Look at the following sentence:

   *The number of people on waiting lists is forecast to rise steadily in the coming years.*

   Rewrite the sentence and begin: **It ...**

   9.   Is it correct to say the following:

   *The projected number of people on waiting lists is set to rise steadily in the coming years.*

   10.  Is the word interesting in the sentence below objective or subjective?

   *The most interesting characteristic in the chart is the variation in temperature during the period.*

   If you replace the word interesting with significant, is there any change in the subjectivity/objectivity?

---

11. The amount of money invested in science and in training are being compared in the sentence below.

    *The falls in investment in science and training are almost the same.*

    What other ways can you compare the two items? You cannot use *'while'* etc (*see* Exercise 15, number 5).

12. All of the sentences below are correct. Which do you prefer and why?
    (a) *The rates of the decline in investment in science and training are not the same.*
    (b) *The rate of the decline in investment in science is not the same as that for training.*
    (c) *The rate of the decline in investment in science does not quite mirror that for training.*
    (d) *The rate of the decline in investment in science differs slightly from that for training.*
    (e) *The rate of the decline in investment in science is practically the same as that for training.*

13 Rewrite the sentence below using the word **not**.

    *The fall in investment in training is slightly smaller than that for science.*

---

**Exercise 17:** Tables

---

It is usually harder to describe tables than graphs and pie charts, mainly because they lack the visual organisation in the latter. However, the same principles apply to tables as to graphs: look for patterns. In addition, it might help you to draw a simple line graph next to each line of data, if it is too long to see a visual image immediately.

Study the table below and look for patterns in the data relating to **land transport only** i.e. excluding Foot, Water and Air.

**Passenger death rates: by mode of transport**

| Great Britain | | | | Rates per billion passenger kilometres | | |
|---|---|---|---|---|---|---|
| | 1981 | 1986 | 1991 | 1992 | 1993 | Average 1983-1993 |
| Motorcycle | 115.8 | 100.3 | 94.4 | 97.0 | 94.6 | 104.0 |
| Foot | 76.9 | 75.3 | 62.5 | 58.5 | 56.2 | 70.5 |
| Pedal cycle | 56.9 | 49.6 | 46.8 | 43.4 | 41.3 | 48.8 |
| Water[1] | 0.4 | 0.5 | 0.0 | 0.5 | 0.0 | 9.2 |
| Car | 6.1 | 5.1 | 3.7 | 3.5 | 3.0 | 4.6 |
| Van | 3.8 | 3.8 | 2.2 | 2.2 | 1.7 | 2.7 |
| Rail | 1.0 | 0.9 | 0.8 | 0.4 | 0.4 | 0.9 |
| Bus or coach | 0.3 | 0.5 | 0.6 | 0.4 | 0.8 | 0.5 |
| Air[1] | 0.2 | 0.5 | 0.0 | 0.1 | 0.0 | 0.2 |

[1] Data are for United Kingdom

Source: Department of Transport, Social Trends 1996, Table 12.15

Now look at the jumbled model below. The sections of text on the left are in the correct order and those on the right are jumbled. Using the table above to help you, recreate the model answer by matching the two sides.

**Example:** 1. matches (d); and 2. matches (e)

| | |
|---|---|
| 1. The data in the table relating to passenger | a. under review. Nevertheless, buses and |
| 2. in Great Britain between 1981 and 1993 | b. motorcycles and rail, the rate dropped |
| 3. The first group, consisting of cars, vans | c. the second most dangerous type of land transport. |
| 4. reduction in the rate of road death over | d. death rates by mode of land transport |
| 5. death among the car and van users | e. can be divided into three categories. |
| 6. from 6.1 per billion passenger | f. than twice as many fatalities as cycling, and more |
| 7. respectively. Cycling, however, | g. safest type of vehicular transport. |
| 8. 56.9 per billion to 41.3, remained | h. despite a significant decrease from |
| 9. In the second category, comprising | i. and bicycles experienced a significant |
| 10. slightly between 1981 and 1993. | j. kilometres to 3.0 and 3.8 to 1.7, |
| 11. type of transport averaging more | k. the period under study. For example, |
| 12. than twenty times as high as cars. | l. and coaches, the road death rate |
| 13. Regarding the third group, buses | m. declined by more than half, falling |
| 14. almost trebled over the period | n. Motorcycling was the most dangerous |
| 15. coaches were still the second | |

Compare your answer with the Key.

---

A book for **IELTS**

**Exercise 18:** Map language – and verbs and tenses

In this exercise, you are going to look at the language that is used in describing maps. Study the two maps below, which show the area of Barton Bingham in 1937 and 1995. Then look at the text on the page opposite which has no verbs. Read the text with the maps and put the verbs from the **Verb box** into the most suitable places in the text. You may use each item in the **Verb box** once only. One of the verb phrases (No.17) has been done for you as an example.

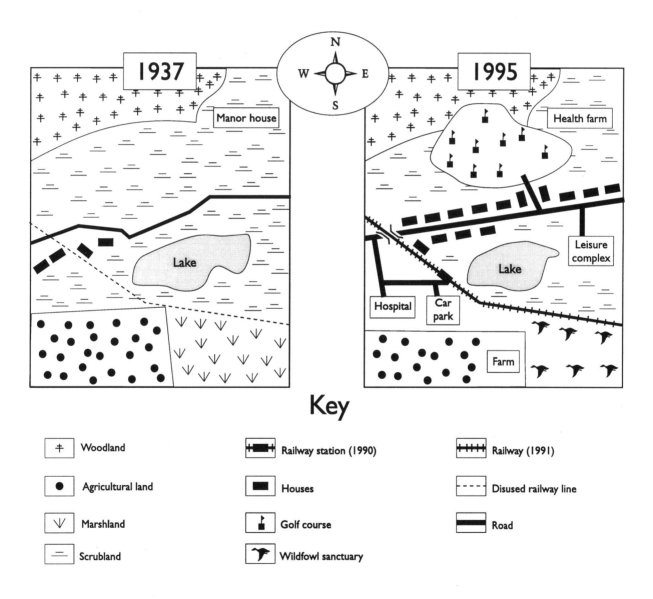

## Key

| | | | | | | |
|---|---|---|---|---|---|---|
| + | Woodland | ▬■▬ | Railway station (1990) | +++ | Railway (1991) |
| ● | Agricultural land | ■■ | Houses | ----- | Disused railway line |
| ∨ | Marshland | ⬩ | Golf course | ▬▬ | Road |
| — | Scrubland | ⟜ | Wildfowl sanctuary | | |

## Changes in Barton Bingham

As **can be seen** from the maps, the area of Barton Bingham significantly between 1937 and 1995. The road bisecting the area and on both sides various developments. On the north side, the manor house into a health farm and part of the surrounding scrubland and adjacent woodland a golf course. The area immediately adjacent to the road to housing along its entire length.

On the south side of the road, a railway station in 1990, which by a minor road to the main thoroughfare. In 1991, the disused railway line, with a bridge across the road. In the scrubland to the east of the lake, a leisure complex in 1995. In addition, the area of agricultural land which in 1937 to make way for the construction of a new hospital and a car park both also with road access to the main highway. A farmhouse the remaining agricultural land. Next to the agricultural land, the marshes that there in 1937, to a wildfowl sanctuary.

### Verb box

| | | | |
|---|---|---|---|
| 1. | became | 10. | was reopened |
| 2. | existed | 11. | was completed and opened |
| 3. | gave way | 12. | were |
| 4. | being built | 13. | was halved |
| 5. | was constructed | 14. | was built on |
| 6. | changed | 15. | was connected |
| 7. | took place | 16. | was straightened |
| 8. | was converted | **17.** | **can be seen** |
| 9. | were turned over | | |

**Exercise 19:** Process language?

And now for the language necessary to describe processes. Look at the timeline below which shows the steps taken to produce a TV documentary on Lenin.

Then read the list (a-o) below diagram and choose the sentences you need to describe the sequence of events that led to the production of the documentary.

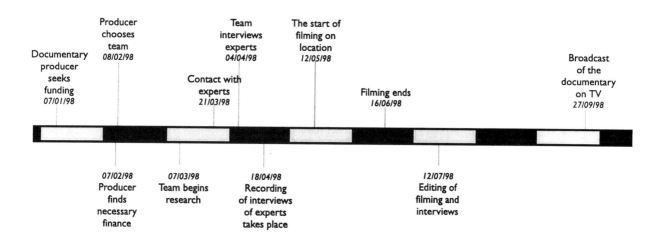

Please note that five of the sentences are not suitable.

a      The next stage was the fact finding which was begun on 7 March.

b      Not long afterwards the programme was edited.

c      and the interviews were finally recorded two weeks later.

d      The required funding was secured just over four weeks afterwards.

e      The film crew were briefed.

f      All the necessary research was done on 7 March.

g      The documentary was then televised at the end of September.

h      At the beginning of 1978, funding for the documentary on Lenin was applied for.

i      The next phase, filming on location, began on 12 May and came to an end just over four weeks later.

j      Contact was then made with experts on Lenin.

k      The experts were interviewed

l      The producer applied for funding of the documentary at the beginning of 1998.

m      and the interviews were finally recorded three weeks later.

n      The producer was chosen by the team.

o      The production crew were selected by the producer the following day.

---

Exercise 20: The process of making a newspaper

---

Look at the diagram below. Then read the brief explanation on the next page, which a printer gave to a group of teenagers about making a daily newspaper.

Below the printer's explanation is an outline for a written version of what the printer said. Using the explanation, complete the report. Then compare your version with the Key.

# Making a daily newspaper

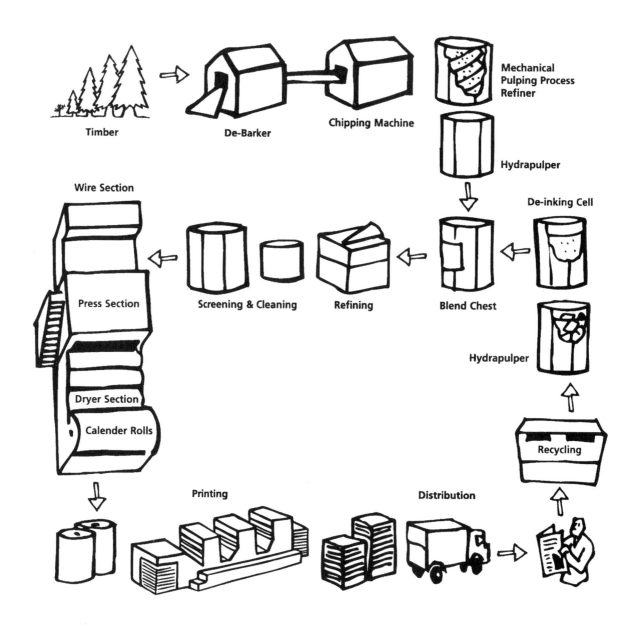

# Printer's explanation

*'Well, if you look at this diagram here, you can see that we take material from two places, timber from trees and recycled paper, and then we pass it through some machines to create the newspaper.*

*We put the wood into this machine here to remove the bark and then we chop the timber up into little tiny pieces in this one here. These tiny pieces we then put into this mechanical refiner, and after that it goes into the hydrapulper over there.*

*And then we mix the chippings with water and make them into a pulp, which we put into this blend chest where we mix it with pulp from recycled paper, which I'll talk about in a minute. We then refine, clean and screen this mixture before it goes into this large piece of machinery here where we press the pulp, dry it and then make it into rolls of paper.*

*Once we print the newspaper, it is sent to your newsagent. After you have finished with the paper, it hopefully goes into a recycling bin.*

*The recycled paper goes into this hydrapulper here and we remove the ink in that de-inking cell over there. This is added to the blend chest: and the whole process is repeated. Any questions?'*

# Written report

To create daily newspaper the necessary material is taken from two sources,

_____.

Trees are cut down to provide timber. In the first machine, _____

_____.

These chippings _____, and subsequently a

hydrapulper _____. At the next

stage, the pulp _____

_____. This mixture _____

_____

_____into rolls of paper.

Once the newspaper has been printed, it _____. After the reader ___

_____. The recycling process first

involves _____

_____into a pulp. A de-inking cell then extracts the ink. After that, the solution is put into the blend chest: and the whole process is repeated.

# Essay Writing for Task 2

**Exercise 21:** Understanding essay titles

Candidates often score badly in the Task 2 of the writing module in IELTS, simply because they do not understand what the essay question is asking them to do. Look at the following:

*Charges for entrance to museums is seen by many as a tax on education.*
*What do you think the consequences of such charging would be?*

The focus of this question is the word consequences and your opinion is involved in the selection of the consequences. So you should organise your essay around the focus word, perhaps using variations like effect and result.

Now look at the ten essay titles below and the explanations which follow. Match the explanations to the titles. Note that there are more explanations than titles and some of the explanations are wrong or not complete.

*The answer to number one is: B*

**Essay titles**

1. *Charges for entrance to museums is seen by many as a tax on education. How far do you agree with this statement?*

2. *Many people believe that the next world war will happen as a result of conflicts over water. Is this fear justified? Give reasons for your answer.*

3. *Success in life is more often than not elusive. What factors help to make an individual successful?*

4. *Some people believe that it would be better if there were only one language in the world. Others are of the opinion that if this ever occurred it would cause more problems than it solved. Discuss the problems that might arise if, in fact, there were only one language in the world and give your own opinion.*

5. *Some people believe that the influence that television exerts over society is largely detrimental and are calling for it to be more strictly controlled. Should television be more tightly controlled to protect society and, if so, how? Or should it have even fewer restrictions placed on it?*

6. *Noise pollution is most certainly increasing at an alarming rate in many industrialised countries. In what ways can this problem be overcome?*

7. *People point to the number of presidents and other rulers who come to power at an advanced age, or artists and famous people who achieve success late in life as one of the arguments against age discrimination in the work place. What are the dangers of such discrimination? Do you feel age discrimination should be banned or do you feel that there are certain jobs that should only be open to younger people?*

8. *As people live longer and longer, the idea of cloning human beings in order to provide human spare parts is becoming a reality. The idea horrifies most people, yet it is becoming a reality rather than mere science fiction. To what extent do you agree with such a procedure? Have you any reservations?*

9. *Money has always been a prime driving force for people, but as we move into the technological age we seem to be driven more and more by the pursuit of money. Discuss the arguments for and against this idea and give your own views.*

10. *People generally believe that knowledge is power, but rather it is the ability to manipulate knowledge not knowledge itself, which bestows power. How far do you agree?*

## Explanations

A.  The title makes a distinction between the use of knowledge and knowledge. It says that the latter gives an individual power. You have to give your opinion about this distinction, i.e. which is more important?

B.  This title asks you how far you agree with the idea that museum charges are a tax on education. You can state your opinion and give your reasons. Or you can state your own opinion generally, then give other people's views and then demolish them by supporting your own opinion. Or you can give other people's views and then demolish them by giving your own.

C.  You are being asked to describe what contributes to making an individual successful.

D.  This title asks what you think about the next world war being fought over water. You can state your opinion and show the consequences.

E.  Describe the arguments against about money being the main driving force for human beings.

F.  This title asks your opinion about whether we should be afraid of a war resulting from fights over water supplies and also asks you to give your reasons.

G.  The question is asking you to state your opinion about the positive effects of TV on society.

H.  Describe the risks of age discrimination in the work place and state whether it should be banned. Also do you feel that certain jobs should be done by younger people?

I.  You are being asked to describe why people more often fail than achieve success.

J.  You are being asked to state how far you agree or disagree with cloning human beings to provide spare parts and also to say whether you have any doubts about the subject.

K.  You are being asked to describe the problems involved if there were only one language in the world and what your opinion is in this matter.

L.  You are being asked to state how far you agree or disagree with cloning human beings to provide spare parts.

M.  You are being asked to describe the advantages and problems involved if there were only one language in the world.

N.  Describe the arguments for and against and also give your opinion about money being the main driving force for human beings.

O.  The question is asking you to state your opinion about whether television should be restricted or not. It also asks you to describe how to control TV, if you agree.

P.  Describe some measures to reduce noise pollution.

Q.  Discuss the problems faced by industrialised nations.

R.  The title makes a distinction between knowledge and the use of knowledge. It says that the latter gives an individual power not knowledge itself. You have to give your opinion about this distinction, i.e. which is more important?

S.  Describe the arguments for and against age discrimination in the work place and state whether it should be banned.

---

> **Exercise 22:** Plans for essays

For many students deciding how to plan an essay under the stress of the exam causes many problems. However, you should note that, while the range of general subjects is wide, there is a limit to the type of question you can be asked to write about.

This exercise shows a range of essay types. Look at the titles below and then at the plans which follow. Decide which basic plan, or plans, is suitable for each essay.

*Note that two of the titles do not have plans.*

1.   A growing number of people feel animals should have the same rights as humans. Discuss the difficulties that the adoption of such a policy would have for humans. What is your own opinion on this matter?

2.   A growing number of people feel animals should have the same rights as humans. Others feel that humans must always come first and accuse animal rights activists of being overly sentimental. How far do you agree or disagree?

3.   The wealth of a nation depends primarily on the level of education of its workforce. How far do you agree with this statement and what other factors do you think might be involved?

4.   The primary concern of architects should be to create buildings that are pleasing to the eye rather than just being functional. What would be the benefits to society if architects adopted such a principle?

5.   Education is not a luxury, but a basic human right and as such should be free for everyone irrespective of personal wealth. Discuss the difficulties of applying such a principle.

6.   The extinction of animals is part of a natural process that we as human beings should not interfere with. What are the arguments against this statement and how far do you agree with it yourself?

7.   For a long time, there has been concern about the quality of the food we eat what with food additives and contamination from pesticides and pollution. Now the advances in genetically-engineered food are causing concern among the general public. Is this concern, in your opinion, justified or are we all just looking for something to worry about?

8.   Prisons are basically universities of crime, fostering the kind of behaviour they aim to eradicate. In what ways can prisons help criminals to function normally when they return to society? Do you think such attempts at rehabilitating criminals are effective?

9.   The cloning of human beings is an inevitable consequence of human development. Should such cloning be banned? Or should scientists be allowed to continue developing this field of research?

10.   Cloning is an inevitable consequence of human development. What are the dangers if it is allowed to develop unchecked? Should it be banned totally?

---

A book for **IELTS**

## Plan A

_____ has been an issue about which there has been considerable hostile debate. There are, of course, a number of problems involved in adopting such a policy. The main difficulty is _____ _____. _____ is yet another obstacle.
As far as I am concerned, _____ _____.

## Plan B

Whether_____ _____. I personally _____.
My main reason is _____ _____.
Another justification is _____ ___ _____.
Last but not least,_____ _____.

## Plan C

Whether_____ _____. (I personally _____.)
Some people feel _____ _____.
Others _____ _____.
In my opinion, _____ _____ _____.

## Plan D

_____ is a matter of debate. There are, however, several strong arguments against this.
_____ is obviously the main argument.
Another justification is _____ _____
From my point of view, _____ _____.

## Plan E

Whether _____. From my point of view,_____ _____.
_____ is, in my opinion, the main contributing factor.
Another _____.
Finally, _____ to be considered.
As we have seen, _____ _____.

## Plan F

Many people are expressing concern about _____. Other people, by contrast, _____ _____.
There are, of course, several risks inherent in such a development.
The most obvious danger is _____ _____.
_____ _____ is another hazard.
Having said that, however, I believe _____ _____.

## Plan G

Whether_____. From my point of view, _____ _____.
_____ is, in my opinion, the main measure.
Another course of action would be to _____ ___ _____.
I am personally of the opinion _____ _____.

## Plan H

_____ is a matter of debate. There are, of course, several strong arguments for/against doing this.
_____ is obviously the main argument for/against. However, in my opinion, _____ _____.
Another justification for/against is _____ _____. Having said that, however, I feel _____.
From my point of view, _____ _____.

---

**Exercise 23:** Same general subject – different focus

---

This exercise gives you further practice in interpreting essay titles. Below there are ten essay titles all with the same general subject, but the focus of each essay question is different. Following the titles, there are some explanations. Match the explanations to the titles. Note that there are more explanations than titles; some of the explanations are wrong or not complete. In one or two cases there may be more than one correct answer.

## Essay titles

1.  *Some people feel that media like the press, television, and the Internet should be more strictly controlled. Others believe that, if anything, the controls should be loosened to give people freer access to information. Where do you stand on this issue?*

2.  *Some people are of the opinion that media like the press, television, and the Internet should be more strictly controlled. Others feel that the controls should be loosened to give people freer access to information. How far do you agree with loosening the controls?*

3.  *Some people are of the opinion that media like the press, television, and the Internet should be more strictly controlled. Others firmly feel that, if anything, the controls should be loosened to give people freer access to information. Discuss the dangers and advantages if media controls were further relaxed.*

4.  *Some people believe that media like the press, television, and the Internet should be more strictly controlled. Others feel that, if anything, the controls should be loosened to give people freer access to information. What are the disadvantages of not relaxing media controls further? And where do you stand on the issue?*

5.  *Some people think that media like the press, television, and the Internet should be more strictly controlled. Others feel that if anything the controls should be loosened to give people freer access to information. Discuss the problems that might arise if the controls were relaxed and give your own opinion on the issue.*

6.  *Some people fear that media like the press, television, and the Internet will cause irreparable damage unless they are more strictly controlled. Others feel that, if anything, the controls should be loosened to give people freer access to information. Is this fear really justified? Give reasons for your answer.*

7.  *Some people believe that media like the press, television, and the Internet should be more strictly controlled. Others feel that if anything the controls should be loosened to give people freer access to information. What are the dangers of such freedom? Do you feel there should be more controls over the media or do you think that the restrictions in place are too tight?*

8.  *Some people believe that media like the press, television, and the Internet should be more strictly controlled. Others feel that if anything the controls should be loosened to give people freer access to information. To what extent do you agree with the idea of reducing media controls? Have you any reservations either way?*

9.  *Some people believe that media like the press, television, and the Internet should be more strictly controlled. Others feel that if anything the controls should be loosened to give people freer access to information. Discuss the arguments for and against the latter idea and give your own views.*

10. *Some people believe that media like the press, television, and the Internet should be more strictly controlled. Others feel that if anything the controls should be loosened to give people freer access to information. Should the controls be made tighter? Or should there be more freedom for the media?*

---

## Explanations

A.   The question is asking you to describe what the drawbacks could be if controls over the media are relaxed. You also have to give your own opinion. The question has two main parts.

B.   You are being asked to discuss the risks involved in relaxing control of the media. There is another part to this question i.e. you have to give your opinion about whether controls need to be tightened or whether they are already too restrictive.

C.   This title asks you whether you agree with relaxing or tightening media controls. You can state your opinion and give your reasons. Or you can state your own opinion generally, then give other people's views and then demolish them by supporting your own opinion. Or you can give other people's views and then demolish them by giving your own.

D.   You are being asked to give your opinion i.e. which side of the issue do you agree with or are you in the middle?

E.   This title asks to write about the risks involved in having media controls. You should also give your opinion.  The question has two parts.

F.   You are being asked to describe the problems involved if media controls were relaxed and to give your opinion.

G.   This title you asks you to write about the risks involved and the benefits in having looser media controls.

H.   The question is asking you to describe what the drawbacks could be if controls over the media are not relaxed. You also have to give your own opinion.

I.   You are being asked to describe the problems involved if media controls were relaxed. You are not being asked to write about anything else.

J.   Note the question has three elements. You are being asked to describe the arguments for and against relaxing media control and also to give your opinion.

K.   Note the question has two elements. You are being asked to describe the arguments for relaxing media control and also to give your opinion.

L.   Should we be afraid of relaxing controls governing the media?  This also means that you should ask yourself: Or should we not be afraid?   Then you are asked to give the reasons for your opinion.

M.   You are being asked to state how far you agree with relaxing media controls and also whether you have any doubts either way regarding the issue.

N.   You are being asked to state how far you agree with relaxing or tightening media controls. Note the question has only one part.

---

**Exercise 24:** A model essay

---

Look at two different answers for the essay title below and see if you can spot the difference between the two versions. Then when you have done this, decide which one is the better of the two.

### Essay title
*Should museums and art galleries be free of charge for the general public or should a charge, even a voluntary charge, be levied for admittance?*

## Version A

1. In many countries, a charge is levied for entrance to museums and art galleries, but, in some instances, entrance is free.

2. The up-keep of such institutions is not cheap and it is only fair that some contribution should come by way of an entrance fee or, at least, a voluntary contribution. An exception is usually made for certain categories of people.

3. If people are made to pay to visit museums and art galleries, then this is effectively a tax on education. People should be encouraged to visit such institutions.

4. Moreover, children who have visited a museum or a gallery with their school may not be able to go again with their parents. A fee would act as a deterrent to people wanting to visit a museum.

5. Often people want to spend maybe only half an hour in a museum rather than spending a long time to justify paying a fee.

6. People should not have pay to visit museums and art galleries.

## Version B

1. In many countries, a charge is levied for entrance to museums and art galleries, but, in some instances, entrance is free.

2. Where a charge is, in fact, levied, the argument is that the up-keep of such institutions is not cheap and while the tax-payer might be expected to provide some funds, it is only fair that some contribution should come by way of an entrance fee or, at least, a voluntary contribution. An exception is usually made for certain categories of people, like the unemployed, the elderly, the disabled, school children and students on the grounds of financial hardship.

3. Personally, however, I believe that, if people are made to pay to visit museums and art galleries, then this is effectively a tax on education. People should be encouraged to visit such institutions, as they contain a wealth of material relating not only to the history and culture of their own countries, but also of other civilisations. They can, of course, obtain information from books films etc, but this is nothing to seeing the real objects.

4. Moreover, children who have visited a museum or a gallery with their school may not be able to go again with their parents, if there is an entrance fee. So a fee, in my opinion would act as a deterrent to people wanting to visit a museum.

5. Often people want to spend maybe only half an hour in a museum rather than spending a long time to justify paying a fee. This would deter many people, myself included, from visiting museums. Having said this, however, I am not against voluntary charges or people being encouraged to make donations.

6. So, all in all, my personal view is that people should not have pay to visit museums and art galleries.

---

**A book for IELTS**

# Writing Tests

## TEST 1

### Writing Task 1

You should spend about 20 minutes on this task.

> *The bar chart below shows the projected sales in the UK of private cars and company cars from 2003 to 2014 and the graph shows the projected motorcycle sales for the same period.*

Write a report for a university lecturer comparing and contrasting the data from the year 2003 onwards.

You should write at least 150 words.

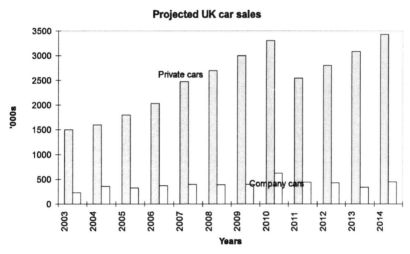

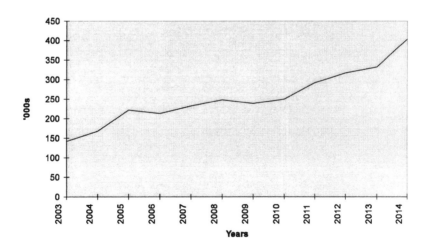

## TEST 1

### Writing Task 2

You should spend about 40 minutes on this task.

Present a written argument or case for an educated reader with no specialist knowledge of the following topic:

> *Some people are of the opinion that prisons are basically universities of crime, fostering the kind of behaviour they aim to eradicate, and are, therefore, not effective. Others feel that prison life is not*

*hard enough. Discuss the arguments on both sides of the issue. What is your own opinion on the matter?*

You should write at least 250 words.

Use your own ideas, knowledge and experience and support your arguments with examples and with relevant evidence.

## TEST 2

### *Writing Task 1*

You should spend about 20 minutes on this task.

The charts below show the result of a public survey on the use of mobile phones.

Write a report for a university lecturer describing the data.

You should write at least 150 words.

**Generally speaking, do you approve of mobile phones?**

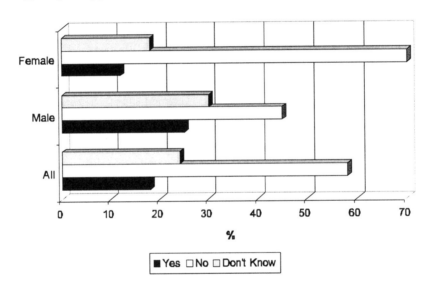

**Do you think that mobile phones could be detrimental to your children's health?**

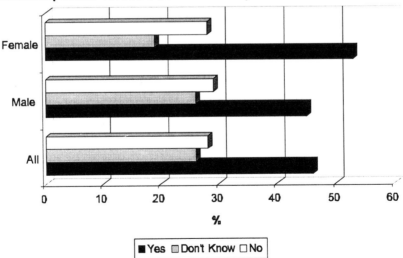

A book for **IELTS**

## TEST 2

### Writing Task 2

You should spend about 40 minutes on this task.

Present a written argument or case for an educated reader with no specialist knowledge of the following topic:

> *Euthanasia, or mercy killing, has been in the news more and more recently. Many people are strongly against such a practice, but there is a growing demand to have it legalised. How far do you agree with euthanasia being made legal?*

You should write at least 250 words.

Use your own ideas, knowledge and experience and support your arguments with examples and with relevant evidence.

## TEST 3

### Writing Task 1

You should spend about 20 minutes on this task.

> *The pictures below show the changes that took place at Laguna Beach from 1950 to 1990.*

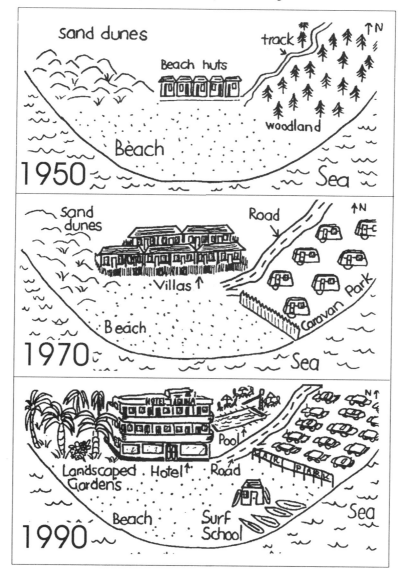

Write a report for a university lecturer describing the information shown below.

You should write at least 150 words.

## TEST 3

### *Writing Task 2*

You should spend about 40 minutes on this task.

Present a written argument or case for an educated reader with no specialist knowledge of the following topic:

> *In recent years, life has become more stressful than it has ever been. As a consequence, more and more people are suffering from stress-related problems. What factors are contributing to this increase and what do you think can be done to overcome the current problems?*

You should write at least 250 words.

Use your own ideas, knowledge and experience and support your arguments with examples and with relevant evidence.

# Section on Speaking

# Introduction to the Speaking Module

The speaking section of the IELTS lasts between 10 and 15 minutes. During the examination you will have a conversation with an examiner, which is recorded. There are 5 main parts within the oral exam:

| | |
|---|---|
| **1. Introduction** | You and the examiner introduce yourselves to one another. The examiner will try to put you at ease and encourage you to talk about your family life, your home, work and interests, etc. |
| **2. Extended discourse** | You will have a conversation with the examiner about a familiar topic, which is of general interest, or which is relevant to your culture, place of living or country of origin. This will include an explanation, description or narration. |
| **3. Elicitation** | The examiner will give you a Candidate's Cue Card, which contains information about a situation and 4 or 5 prompts. Your task is to ask the examiner questions regarding the prompts to find out information. You may instead be given a problem to solve by asking questions. |
| **4. Speculation and Attitudes** | The examiner will usually ask you about your future plans and your proposed course of study. He or she may also ask you to talk about an earlier topic which you brought up. |
| **5. Conclusion** | The examiner will end the conversation. |

*NOTE*

**A.** In the Speaking Module, the examiner is assessing whether you have the knowledge and skills to communicate effectively with native speakers. The examiner is, therefore, not just assessing your grammatical accuracy, but the communicative strategies you use, and whether your grammar and vocabulary are appropriate and flexible.

**B.** Students often make the mistake of learning by heart chunks of information relating to stages 2 and 4 above. This causes problems, because it is very easy for an examiner to see if you are doing this. All the examiner has to do to check your fluency is to ask a question you are not prepared for!

**C.** You may think this is unfair, but remember the IELTS tests your ability to use the language, not your ability to produce speeches from memory.

**D.** Remember that in the exam, you need to give the examiner enough evidence of your ability to use the language. Otherwise, you will probably not receive the score you deserve.

**E.** You should, therefore, learn to develop your answers. Look at the following example:

> **Examiner:** What do you like about Sydney?
>
> **Candidate:** The people.

The examiner is speaking more than the candidate! The candidate could expand on his/her answer:

> The people, because, since I have been here, they have been very friendly and helpful and ...

So remember to give the examiner evidence of your ability to use the language.

**Exercise 1:** Eliciting information

Look at **Cue Card A**, which contains a number of prompts for asking questions, and the **Examiner information** below. Then look at the list of **Questions** on the right, some of which contain mistakes. Match each prompt with a correct question.

**Candidate's Cue Card A**

You are a first year student at a university. You would like to book a computer in the new Open Learning Centre. Your examiner is a librarian.

*Ask the examiner about:*

(a) The Process for reserving a computer

(b) Advance booking

(c) Help available

(d) The length of a computer session

(e) Facilities on computer, e.g. Internet access, e-mail.

**Questions**

1. How do you get a computer?
2. Can you tell me how far in advance do I have to book?
3. What facilities are available on the machines, like Internet access, e-mail and so on?
4. How do I go about booking a computer?
5. How far in advance do I have to book?
6. Shall I book a computer?
7. What length of time is that I reserve it for?
8. What technical help is available?
9. How long can I reserve the computer for?
10. Are there someone around to help if needed?
11. What are the available facilities on the machines, like Internet access, e-mail and so on?

**EXAMINER INFORMATION**

**(a) The Process for reserving a computer**

Students need to have a library card and pay a refundable deposit of £25.

**(b) Advance booking**

The use of computers is very heavy, so advance booking is necessary.

**(c) Help available**

There is always a computer technician or supervisor available to sort out problems.

**(d) The length of a computer session**

One hour, but if a computer is free, the time can be extended.

**(e) Facilities on computer, e.g. Internet access, e-mail.**

There is Internet access, but students must pay an extra fee of £2 per week for e-mail.

# Candidate Cue Card B

Look at **Cue Card B**, which contains a number of prompts for asking questions, and the **Examiner information** below. Then look at the list of **Questions 1–24** and decide which one is the correct question for each prompt.

**Candidate's Cue Card B**

You are planning to stay in a youth hostel, while you are on holiday. The examiner is the receptionist at the youth hostel.

*Ask the examiner about:*

(a) Rates for bed and breakfast

(b) Number of people per room

(c) Visitor regulations

(d) Vacation of the hostel during the day

(e) Security of belongings

(f) Payment options

## EXAMINER INFORMATION

(a) **Rates for bed and breakfast**

   *Bed and breakfast costs £12 per night.*

(b) **Number of people per room**

   *Accommodation is in single-sex dormitories with between 4 and 12 beds to a room, many of these being bunk beds. Some twin-bedded rooms are available, but are full at present.*

(c) **Visitor regulations**

   *No visitors whatsoever are allowed in the dormitories. Hostel residents may receive visitors in the common room and entertainment rooms, but all visitors must leave the premises by 10 p.m.*

(d) **Vacation of the hostel during the day**

   *All residents must vacate the hostel by 10.30 a.m. and no entry to the hostel is allowed until 4.30 p.m.*

(e) **Security of belongings**

   *Property is left in the hostel at the owner's risk. Residents are advised to carry their valuables with them at all times or ask hostel staff to secure belongings in the safe where necessary.*

(f) **Payment options**

   *By cash, travellers' cheques, or credit card.*

## Questions

(a) *Rates for bed and breakfast*

   1. What is the cost of bed and breakfast?
   2. What means bed and breakfast?
   3. I'd like to know how much does bed and breakfast cost?
   4. Can you tell me what the rate for bed and breakfast is?

(b) *Number of people per room*

   5. May I have an idea about the kind of room?
   6. Are the rooms single or sharing?
   7. Who are the room occupants?
   8. How many you get into a room?

(c) *Visitor regulations*

   9. Are there any rules regarding visitors?
   10. Visitors are a possibility, isn't it?
   11. Are visitors regulated?
   12. I am a visitor, so I need regulations.

(d) *Vacation of the hostel during the day*

   13. When we should leave the hostel during the day?
   14. Is this hostel a vacation one during the day?
   15. At what time do I have to leave the hostel each day?
   16. Is there daily vacation?

(e) *Security of belongings*

   17. Can you offer me security?
   18. Will my things be safe?
   19. I'd like to know about belonging and security.
   20. What about possessions security?

(f) *Payment options*

   21. How do I have to pay?
   22. Do I have to pay?
   23. How can I pay?
   24. Can I pay in options?

# Candidate's Cue Card C

Look at **Cue Card C**, which contains a number of prompts for asking questions, and the **Examiner information** below. Then look at the list of **Questions** (A-S) and choose the most appropriate questions for each prompt. There may be more than one suitable question for each prompt.

## Questions

A. Can I lend my permit to someone else?

B. You have provided student car parks, haven't you?

C. What restrictions are there on student parking?

D. How much you want me to pay?

E. How about opening times?

F. Where exactly are the student parks?

G. How much costs parking?

H. What time does it open the car park?

I. Can anyone else use my permit?

J. Where can students park?

K. Is the permit transferable?

L. Can you tell me when students can park on campus?

M. What does a parking permit cost?

N. Where can I place my automobile?

O. Are the student car parks open round the clock?

P. How much is a parking permit?

Q. What about fines for illegal parking?

R. Is it okay for me to park in other Colleges?

S. Could you tell me about parking for students at the university?

---

**Candidate's Cue Card C**

You are a student who has recently started university. You would like to use your car to come to College every day and want to find out about parking on the campus. Your examiner is a student services officer.

*Ask the examiner about:*

1. Places for students to park
2. Cost of permit
3. Parking restrictions on campus
4. Transfer of permit
5. Penalties

---

## EXAMINER INFORMATION

| | |
|---|---|
| **1. Places for students to park** | Places to park are very limited, as it is a busy urban area and there are many red routes. Also the parking meters are very expensive. However, there are two student car parks. |
| **2. Cost of permit** | The cost is £1 per day. A weekly or termly permit works out cheaper in the long run. |
| **3. Parking restrictions on campus** | Outside the car parks, parking spaces are very limited. |
| **4. Transfer of permit** | Permits cannot be used for other cars. |
| **5. Penalties** | Vehicles parking illegally are clamped and the unclamping fee is £100. |

# Candidate Cue Card D

Look at **Cue Card D** below, which contains a number of prompts for asking questions, and the **Examiner information** below. Then look at the list of **Questions** on the left and match the questions to a prompt. Most prompts have more than one question.

## QUESTIONS

I. Can you suggest what we should charge for membership?
II. Is help with things like photocopying and publicity available?
III. Any idea what we should charge for membership?
IV. Do we have to pay for the hire of rooms and other facilities?
V. What do we have to do to get the club up and running?
VI. Do we need to register the club somehow?
VII. What help can we get from the Students' Union?
VIII. Do all clubs have to be registered?
IX. How do we go about setting up the club?
X. Can we get any help with photocopying and advertising?
XI. Are rooms and other facilities free of charge?

---

**Candidate's Cue Card D**

You are a first year student at a university. With some friends, you are planning to set up a club. Your examiner is a student Union Official.

*Ask the examiner about:*

A. Process of establishing club
B. Registering the club
C. Union support
D. Paying for facilities
E. Photocopying/ advertising
F. Recommendations on charging membership fees

---

## EXAMINER INFORMATION

### A. Process of establishing club

You need only three members to establish a club. And a set-up fee of £5 is required.

### B. Registering the club

All clubs have to be registered with the Students' Union. You have to complete a form and the first three members have to sign it.

### C. Union support

Yes

### D. Paying for facilities

No. Registration means you get rooms and furniture free. Any specialist equipment you have to hire yourself.

### E. Photocopying/ advertising

Any photocopying etc has to be paid for by the club, though there are small grants available for special circumstances.

### F. Recommendations on charging membership fees

It is difficult to suggest, but you should look at the fees paid in other clubs and think about the need to cover special costs.

**Exercise 2:** Example of extended discourse No.1

Look at the dialogue below which has been split between Examiner and Candidate. Complete the examiner's questions using no more than three words in each case. Practise reading the answers given by the candidate and then try to give your own answers. Or you can practise with a friend.

Examiner

A. _____ to tell me a bit about yourself?

B. Not yet, but I hope to before I leave. ____ __ _____ to see there?

C. Mmm, sounds very interesting. _____ best way of getting there from this side of the city?

D. I see. Well, that's very helpful. Now _____ to hear some more about you. Have you graduated or are you still studying?

E. _____ you to tell me more about your life here in Delhi. Have you any brothers or sisters?

F. So that means a lot of work for your mother!

G. Can you_____ about your festivals? Which is your favourite holiday?

Candidate

i.  I live here in Delhi with my family. Actually, I live the other side of the town from here, in Old Delhi, near Kashmiri Gate just by the Interstate Bus Terminal. Have you been to Old Delhi yet?

ii. I'm sure you have heard of the Red Fort haven't you, and Jami Masjid, the biggest mosque in India? They are in the old city and they are very beautiful, very old and very interesting. Also Chandni Chowk bazaar is there.

iii. I think by scooter, that is the motor rickshaw – you must have seen plenty already – they are yellow and black and also very noisy, but as they are small they can move about quickly and also they are quite cheap. But you must agree the price before you start.

iv. I am still at the university, Delhi University, and I am studying engineering. I have one more year before I finish.

v.  Oh yes, we have a very big family and my two brothers and one of my sisters live at home and also my grandparents – that is my father's parents. My other sister is married and has gone to live with her husband and his parents. My two brothers are both working, but my younger sister is still at school.

vi. Yes. She is always cooking.

vii. I think the one we call Holi. Have you heard of it? It comes at the end of winter and all the young people especially enjoy it, because we can do things you would not normally be allowed to do. Everyone puts on their oldest clothes, as the tradition is to throw coloured water or powder at each other and, of course, everyone gets into a terrible mess.

H. _____ special day within the next two weeks while I am here?

viii. At the end of January? Let me think. Of course. Republic Day on 26 January. There is always a huge military parade and all the different regiments march down Raj Path, wearing their special uniforms with such a variety of colours and different turbans, some on horseback, some on camels and some on foot as well as the modern tanks and armoured cars. I am sure you will never have seen such a sight before.

I. _____ to get a special ticket to watch this?

ix. You don't have to but I think that there are some enclosures with a good view and you can get tickets for a place in one of them.

J. It sounds wonderful. _____ any short trip I could make out of Delhi on my last weekend?

x. You must have heard of the Taj Mahal?There's a fast train to Agra from Delhi and you can spend the whole day visiting the Taj and Agra Fort and there are various other sites to see by the Yamuna river. Then you can just get the train back again in the evening. It really is quite easy.

K. Well, thank you for your good advice. I shall have to apply for another opportunity to come and work here

**Exercise 3:** Example of extended discourse No.2

Look at the dialogue below. The Examiner's questions on the left are not in the correct order, but the candidate's answers are. Match the questions and answers in the dialogue. The first question of the examiner is marked in bold.

When you have finished try to give your own answers to the examiner's questions.

*1. Such as?*

*2. So, in what ways would you criticise the British way of life?*

*3. More marked, in what way?*

*4. And is that always a bad thing?*

*5. But how can young people become independent if they aren't given the chance?*

**6. I expect family life is different in your home country?**

*7. Can you give me an example of this bond?*

*8. What about differences between parents and, say, teenagers, are there differences there too?*

*9. So you think children should live at home as long as possible?*

*10. And what are the advantages of having people around all the time?*

A. Well, there are several differences that I have noticed. First of all, where I come from, the bond between each generation seems much stronger than in Britain.

B. Yes, for example the older generation, the grandparents are looked after by their grown-up children, and more often than not they live with them.

C. Well, for one thing, it means that there is always someone around to help with the children, the housework, the shopping or just to provide company for another member of the family.

D. Oh yes and in many ways they are even more pronounced.

E. Well, for instance in my country teenagers would never dream of leaving home to live somewhere else, but, in the UK, it's almost the norm.

F. Yes, if it is possible, because they need their parents both financially and, in other ways, too, for example, in an emotional or educational capacity.

G. Independence is something that comes gradually to young people in my country, but here it seems to be an instant thing. At home, young people tend to leave their parents home only when they get married and not always then either.

H. Well, to start with, I think one of the disadvantages of there being weaker family ties than in my country is that children are more easily influenced by forces outside the home rather than by their parents.

I. Like films, their peers, the media in all its forms.

J. No not necessarily, but I do feel that in the UK there is a lack of respect generally for parents as far as teenagers are concerned.

---

**Exercise 4:** Your future plans

---

In the fourth part of the Speaking Module, you need to be able to talk about your future plans. You should think beforehand about what you are going to say, but you should not learn a speech by heart. Remember the examiner is testing your ability to use the language, not to remember it.

This exercise looks at some of the ways you talk about the future in English.

The future in English is expressed in many ways. Study Questions (i-vii) below, which ask you about what way you look at the future.

### Do you

    *i.*   *make firm plans for the future?*

    *ii.*  *plan to finish something before a particular time?*

    *iii.* *dream about doing something at a particular time in the future?*

### Or do you

    *iv.* *run your life according to a timetable or calendar?*

    *v.*  *intend to do things, but can't make firm decisions?*

    *vi.* *make decisions about your future without really thinking?*

### Or are you

    *vii.* *very indecisive about your future?*

Now look at the statements below and match them with the categories above.

A. I am going to start working once I finish university

B. When I have graduated, I intend to find a good job.

C. I am planning to go to university in the future.

D. I am intending to go to university in the near future.

E. If I am successful in the IELTS, my plan is to do a postgraduate course.

F. I'm starting university next October.

G. I'll have finished university in three years' time.

H. I am having a small party to celebrate the completion of my IELTS exam.

I. This time next year I'll be studying at university, I hope.

J. The next step in my career, after this one year course, is to find a good job.

K. Mmm, I'll become a doctor!

L. In ten years' time, I'll be writing full-time, I hope.

M. I might be going to university next autumn, I don't really know.

---

**Exercise 5:** Put meaning into your future

Now look at Questions 1-10 below. You can see that there are four alternative answers for each question. Decide which answer is the most appropriate in each case. Note that more than one answer may be suitable.

1. **What are you going to do once you finish university?**
   (a) Well, I intend to spend a year travelling round the world.
   (b) Well, I think I'd like to spend a year travelling round the world.
   (c) Well, I am intending to spend a year travelling round the world.
   (d) Well, I'll be taking a year off to travel round the world.

2. **When you have graduated next year, what do you intend to do?**
   (a) My plan is to take time off before starting work.
   (b) Mmm, well, I'll take time off before starting work.
   (c) I am planning to take time off before starting work.
   (d) Yes, I take time off before starting work.

3. **Any plans for after graduation?**
   (a) Yes, I start work immediately.
   (b) Mmm, I know, I'll go abroad for a few months.
   (c) Mmm, I'll be going abroad for a few weeks.
   (d) I'll hope to go abroad for a few months.

4. **Are you intending to go to university in the near future?**
   (a) Yes, next September.
   (b) Yes, I start next September.
   (c) Yes, I'm starting next September.
   (d) Yes, I might start next September.

5. **Do you have any thoughts about where you'd like to work?**
   (a) I was thinking of applying for a research post in China.
   (b) I like to work somewhere in South-east Asia.
   (c) I'm really not decided yet.
   (d) I'll like working in Australia or New Zealand, I think.

6. **What do you hope to have achieved in two years' time?**
   (a) I hope to qualify as an accountant.
   (b) I hope I'll be finally working as an accountant.
   (c) I hope I finish all my accountancy exams.
   (d) I hope I'll have finished all my accountancy exams.

**7. Are you doing anything to celebrate the completion of your IELTS exam?**

    (a) I'll be having a rest.

    (b) Yes I have a small get-together with some friends.

    (c) Yes, I think I'll have a small get together with some friends.

    (d) I'll have had a small get-together with some friends and we'll probably do something.

**8. What do you think you'll be doing this time next year?**

    (a) I hope to start my degree course.

    (b) I hope I'll start my degree course.

    (c) I hope I get on my degree course.

    (d) I hope I'll be studying at university.

**9. What is the next step as far as your career is concerned?**

    (a) I'll apply for a job.

    (b) I start a postgraduate course immediately, once I get through the entrance exam.

    (c) If I pass all my exams, I can start work immediately.

    (d) I'm starting work immediately.

**10. Where do you see yourself in ten years' time?**

    (a) Hopefully, I'll be working as a teacher.

    (b) Hopefully, I'll have been working for quite a number of years.

    (c) I'll be a politician!

    (d) Happily living in a cottage in the countryside, writing books and making jam.

# Listening Module

## Key to Tests 1-4

---

```
┌─────────────────────────────────────────┐
│                                         │
│  Practice Test 1          Section 1     │
│                                         │
└─────────────────────────────────────────┘
```

## Questions 1–5

SA: ...versity Bookshop, Bridge Street, Doris speaking, can I help you?

S: Is that the University Bookshop?

SA. Yes, it is.

S: I'd like to place an order for some books, if I may.

SA Have you got an account with us?

S: No, not yet. I haven't started university yet. I'll be starting in October, but I'll be coming in early to have a look round and to get settled in and wanted to order some books.

SA: Right. I see. Would you like to open an account?

S: Mmm, I don't know.

SA: Well, you get a student discount on all book purchases.

S: Oh! And how much is that, then?

SA: **15% for first year students.**

S: **15%!** That sounds all right.

SA: You just have to make sure that you settle your account at the end of each month.

S: OK. Well, mm, I might as well open one, then.

SA: I just need to take down some details. Do you want the account to be at your term time address or your home address?

S: They're the same.

SA: Right. First of all, can I have your name?

S: Nasreen **Kerrigan.**

SA: Is that, K , I ...

S: No, I'll have to spell it for you. It's **K, E for everyone, double R, I , G for Go, A and N for Nobody.**

SA: **A ...; N for Nobody. ...Kerrigan.**

S: Yes. That's it.

SA: And your address?

S: It's **127a Adelaide Mansions** ...

SA: Hold on. 117a ... Ade ...

S: No, **127a** ...

SA: Ok, Right. And **Adelaide, that's A, D, E for everyone, L, A , I , D, and E for everyone.**

S: Yes, that's it. Then Mansions.

SA: Mansions. Right.

S: Compton Street.

SA: Right.

S: London.

SA: London. And the postcode?

S: **SE 19.**

SA: **SE ...19.**

S: **7FT**

SA: 7?

S: Yes 7 **F for Freddie and T for Tommy.**

SA: FT. Right. So let me just check that. Mm **127a Adelaide** Mansions, Compton Street, London **SE19 7FT.**

S: That's correct.

SA: And are you on the telephone?

S: Yes, it's 0181 **797 4882.**

SA: **797 ...**

S: **4882.**

SA: **4882.**

S: Yes, that's it.

```
┌─────────────────────────────────────────┐
│   1.    15%/ fifteen percent/per cent   │
│   2.    Kerrigan                        │
│   3.    127a Adelaide                   │
│   4.    19 7FT                          │
│   5.    797 4882                        │
└─────────────────────────────────────────┘
```

## Questions 6–10

SA: Right, that's that out of the way. And which books would you like to order?

S: Well, I just want four books to start off with.

SA: Hmm.

S: Have you got Physics in the Age of Technology by Adrianna Stern.

SA: Physics in the Age of ... it's out of stock, I'm afraid.

S: Oh, OK.

SA: Would you like me to order it for you?

S: No, what about mm. Mathematics in Physics by Professor I Lovatt. Experimental ...

SA: Just, just wait, **Mathematics in ... Physics by ... Professor I Lovatt.** Let's just check that. Right, here we are. Yes, .... we've got it in stock. **It's £27.95.**

S: £27.95! With the discount?

SA: I'm afraid, yes. Ah, the next one?

S: **Experimental Physics by Simon Blair and Violet Boyd.**

SA: **Experimental Physics by Simon Blair and Violet Boyd.** OK, let's see ....That's £29.50.

S: OK and **Physics for the first year student by A. Laska.**

SA: Physics for the first year student ... That's ... **£25.**

S: OK. I'll stick with these three for the moment.

SA: Right. Would you like to have the books posted to you?

S: No, No it's it's okay. I'll come in one day this week and pick them up.

SA: Right. When you come in, can you bring **two forms of identification**.

S: OK, Like what?

SA: **A credit card, ... driving licence, ... a cheque card and ...**

S: Oh, OK.

SA: **... and your letter confirming admission to the university.**

S: Yeah, OK. What time do you close?

SA: We're open until 6pm every day except Thursday, when we close at 7.30.

S: And you're on which floor?

SA: **The Physics Department is in the basement. The books will be kept here** and as you're paying by account we'll post the bill to you.

S: Thanks. Bye.

SA: Bye-Bye.

```
┌─────────────────────────────────────────────────────────┐
│  6.  ✓      7. Physics    8. £25    9. D     10. B       │
└─────────────────────────────────────────────────────────┘
```

A book for **IELTS**

Note: **Section 1** usually tests your ability to extract basic
information from a dialogue. It is easy to pick up marks
in this Section. However, it is also easy to lose them. If
you need a high grade you should be aiming to get all
of the first section correct.

---

| **Practice Test 1** | **Section 2** |

## Questions 11–14

Good morning. My name is Dave Eastman and I'm one of the
**five student counsellors** in the university. And I'm here today
to introduce myself to you briefly and to say just a few words
about the **Student Welfare Service**. But before I begin, I'd like
to thank your Faculty Head, Professor Anwar, for inviting me
here to talk to you. At the end, I'll throw questions open to the
floor.

The service we offer is available on all six sites of the university
campus. **The three main sites** have a counsellor available
week-days, Monday to Thursday, between 9.30 am and 4.00
pm. On this site, the office is situated in the **Queen's Building,
on the first floor**. I understand that all of you are based on this
site, so I won't go into details about the others.

| 11.   C | 12. B | 13. A | 14. D |

## Questions 15–20

Information about the service and the other offices is contained
in this leaflet, which you can pick up practically **everywhere on
campus.** We also run a Helpline, which is open after the office
is closed. The number for the line is 0345 1607 2390. This
number with all the others, my own, included, is contained in the
leaflet. Obviously, we would like to make the Helpline available
24 hours a day, but the money simply isn't there, so we have to
rely on the **generosity of volunteers.** I can say on average the
line is open about 3 hours per evening most evenings and
**roughly 8 hours** at weekends. If there is no-one to take your
call, or in the event of an emergency, there will be a message
on the answering machine which will give you other contact
numbers.

You might be thinking why not just give us the leaflet and get on
with the lecture. Well, the answer to that, as you probably well
know, is that people don't always read leaflets; they look at them
and say: That's not for me.

People contact us for a **variety of reasons**. They may come to
see us if they feel isolated, because it's the first time many have
been away from home; or they may have personal relationship
problems; or money problems. Certain times of the year bring
increased pressure to bear on students, the exam time being
the main one and I'm not just talking about Finals. Preparing a
paper for a tutorial or a seminar can also be a stressful exercise.
On occasions like this, we are available to help you.

We don't pretend that we have an answer for every problem,
but we can try and help; and if we can't we can usually refer you
to **someone who can.**

I would also like to take this opportunity to ask for volunteers for
our advice Helpline. You don't need any previous experience
and, because you are newcomers to the university, it does not
mean that you do not have anything to offer. We provide
**training and support** for all volunteers. So if you'd like to get
involved see me at the end of this session.

I'd like ...
some ...
T-shirt.

15.
16.
17.
18.
19.
20.

Key to Listening Practice Tests

Now, near the beginning
present day fears ab
Yeah.
and the 19th
but don't
Luddit

**Note:** You can
this secti
number 1 ............................ down the answer for
the first nu ............. near, i.e. **A** six.

Note that the answers for 16 and 17 come close together.
Always be ready to write down the next answer. Do not
assume that the answers will be wide apart.

It is also easy to lose concentration as you are listening.
You need to practise holding your concentration. There
is quite a big gap between the information in 17 and 18,
which tests your ability to concentrate as you listen.

Note that to answer the questions you do not need to listen to
all the information in the speech. Try to learn to treat
the questions as markers and listen only for that
information. When you are talking to someone in your
own language or in English, you hear every word, but
you do not listen to all of them!

---

| **Practice Test 1** | **Section 3** |

## Questions 21–23

L:  Come in!

J:  Hello, Dr Townsend.

L:  Ah – hello Jim, come and sit down. Now – it's about this
essay of yours, am I right?

J:  Yes, the one on **global employment.**

L:  Ah yes, global employment, let's see ...What was the exact
title again?

J:  'Information Tech ...

L:  Right, here it is: " '*Information Technology will put millions
of people out of work throughout the world in the
coming decades*'. Explore the arguments on both sides
of this debate and give your opinion.'

J:  Yep, that's it.

L:  Yes, on the whole, I was very pleased with what you wrote
... mm ...You've presented the different points of view
clearly.

J:  Thank you.

L:  Did you give the sources for your statistics?

J:  Yes, I ...

L:  Ah, yes, I see, **the World Bank** and the OECD.  Where
did you get the figures from?

J:  On the Internet.

L:  Right, I see. OK – well, let's have a closer look.

J:  OK.

... you draw a parallel between ...ut **machines replacing people,**

...Century Luddites. It's an appropriate parallel, ...u think it might be better to explain who the ...s were?

...ll, I mm did think about it, but ...ah ..

...Yes?

...: I thought it might be a little bit simplistic.

L: Well, yes, maybe, but a short sentence might help just to show the connection between then and now.

21. **global employment**
22. **The World Bank**
23. **machines replacing people**

*The test is just checking discrete points of information as in Sections 1 and 2. You just have to use the questions in the exercise as markers for the informatio on the tape.*

## Questions 24–27

L: Good. Let's move on then.

J: Right.

L: So, in the first paragraph you describe three reasons for people's fears: IT is more pervasive in its impact than the effect of steam power or electricity, affecting service industries as well as traditional manufacturing. **Second, IT is being introduced faster than earlier new technologies and thirdly, ... that it makes it possible for jobs to be easily moved from one place to another.** Could you have described any other reservations?

J: Well, I suppose I could have said that the richer industrial economies fear the easy transfer of their jobs to poorer and, therefore, cheaper economies, but I felt it was too restricted a fear. You could also blame the media for their coverage of large job losses at big firms without publicising small business creation.

L: I see – fair enough. So then you continue with two paragraphs saying why people need not be afraid. I see you start with the historic evidence, **that over the past 200 years of huge technological advance, employment and real incomes in rich industrial countries have risen fairly continuously,**

J: Yes ....

L: and you illustrate it by an OECD chart. Then you state that although jobs <u>are</u> destroyed by new technology, **new ones are constantly being created which offset the losses** – I liked your example here: that as blacksmiths and coachmen disappeared, mechanics, drivers and car salesmen took their place.

| 24. b | 25. b | 26. a | 27. b |
|-------|-------|-------|-------|

*This part of Section 3 is more difficult than any of the previous Questions 1–23. The nature of the questions has begun to change. Instead of just giving information straight from the conversation, you are being asked to summarise what is being said. Also the detail is quite close together, so you need to be very quick.*

## Questions 28–30

L: Now, where were we?

J: We were ...

L: Yes, you said that although new technology may reduce the amount of labour necessary to produce a given volume of output, this doesn't necessarily reduce overall unemployment,

J: Employment,

L: Sorry, yes, employment, because technology can boost output **and create new demand** and new products.

J: Yes.

L: Perhaps you could have given some examples here of products which didn't exist 20 years ago?

J: You mean things like VCRs, mm ... personal stereos, soft contact lenses! Yes, mm, I suppose I should have done.

L: And, of course, computers themselves, both personal and industrial! Good! So let's have a look at your conclusion – so you believe that on balance, given a favourable business climate, and **a well educated, high-skilled workforce, there's no reason why IT should destroy jobs.**

J: Yes.

L: You haven't ah explained what you mean by a '**favourable business climate**'.

J: Mmm well I I mean an environment where there aren't **too many restrictions,** rules and regulations like protectionism over goods and restrictions on work practices and, perhaps, minimum wage levels that are too high.

L: I see. Well, you've certainly thought through the issues, but they are complex and perhaps you could have gone into them rather more deeply. However, as I said at the beginning, you're good and clear about your points, so I've marked it ...............

| 28. C | 29. D | 30. A |
|-------|-------|-------|

*This sub-section is testing understanding of points in the conversation*

| **Practice Test 1** | **Section 4** |
|---------------------|---------------|

## Questions 31–37

Good afternoon, and welcome to everybody. My name is Dr Paulette Southfield and I specialise in **European product design** in the Department of Product and Furniture Design. It has fallen on me to kick off your first term with **the introductory lecture.** And after much thought looking for a fancy title, I decided to call my talk today, simply: What is **design** for?

What is design for? is one of the most important questions that we seek to answer in this department. After all, an electric kettle is no more than a vessel with a heating element, a chair – no more than a seat and back with enough legs for support, and a motor car no more than a box with seats, four wheels and an engine. But, we all know that a kettle can pour badly and be awkward to handle, a chair uncomfortable and ugly to look at and a car unreliable and unattractive. The answer to my question is, of course, implicit in these examples: good design makes for **efficient products**, like an efficient kettle, maybe cordless and manageable by arthritic or elderly hands; a well designed chair is comfortable and an inviting asset to our living-rooms and a carefully designed car combines maximum

**A book for IELTS**

safety, comfort and elegance. The conclusion we can draw from this is that the role of design – to paraphrase Terence Conran – is to ensure that things do the job they were **intended to do**; that they are well made and efficient and that they are pleasing to use and to look at.

There are, however, other reasons for the importance of design. **Advertising and the media** fuel the acquisitive nature of consumerism but, together with greater choice, they encourage a more discerning approach from the public who can compare the qualities of one product with those of another. The aesthetic appeal of a bold new table lamp can be weighed against the charms of a dozen others – while the choice of a new personal stereo may involve its stylish appearance as much as its **efficient function**.

31.     **European product design**
32.     **introductory lecture**
33.     **design**

*You can see that the first three answers (31–33) are fairly straightforward and give a very broad summary of the lecture.*

34.     **efficient products**
35.     **intended to (do)**
36.     **advertising/adverts (and) the media**
37.     **efficient function**

*You can see that after the introduction, the amount of detailed information in the speech has increased. The type of checking in the listening has changed from seeing if you understand specific points to understanding chunks of information. Compare this with the basic information check in Section 1 of the Test. Again, it is not important that you understand every piece of information but that you understand the overall meaning.*

## Questions 38–41

And yet there is another reason for the enhanced role of the designer in today's world of rapidly advancing technology. **As the life cycle of every product grows ever shorter, the designer has to be working on an updated model as soon as the latest one is off the drawing board.** Nowhere is this more evident than in the design of motor cars. The same technological advance has also made a huge impact in the field of medicine and here the designer is involved **in the development of new equipment, from the endoscope, the increasingly sophisticated dentist's chair and the robotic hospital 'porter', to the artificial hip replacement and other prostheses.**

Finally, we should not forget the role of design in the marketing wars. **As manufacturers battle to enhance the desirability of their products over those of their competitors, the talents, imagination and training of their designers are paramount.** A proper appreciation of this factor can even be significant for national economies and their export markets.

I would like to end, though, with a few words on the relationship between good design and that elusive factor – quality of life. If we start by agreeing that living is more than just existing, **we must admit that living with everyday things that are aesthetically pleasing as well as effective, enhances that quality.** Most of us react against things which are coarse, feeble or pretentious, but are drawn towards things which embody efficiency, imagination and style. In the words of French designer, Roger Tallon, design is *first and foremost an attitude.*

Now if anyone would like to ask any questions, or raise any further points ...

| 38.  D | 39.  A | 40.B | 41.  C |

*The answers here are more difficult as they paraphrase and summarise parts of the lecture. Compare this with questions 34–37 where the summaries were in the speech.*

| **Practice Test 2** | **Section 1** |

## Questions 1–4

C:     I'd like to send some flowers and some chocolates.

SA:    Ok, I'll just get the com ... puter on ... Right. Can I just take your details?

C:     Yes, certainly.

SA:    Your name?

C:     Angela Love.

SA:    Angela Love. And your address?

C:     144a Orchard Heights, Marsh Drive, Edinburgh.

SA:    Right. And the postcode?

C:     Ah, I don't know ... I'm just staying here for a while.

SA:    Oh It doesn't matter. What ... What exactly is it you'd like to send?

C:     Ahm, **a bouquet of flowers**.

SA:    And how much would you like to spend?

C:     **£30.**

SA:    Any particular flowers?

C:     I don't know  mmm, something exotic perhaps.

SA:    OK. And you wanted a box of chocolates?

C:     Yeah.

SA:    To what value?

C:     Oh, say **£25.**

SA:    Right, **£25.** And the chocolates, what would you like ah dark, white, milk, liqueurs, or a mixture?

C:     **Well, a mixture, I suppose, but no liqueurs. And more white chocolates than the others.**

SA:    I'll just write this on the order form: mixture – mostly white/no liqueurs.

C:     That's it.

SA:    And these are to go within Edinburgh?

C:     No, they're to go to Cardiff, in Wales.

SA:    There'll be a delivery charge of **£19** for both items, I'm afraid.

C:     For both, not each?

SA:    Yes. That's right.

| 1.  A | 2.  D | 3.  D | 4.  C |

## Questions 5–10

SA:    And how would you like to pay, madam?

C:     By Switch Card, if I may.

SA: Of course, that's fine. And the number?

C: It's 569 000

SA: 569 000

C: **212 897**

SA: 212 897

C: 884 223

SA: 884 223

C: 7.

SA: 7.

SA: Can I just check that? 569 000 **212 897** 884 223 7.

C: Yes, that's it.

SA: So, the total amount to be debited is £74.

C: OK.

SA: And to whom would you like them sent?

C: **To Mrs Easter**

SA: That's **E A S T E R**?

C: Yes.

SA: And the address?

C: 27

SA: 27

C: **Rowntree Road**

SA: Is that **R O W N T R Double E**.

C: Yes. That's it. Cardiff.

SA: Cardiff.

C: CA13 8YU.

SA: CA13 8YU. And did you want any message to go with the flowers and chocolates?

C: Yes, mmm, *Congratulations on **passing your test**! Just let me know when you're out on the road! Love Angie.*

SA: Someone's just passed their driving test, then.

C: Yes, my mother.

SA: Your mother?

C: Yeah, it's her sixth attempt.

SA: Oh, right; that is a cause for celebration!

C: Yes.

SA: And, when would you like them delivered?

C: The day after tomorrow, between 9 and 11 am.

SA: That's the **17**th in the morning **between 9 and 11**. I just need to take a daytime contact number.

C: I'll give you my mobile number; it's 0963 371 555

SA: 0963 317

C: No 371 555

SA: 371 555. I'll arrange this for you now.

C: OK, thank you.

SA: Thank you. Good-bye. Have a nice day.

C: You too. Good-bye.

---

5. **212 897**

6. **Easter**

7. **Rowntree Road**

8. **passing your test**

9. **17th/seventeenth**

10. **9 [and] 11/ nine [and] eleven**

*Just like the first section in **Test 1**. The exercises are testing your ability to extract basic information from a simple dialogue.*

---

| Practice Test 2 | Section 2 |
|---|---|

### Questions 11–13

Good afternoon, my name is Mick Clarke and I'm the sports rep from the Students' Union. As well as these talks on the university sports facilities, information will be put up on **notice-boards all over the campus**, so you will definitely all know where to find us.

Well, as you have probably realised the university is spread all over the place and the sports facilities are, I'm afraid, no different. **If you look at the map here on the screen**, you'll see we we are here on Thames Street opposite the city Library. If you look down at the bottom of this map on the right you'll see **Burse Road**. On the left of the police station, between the shopping complex and the theatre, and the Phoenix theatre, is the university sports complex.

| 11. B | 12. A | 13. A |
|---|---|---|

*This is just a test of basic information.*

### Questions 14–17

The complex is arranged over four floors; two above ground and two below. The buildings were just completed last year funded by an anonymous donor. The swimming pool is on the lower ground floor and we are very lucky in **that a full-sized Olympic pool is to be built by the end of this academic year along with a new sauna**. In addition, there are a number of other facilities, including various courts, and I would strongly advise you to book well in advance if you want to use any of these courts, as they are very much in demand. Mm, We have, full changing facilities, three large halls for aerobics and other classes, three squash courts, and two badminton courts. And **two other exciting developments in the pipeline are a state-of-the-art gym and an ice-skating rink**. There are also courts for playing softball and basketball. And there is, of course, a cafeteria, which is run by the Students' Union, so the prices are reasonable. **A welcome addition is the bar, which is due to open shortly.**

| 14. D | 15. F | 16. G | 17. K |
|---|---|---|---|

*You need to be careful here. We do not always talk about the future by using the Simple Future. This is a good test of comprehension. Notice the different ways the speaker talks about the developments: is to be built/is in the pipeline; is due to open shortly.*

### Questions 18–20

For outdoor sports, I'm afraid, we have to go further afield. The university grounds for rugby, football, hockey and cricket are **on the edge of the city centre in the southwest, on the north bank of the river** as you can see from this map. The rowing and canoeing clubs, which are very popular, also run from there.

The only bus that goes to the university sports fields directly from here is the 553; **no sorry, it's the 53**. It is fortunately very frequent and runs late into the night; the last buses either way are **around 12.30**. But there is also a mini-bus service, which is pretty frequent and reliable, and the times are posted at the Students' Union office.

If you want to join up for any of the clubs, you just have to see the reps on the stalls at the different Societies' stalls outside.

Anyway, thanks for taking the time to come in and listen and I wish you every success whether you decide to take up some form of sport or not.

| 18. B | 19. D | 20. A |
|-------|-------|-------|

---

| | Practice Test 2 | Section 3 |
|--|-----------------|-----------|

## Questions 21–26

L = Dr Warner; S = Sandra; D = Derek

**Knock**

L: Come in! .... ah Sandra and Derek. Come in, come in.

S: Good morning, Dr Warner.

L: Good morning, Sandra.

D: Good morning, Dr Warner.

L: Good morning Derek.

D: We know you're busy, but have you got a moment?

L: Yes, for the moment, I'm free. What can I do for you?

S: We just wanted to ask your advice about applying for awards

L: Oh, right. Ah. Which awards are you interested in?

D: Well, I'm interested in the FBT Award for a grant **to travel abroad**.

S: And I'd like to apply for the Bisiker Travel Award for a research grant in Entomology in Jordan.

L: Okay. Ah. You do know that you have to satisfy a number of criteria to be eligible for each award.

S: Yesss ...

L: The book is here somewhere. ... Right, here it is. Ah. For you Derek, ... Ah. Let's see, The FBT Award. Mmm. The conditions for that are ... **You have to be in your fourth year**, ... as you are.

D: Okay.

L: You have to be a British or Commonwealth citizen. So you're okay on that one, as well.

D: Yes.

L: **And you have to come in the top five students in your year in your Finals.**

D: Ahh. Right. Well, obviously, that I won't know until I've taken my exams.

L: No, but you should put in the application now, **as the deadline is the end of June, no sorry it's May** ... and that's before the exams even start. So they expect you to tell them afterwards.

D: And are there any other criteria?

L: Let's see. Mmm ... Well, it says here you have to be **under 25 years of age at the end of your final year**. Are you?

D: I won't be 25 until September 27th. So that's okay. And do I need any referees?

L: Yes, Ah, **two**. And I am happy to do one for you and ...

D: I was also thinking of asking Dr Jameson.

L: Yes, I'm sure he'll gladly do one for you.

---

| 21. | travel abroad |
|-----|---------------|
| 22. | 4th/fourth |
| 23. | top five/5 students |
| 24. | end of May |
| 25. | twenty-five/25 |
| 26. | two/2 |

*The information relating to the conditions for the award comes in quick succession. You need to learn to practise processing information quickly as you listen.*

## Questions 27–30

L: And Sandra ...

S: Yes.

L: **The Bisiker Award is a lot stricter, as it's for a much larger sum of money. And you must realise that the competition is very stiff indeed.**

S: Yes, I've heard it's not easy to get one as there are only three per year,

L: Yes, you're right. Unlike the FBT award, for which there are 10 bursaries. The first thing you have to know is that application is by way of a **5,000 word summary outlining how you intend to use the money; of course, accompanied by a covering one page form with all your personal details**.

S: Yes, I know about that, but what I wanted to know is whether there are examples of other applications I can look at.

L: Well, not really. Ah. **The summary has to be very much an original piece and that I cannot emphasise enough**. If there are any signs of it having been copied, then ...

S: I see, but will you be able to read it through for me?

L: Oh I don't see why not.

S: Oh that's alright, then. What do you think my chances are of my getting one of the grants?

L: It's difficult to say. Ah. There's usually about 20 to 30 people applying every year.

S: And this year?

L: Well, I'd imagine it's about the same.

S: Who decides?

L: Well, there is a panel of five trustees and once you have submitted everything ...

S: Mhmm

L: to the Departmental secretary, they each receive a copy of your full application.

S: But do you think I stand a chance?

L: Well, as I said it's not easy to say; it's up to the Trustees.

S: Okay.

L: **Another thing that I would stress is that the applications must be typed, very tidy and properly bound.**

S: With a ring binder?

L: Yes ... There have been complaints in previous years about the lack of care taken in completing the forms and essays. Ah. This applies to you too, Derek.

D: Yes. Well, it's only fair; after all we are asking for help.

L: Yes. Is there anything else I can help you with while you're here Sandra?

---

S:  No. Thank you very much for all your help.
L:  Derek?
D:  No. And thank you for your help.

| 27. D | 28. B | 29. A | 30. D |
|-------|-------|-------|-------|

*Questions 27 and 28 check basic detail regarding the award Sandra is applying for. The next questions check your interpretation of the function/meaning of what the lecturer says. We would advise you for all parts of the IELTS test, not just the listening, to study modal verbs, e.g. to have to, should, may etc, and complex tenses. You need to understand more than just the simple tenses like the Simple Present Simple Future, Simple Past etc. Compare Questions 14 -17 in Section 2 of this Test.*

---

## Practice Test 2        Section 4

---

## Questions 31–36

Thank you for inviting me here to speak to you today at your department of Social Sciences. As I'm sure you already know, the title of my talk, *Europe goes grey,* relates to the **marked demographic change** which has taken place in Europe since the 1960s. Just a few statistics showing the projected trends will illustrate this.

**By the year 2029, almost one in four of the population of the UK** will be over the present retirement age of 60 years for women and 65 for men. **By the year 2020, Italy, for example, will have both the oldest population with 23.2% aged 65 and over**, and at the same time, the lowest fertility rate. Furthermore, a 1997 report from the UK Office for National Statistics notes that since 1950, the number of centenarians **has increased at the rate of just under 7% a year** – faster than for most other age groups – **and will continue to do so into the next century**.

The main reasons for the generally increased life-span are self-evident. These are, simply, a better diet, better housing and above all, **the ever-improving standard of health care**.

The social reasons for the changed demographic profile of Europe – that is, the increasing proportion of the elderly, relative to the middle and steadily diminishing young generations – are, of course, the falling birth rate, as a result of **widespread birth control** and the education and increasing participation of women in the workforce.

| 31. | [marked] demographic change |
|-----|------------------------------|
| 32. | twenty-five/25 |
| 33. | Italy |
| 34. | just under 7 |
| 35. | ever-improving standard |
| 36. | (widespread) birth control |

*The information comes thick and fast in this lecture. The questions relating to the Projections are fairly straightforward. However, you need to be able to process the information rapidly. The layout of the question prepares you for the information need to fill 35, but for 36 you have to be on the alert as it is the first one in the sequence. If you find it difficult to catch the answer to 36 at the first attempt, listen several times and try to catch the information. Again, remember that you do not need to understand everything that is being said.*

## Questions 37–40

This change raises two profound questions - one social and one economic – and it is these that I propose to examine here today.

At the end I intend to share with you a few thoughts on how we can help to make the lives of those in the third age, more fulfilling and rewarding.

Firstly, we need to recognise that **the elderly are not a homogeneous group**. They can range from a fit, active and independent 85-year-old, to a 65-year-old with rapidly advancing Alzheimer's disease, to a retired 55-year-old with both a dependent parent and still dependent student children. The social aspect I referred to earlier is, of course, the big question: who will care for the elderly? The question is a complex one and I would like to illustrate this by making a few comparisons with the past. **In earlier times, large extended families living in the same area, were the norm. This meant the sharing of care for the grandparents' generation was usual. Now, however, the mobility of the population combined with smaller families often means there are, quite simply, no family members to take care of an older person**. The breakdown of traditional family structures and the increase in divorce has exacerbated this.

The other big question, the economic one, involves the increasing cost of adjustment to this situation, and how the burden of this cost can most equitably be shared between, on the one hand, the elderly and their families and, on the other, the relatively smaller number of people of working age whose tax contributions have to be used to fund pensions and services for an increasingly elderly population as well as all the other demands on the public purse.

The questions raised by this demographic change are exercising Governments all over Europe, **and there is naturally, widespread debate about how best to help financially those who can remain independent**, while supporting those who cannot, and ensuring that they continue a sometimes failing life, with dignity.

I promised to finish with a few thoughts about how we might come closer to achieving this. More imaginative use is being made of existing property by adapting it for elderly, often less able people, and their needs are now being kept in mind by planners, Local Authorities and transport providers. But not forgetting the cry – where does the money come from – we need radically to rethink the arrangements for funding pensions and younger people's planning for retirement. **Innovative insurance schemes should be developed to assist people in providing for the future,** and financial institutions ought to be thinking about these.

So I will close by repeating that I believe we should do everything to enable the elderly to live meaningful and rewarding lives. After all, we will be in the same situation, all too soon.

Thank you, and I would welcome any questions or comments from the floor.

| 37. C | 38. C | 39. B | 40. A |
|-------|-------|-------|-------|

*These questions are much more difficult than the earlier part of this section, because they are analysing much larger chunks of text. The two tests so far, it is hoped, show you how the listening test in the IELTS exam becomes progressively more difficult.*

A book for **IELTS**

## Practice Test 3      Section 1

### Questions 1–7

**PGS** = postgraduate student; **UGS** = undergraduate student

PGS: I'm a research student in the Social Sciences department

UGS: Yes?

PGS: Would you mind if I ask you a few questions to help me complete this questionnaire?

UGS: Mmm , well ...

PGS: Are you an undergraduate?

UGS: Yes. I'm in my second year. Is this going to take long?

PGS: Well, no it shouldn't. Do you mind?

UGS: No . Not if ... if it's quick. What time is it now?

PGS: It's ten to 11.

UGS I've a lecture at 11.15.

PGS: Well, it shouldn't take more than five minutes.

UGS: Oh, that's OK, then.

PGS: Right, off we go. Ah, you're in your second year, right. Well, the questionnaire is anonymous, so I don't need your name, but I do need some other details.

UGS: OK.

PGS: Which faculty are you in?

UGS: Humanities.

PGS: Oh right; you're in the Hunter Building.

UGS: That's right.

PGS: And what are you studying?

UGS: **Chinese and Oriental Studies**.

PGS: Chinese and Oriental Studies. Oh, right. And what age are you?

UGS: **I've just turned 19**.

PGS: Do you live on the campus?

UGS: Yeah. I'm in one of the students' flats, so I don't have much travelling.

PGS: Ok. And which block are you in?

UGS: **Benbradagh**.

PGS: How do you spell that?

UGS: **B E N for Nobody B again R A D A again; then G for ... grow; and H.**

PGS: Ben ... bradagh. What's that named after?

UGS: It's a mountain in Ireland.

PGS: Oh, right. You' re quite a bit out. It's on the edge of the campus next to the sports complex.

UGS: No. That's Mount Bures House. We're on the opposite side of the campus next to the Student Union building, Cornwall House.

PGS: Oh, yes. I just need to ask you a few social questions, if I may.

UGS: Mhmm.

PGS: Do you play any sport?

UGS: Yeah. Squash, basketball and football.

PGS: How often do you play **squash**?

UGS: Usually once a week.

PGS: So, say 3 to 5 times a month.

UGS: Yeah.

PGS: **And basketball**?

UGS: **Usually twice a month**.

PGS: **Basketball, twice a month**. Right. And how often do you play football?

UGS: I'd say at least twice a week.

PGS: So about 8 times a month. Do you go to the gym?

UGS: No.

PGS: Right. And do you belong to any clubs?

UGS: **Ah, the Film Club and Amateur Dramatics**.

PGS: **The Film Club,** how often do you go?

UGS: Not as often as I'd like. I went loads last year, but this year I don't seem to have much time.

PGS: But how often? Say once a fortnight?

UGS: **More like once a month**.

PGS: **Right one to two times per month**. And **amateur dramatics**?

UGS: Actually, at least once per week. And if we're rehearsing it could be a couple of nights and all day Saturday and Sunday as well.

PGS: Shall we say 6 to 8 times a month then?

UGS: **Mmmm, it's more like 9 or 10 times**.

| | |
|---|---|
| 1. | **Oriental Studies** |
| 2. | **nineteen/19** |
| 3. | **Benbradagh** |
| 4. | **Squash** |
| 5. | **A** |
| 6. | **(The) Film Club** |
| 7. | **D** |

### Questions 8–10

PGS: And how much do you spend on **socialising** per week?

UGS: I don't know.

PGS: Say 5%, 20%, 30% of your income?

UGS: Oh, I suppose I must spend **25%**.

PGS: Is that typical of your friends as well?

UGS: I think so. We stick to the university, so it's cheaper ... and the sports facilities are cheap as well and the bar, of course, is subsidised.

PGS: And books, how much do reckon you spend?

UGS: Mmm. Not more than 10%. I borrow most of the books from the library, when I can get hold of them.

PGS: Right.

PGS: And what about **accommodation and food**?

UGS: I'd say **50%**.

PGS: And what about the rest of your money?

UGS: Well, **it goes on small luxuries ... very** small. What's this for anyway?

PGS: It's part of a study on the change in students' spending patterns, as they progress from first year to postgraduate level.

UGS: Oh right.

PGS: I wish you luck.

UGS: Thanks.

PGS: And thanks for your help.

PGS: No problem. Oh, look at the time I must get a move on. See you!

8. B
9. B
10. D

*The listening is testing your ability to extract simple information from a dialogue.*

---

## Practice Test 3      Section 2

### Questions 11–16

Hello! And welcome to this week's edition of *Science Tomorrow Today*; my name is Bertie Jackson and today we are going to look at three totally unrelated topics.

First, is it a Hovercraft or is it a plane?

The *Hoverplane*, a cross between a boat and a plane with elements of the Hovercraft and Catamaran, is under trial at the moment. The plane-like wings allow the craft to take off in a short distance, and a flexible skirt allows it to operate over water like a Hovercraft, moving on a cushion of air.

The greatest potential for this craft is as a ferry, travelling between one and two metres above the water at up to **250 kilometres per hour**. Its advantages are those of safety and efficiency - safety as it avoids hitting floating or submerged debris and efficiency as it can travel at five times the speed, but **at one fifth of the fuel cost** of a normal ferry. And plans are being drawn up for a large version, big enough to carry **150 passengers** and freight for 2,000 kilometres at over 300 kilometres per hour. Since the Hover plane can carry a 50% greater payload than a similar sized aircraft, but with a 30% lower fuel consumption, and it needs neither special ports nor runways, the craft should be an attractive economic proposition for operators and promises to be a popular ferry in the 21st century.

Our second item is bad news for the criminal, but should provide a reassuringly secure communication system for the overworked policeman. At present, a criminal with a radio scanner can detect **police presence** in the area that he, or indeed she, is operating in. This is now about to change. A new computer-based system will soon replace most radio traffic with **digital text messages**. These messages will be imperceptible, and will allow officers to cover more jobs as they pick up and answer text messages rather than waiting for an operator to spell out commands. What's more, if the initial trial is successful, the system may be upgraded so that even **maps** can be sent to police cars allowing pursuits to be visually co-ordinated. Will this spell the end of the high-speed car chase?

11. 250 kilometres/kms
12. fifth/5th
13. 150 passengers
14. police presence
15. digital text messages
16. maps

*The answers for the first three questions in this sub-section are easier than Questions 14–16. The vocabulary in the part about the Police Communication System is more difficult.*

### Questions 17–20

And now for something quite different: how can chickens provide not only that delicious breakfast egg, but also the power to cook it? The answer lies in that **plentiful by-product** of the chicken farm, namely, chicken dung. An enterprising British company has proved that 'green' solutions to the electric power needs of communities can be profitable. In fact, there are already **three, yes three** dung-fired power stations in use in Britain, which have attracted attention from other European countries and several projects in different places are already at the advanced planning stage. 'We first believed that the only use for our dung was to make electricity,' says the British company's owner, 'but after burning it for power, we are left with a residue rich in potash and phosphate, but nitrogen-free. This provides a far more marketable fertiliser which we can sell as well as the electricity we produce'. In many countries, **agricultural waste** is even more of a problem than industrial waste, polluting even the sea where rivers have carried nitrogen and other agricultural waste to estuaries and inshore waters. By burning dung and producing cheap **electric power** in the process, however, this company is solving two problems in one go.

That's all for today.

Next week: It's *Chips with everything* - a new use for microchips; robots for fixing bridges overnight; hand-held lasers for instant blood tests and the first commercial fully-operational satellite for tracking shifts in climate.

I'll be back next week.

Goodbye.

17. [plentiful] by-product
18. three/3
19. agricultural waste
20. electric power/ electricity

*Students find this type of question rather difficult, because they have to read the summary and listen at the same time. The summary paraphrases the talk and so the words that are written down are not exactly the same as those you hear. You need to practise this type of question as much as you can.*

---

## Practice Test 3      Section 3

### Questions 21–23

**D = Dave; S = Sarah; T = Terry**

D: Hi Sarah. That was actually quite exciting, wasn't it?

S: You really think so, Dave? I'm completely worn out. If I have to take in another piece of information, my head's going to explode.

D: **It was good, though.**

S: **I have to admit it was, mmm,**

D: And it was challenging.

S: Challenging? The last tutorial? It makes me think I learned absolutely nothing at school. **I understood nearly all of it, but a few bits I'm not sure I got at all.** Reading is reading and that's that.

D: Well, it is and it isn't, you know.

S: We all read in the same way.

D: No, we don't!

T: What are you two arguing about?

S: Oh, it's Terry. Hi.

D: Reading!

T: Reading?

D: Yes, reading.

T: It's not exactly a sexy subject to be arguing about. Is it Dave?

D: I don't know; I find it quite exciting, really.

S: You would!

D: **We've just been to this tutorial on study skills as part of the English Literature course** and Sarah's found it difficult to follow.

S: No, Dave. That's not true. It's just there were some things that I'm not so sure about or more importantly sure whether they're important or not.

T: Well, what was the problem?

S: Well, when I read I just read and Dr Pratt was going on about all these different techniques that we need to develop and hone.

---

| 21. D | 22. C | 23. A |
|-------|-------|-------|

---

## Questions 24–30

T: Mmm. How do you read then, Sarah?

S: I just read as I said; like everyone else. I read each word as it comes.

T: How many pages do you read in an hour?

S: About twenty-five/thirty?

T: And what about you, Dave?

D: **Sixty/maybe seventy**.

S: **Sixty to seventy**!

T: That's not a lot.

S: How many do you read, then, Terry?

T: It depends. About 120 ...

S/D: What?

S: Oh, come on, Terry.

T: Yeah and I'm not unusual. One of my friends, doing Medieval European history, **Arnold, he reads about 160 an hour**.

D: But does he remember it all?

T: Yeah, I think so, Dave.

S: **I get through only one book a week**!

D: **Me too**. What about you, Terry?

T: **At the moment 3**.

S: And your friend Arnold?

T: Twenty.

S: Twenty!

T: Yes, but it doesn't matter at the moment. What matters, is that you develop your reading speed to **suit the circumstances**. You could still stick to your reading speed of 25 pages an hour for leisure purposes, but double your reading speed for say reading journals or academic texts. If I'm scanning a text for specific information, I can just whizz through. Then when I find what I want, I'll read through that particular part very slowly.

S: Mm.

T: With forty to fifty or more books to get through in a term you can't afford to read every word.

D: Have you always read like that?

T: No, it's only since I've been here.

S: I find this all very depressing. How did you do it then?

T: In the first week of term, in the first year, we had a tutorial on reading.

D: From Dr Pratt.

T: Yes, and I felt **so inadequate** after the class.

S: Well, what did he tell you?

T: He just gave us a few basic strategies on reading and then over the last two years he's been nurturing us, so that we all now work very efficiently.

S: So he's your tutor too. You can tell us then what he means when he talks about learning to read the content words only.

T: Well, this is obviously just the first step. If you read every a, the, to, from, was etc. it really slows you down.

S: Yeah?

T: But if you train your eye to look at the nouns, verbs, adverbs and adjectives

S: Assuming you know what they are!

T: Well, then the big words. Then you automatically increase your speed.

D: Yeah, that makes sense.

S: Mmmm.

S: Right. I think I'm going off to the library to start. Thanks for the tutorial!

T: Anytime. I'm off to the sports centre.

D: By the way, what was your reading speed per hour when you first came here?

T: **Twenty-five**.

---

| 24. | 60/70 or sixty to seventy |
|-----|---------------------------|
| 25. | 160 |
| 26. | one/1 |
| 27. | three/3 |
| 28. | **suit the circumstances** |
| 29. | **so inadequate** |
| 30. | **twenty-five/25** |

*The listening in Section 3 contains no surprises. However, completing the table may cause some problems. You need to practise doing this kind of question as much as you can in other IELTS books and listening practice for foreign language students.*

---

| Practice Test 3 | Section 4 |
|-----------------|-----------|

## Questions 31–34

Good afternoon to you all again, and thanks for coming for the second lecture in the series Drama after Graduating. For those of you who weren't here last week, my name is Jennifer McKenzie-Davies and I am one of those lucky ones – an actress with a job!

---

I'm going to talk to you today about the difficulties actors and actresses face finding work; not that any of you need reminding! It's a jungle out there and you've got to be very hungry to survive. **Are you hungry?** Well, I'm afraid you're going to have to be, because if you aren't you might as well pack your bags and forget all about acting as a career. **And not just hungry; but also resolute in getting what you want. And, of course, persistent. Not to mention gifted!**

**Between 80 and 90 percent of you will be out of work at any one time.** You are joining a group of people whose **average time in employment is 12 weeks a year for men**, and **7 weeks for women**. Why do we do it? We must be mad! And yet, there are thousands more waiting to take our places, if we fail.

| 31. | C |
|-----|---|
| 32. | B |
| 33. | D |
| 34. | C |

*The answers to the questions in this sub-section follow very closely after one another. It is not the detail itself, which makes the speech difficult to understand, but, again, the speed of processing the information. If you are aiming for a high grade, you should be able to cope with this.*

## Questions 35–40

Still hungry? Good, 'cos this is where the interesting bit starts, now we've got the stats out of the way.

First of all, where do you look for work? Well, there's The Stagedoor, the weekly newspaper which occasionally has a couple of decent jobs in it. And then there's the weekly list of jobs called TCR, but you need to subscribe to that with friends – it's very expensive, especially if you're out of work – about £20, no sorry £25, for five weeks. Then, there's your agent.

You'll discover sooner or later that you need an agent if you want to have access to the best work available. But how do you get an agent?

Well, unless you're really very lucky and get taken on by an agent who just likes the look of you, you have to get an agent to see you in a **live performance**. This could be a good part in a play which shows off your talents, or a film role, or just a show-reel of you performing your **best speeches**. I must say, I don't really know which is harder: getting the part without an agent in the first place or getting an agent interested enough to come and see you; in other words, a real Catch 22 situation. A word of warning: they don't usually travel more than a few hundred yards from their office! They're supposed to be working for you, but they actually behave like it's the other way round. As for show-reels, if you want them to look at yours, you really need to tie them to a chair and force them to watch.

You may find it difficult to get work without an agent, but it'll be **well nigh impossible** without an Equity card. Fortunately, things have changed. In the past, drama school students leaving here in July had what was known as a Registered Graduate Equity Card. This gave you 2 years to get an Equity contract for work – not that easy without experience, an agent or a full Equity Card. But, even when you got your first job paid at Equity rates, you received only a provisional Equity Card. The Union was quite strict about membership, but the alternative was much harder and less likely to result in success. This provisional card could become a full one only after 30 weeks of work. Without it you could forget the West End theatres, top tours and work in television.

Now, however, things are a bit easier. After you finish from here, you automatically get your Equity card. The downside of this is

obviously that there are more people chasing the **same number of jobs**.

But even before you start worrying about Equity Cards and your agent, you've got to establish yourself with photographs: **eye-catching and professional** black and white photos – **small postcard** size for your publicity and CVs. There will be several sessions devoted to choosing the right photos that will show you off the way you are most likely to be cast, and also what to put in your CV and, more importantly with some of you, what not to include. So you see it's not an easy road to fame and fortune.

This has just been an introduction to the trials and tribulations of actors looking for work. Next week, we'll make a start on CVs. But now it's time for a ten-minute tea break, followed by a question and answer session.

| 35. | live performance |
|-----|------------------|
| 36. | best speeches |
| 37. | well nigh impossible |
| 38. | same number of jobs |
| 39. | eye-catching and professional |
| 40. | small postcard |

*The testing in this part of the speech is very different from the first section. You have to listen very carefully for the information. The task is made easier for you, however, by the headings in the notes in the exercise.*

---

## Practice Test 4                         Section 1

## Questions 1–5

**A = Travel agent; S = Student**

A: Good morning. Can I help you?

S: Hello – yes, well, I just want some information actually. I'm trying to work out a trip at the end of the summer holidays

A: Yes.

S: And I wonder if you could help me? I'm a student studying Arabic and I'm heading for **Alexandria in Egypt** to do my language year abroad out at the university there.

A: Right. I just need to get a few preliminary details. I'll put everything on the computer as we go along.

S: Okay.

A: First, when do you want to leave?

S: **I have to be there by 27th September,** and I'd like to leave about a month beforehand so I can do some sightseeing on the way.

A: So ... let's say you want to leave on 27th August.

S: I was planning to leave around the 20th.

A: the 20th of August. Okay. That's a Sunday.

S: **I'd rather leave on the Monday. Right, the 21st then.**

A: **So the 21st.** And did you want to fly?

S: Mmmm, I don't really want to have to fly ah straight there; actually ...

A:  Yes?

S:  I'd like to go by train and ferry to Paris.

A:  What about going through the channel tunnel?

S:  Well, mm, **I don't like the idea of going through tunnels. It scares me.**

A:  Oh, it's just like catching the London Underground!

S:  I never catch the underground.

A:  The ferry trains are pretty frequent, so you won't have to worry about that part of the journey. And where to, after Paris?

S:  Vienna.

```
1. C
2. C
3. A
4. B
5. A
```

## Questions 6-10

A:  **From Paris to Vienna, by plane or train?**

S:  **Train. I'd like to travel overnight, so I'd like a sleeper, if possible.**

A:  Right, a sleeper to Vienna from Paris. Right: there's an early morning train to Vienna, the 7.50, but that won't work because you want an over-night train. But then, there's one at 17.49.

S:  Right.

A:  and you're lucky, because they leave from the Gare de l'Est, which is right next to the Gare du Nord station, where the ferry train comes in.

S:  Brilliant.

A:  So, that gets in to Vienna at 8.35 the next morning. You see that bit of the journey alone costs, er, let me see ... £141.80.

S:  Is that with the student discount?

A:  Yes. And then?

S:  I'd like to spend some time in Vienna; about a week perhaps, before going on to Athens.

A:  Train again?

S:  Well, no. **I was thinking of going by plane via Budapest and stopping off there for a couple of days.**

A:  You do realise that it's going to cost you a lot more going part of the way by plane and part by train. It would work out a lot cheaper if you did it all by train or flew direct.

S:  How much are we talking about?

A:  Probably about at least £250 more.

S:  As much as that.

A:  Well, yes. **You'll probably have to get a scheduled flight from Budapest to Athens** and that's going to cost a lot more than by train.

S:  Well, let's see when we add all up at the end.

A:  **And the last leg of the trip from Athens?**

S:  **I want to go from Piraeus by ferry.**

A:  I see. Okay. Now I'm almost certain there's a ferry service to Alexandria from Piraeus, but I'll have to check ... Mmmm. The computer's not giving me anything.

S:  Can I think this over? I'm maybe making it more complicated than it really is.

A:  Oh, oh, by the way, **have checked the visa requirements for each country?**

S:  **Oh, I hadn't thought of that.**

A:  Right. Can I take a few personal details?

S:  Okay.

A:  Your name?

S:  It's James Weston that's W - e - s - t - o - n.

A:  Right. Fine! OK, then. And a daytime telephone number?

S:  It's 0181 889 4269.

A:  I have logged all these details on the computer. I'll just give you the reference. It's **IAMIFUR2**.

S:  IAMIFUR2.

A:  You just quote this reference when you come in again or telephone. Then it will speed things up a bit.

S:  Okay thanks.

```
6.    H
7.    B
8.    F
9.    C
10.   IAMIFUR2
```
*Be careful with questions 6 – 9.*
*If you find it difficult listen several times.*

---

**Practice Test 4**                    **Section 2**

---

## Questions 11-16

Welcome and indeed welcome every Friday afternoon at 2.15 to Post-bag, your chance as listeners to let us know what you think about our programmes and current issues.

This week our Post-bag has been virtually overflowing - not that we are complaining, mind you! Many of you, in fact, a staggering 4,373 of you to be precise, have completed Radio South's listener phone-in survey. Some general points: **83%** of you think that the radio station has improved over the past year; and only **7%** that it has got worse. Most of you think that the radio station provides an excellent service! That's a big thumbs up for Radio South. Some more statistics: a rather disappointing 64% of you did not like the start of the new international radio soap that began on Wednesday evenings last month. Many of you said that it was too vulgar and puerile, with no plot, no excitement! And only 17% said they liked it.

We passed on your messages to the producer and he said that he had received a number of letters and countless phone calls, saying how innovative and modern the plot was. In fact, those figures for those listening had more than doubled for the second programme! We'll have to wait and see how this one develops!

And for 87% of you, the new starting time of 5 am for the Wake-up show went down really well! Only a small disapproval rating for this one; in fact, only **3%**. Many of you said the earlier time is a **real hit!**

Unfortunately, **The Wine Show** has not gone down well at all. It had a 15% approval rating and 25% who did not like it and 60% don't knows! Sadly, the main comment was that the programme is **downright boring.** Maybe, wine's going out of fashion.

The full survey will be published next month and it is free on request!

And now to our weekly letters slot.

11.   83/ eighty-three
12.   7/ seven
13.   3/ three
14.   a real hit
15.   Wine Show
16.   downright boring

## Questions 17–20

Sharon from Tasmania has written in to say that she has tried to get through on the telephone to our new Message Line to leave a message on the Voicebox, but she finds it too complicated. She says, and I quote: Every time I press a number after the main menu the line won't accept my message. It is so frustrating. Maybe your Voicebox should come with a health warning! Well, I can tell you that you're not the first person to have complained about this; in fact, we had 67 letters this past week alone and **complaints have been going up at the rate of 10% a week recently**. And we're now looking into the problem.

On a more cheerful note, Mary from Sydney, Australia, wrote in to say how refreshing and cheerful she found our station. She says the music and the morning Wake-up show she finds really invigorating. We've had lots of similar letters **from all around South-east Asia** saying the same thing: from Terry in Auckland, New Zealand, Yuko in Japan and Ahmed in Indonesia. Robyn in Australia says it's really an excellent new contribution to the radio scene in the area and encourages us to keep going. Thank you Robyn for your support.

Pangaporn from Thailand wants to know if there are any plans to repeat the English language programme, *English Worldwide*, on Sunday mornings at 9 am or whether we are going to expand the programme. We've had so many letters over the past week about *English Worldwide*; it appears to be hugely popular. Since it started 5 weeks ago, **the number of people tuning in has grown tenfold**. There are no plans at the moment to increase the 2-hour slot on Friday morning, but if numbers keep increasing at the rate they are we may have to.

Many of you have asked when we are becoming a 24-hour service. The answer is as soon as we can. **We now broadcast 19 hours a day** and hope to be on air 24 hours a day within the next six months.

And now it's over to Marco, who's going to look at the latest cinema and video releases

| 17. D | 18. C | 19. A | 20. B |
|---|---|---|---|

---

**Practice Test 4**          **Section 3**

---

## Questions 21–25

**Dr: = Dr Goldfinch; F = Farilla: L: = Lorraine: S = Stevie.**

Dr:   This is our third and last group tutorial of the term. Have you been finding them of any use?

F:   Oh yes. I get a lot out of them.

S:   Me too.

Dr:   And What about you Lorraine?

L:   **Yes, I think so**

Dr:   Okay. Right. Anything for this week? Lorraine?  No? Okay.  Farilla?

F:   **Well, ... you know I have two teenage daughters and I'm a single parent**.

Dr:   Yes?

F:   Well, mm,  I'm finding it less and less easy to study as a mature student and have a teenage family. **The girls have been playing me up.**

Dr:   And what exactly do you mean by that?

F:   Kimberly, the eldest, has a boyfriend and she's taken to staying out later and later. And she's becoming difficult to control. And the younger one, who's fourteen, misses Kimberly, because they were always together.

Dr:   Mhmm and

F:   **and I feel as if I'm letting them down by doing this course.** They don't have a father and all they've got is me. I just don't know what to do.

Dr:   It is a difficult situation this one.

S:   My mum did the same thing, went back to studying when I was 16 and I think at the time I got really jealous ...

L:   Of what?

S:   the course!

L:   the course?

S:   Well, it wasn't just the course. It was the other people and the fact that my mum's time was taken up by other things and people. At the time I did not like it at all!

F:   That's the problem here, I think.

Dr:   And what happened, Stevie?

S:   Well, I started playing up to attract attention and ... doing some pretty stupid things, in fact really stupid things.

L:   Like what? Oh, go on, tell us!

S:   No! Anyway, my mum sat my brother and me down and told us how important the course was for her and us and why she hadn't been able to do it before.

F:   And?

S:   Well, she said that, even though it had cost her a lot of money and she was having to work part-time to keep everything going,  she was prepared to give it up.

L:   And did she?

S:   Of course not, Lorraine! We felt pretty stupid. After that we helped out more **and both of us got a job, a small job, so that she didn't have to give us any pocket money.**

Dr:   **Ah, well, Farilla, maybe you should try the same approach.**

F:   I think I might just give it a try. Thanks Stevie. You're a star.

Dr:   And what about you, then Stevie?

| 21. B | 22. A | 23. D | 24. C | 25. D |
|---|---|---|---|---|

## Questions 26–30

S:   I've got a rather more mundane problem, well, maybe, not that mundane.

Dr:   Mhm.

S:   I had to type **a paper for a seminar** for this Friday and I had everything almost ready and ..

L:   and

S:   **My laptop crashed ...**

**A book for IELTS**

Dr: Haven't you got a copy on disk?

S: No, I ...

L: You're crazy. This isn't the first time it's happened to you; haven't you learnt by now?

S: I know, I know, but that doesn't help me at the moment, does it?

L: You just don't listen, do you?

F: Leave him alone, Lorraine. You're not exactly helping, are you?

L: I ...

Dr: I think Farilla is right. There's no point in crying over spilt milk.

F: **Have you a rough copy?**

S: **Yes,** but

F: You can type it in again,

S: I'm very slow and I'm not going to get it done in time. I also have to get OHPs together as well. They were on the computer and it was just as I was printing them out that the machine went. I also have to hand a typed up **summary in 2000 words,** bound as well, to Dr Johnson the day before. And on top of that I have to hand in the full paper at the end of the seminar. As it goes towards my final grade and **a credit is taken off for handing papers in late**, I have to do it. And it's Tuesday now, so I haven't really got much time. I nearly didn't come today.

F: Don't worry, Stevie, I'll help you do it, if you want; we can start straight after the tutorial.

S: Will you, Farilla?!?

F: Yes,

L: You should let him do it himself!

Dr: Now Lorraine,

F: He helped me, so I don't see why I shouldn't help him. You could lend a hand too, you know. You don't know when you might need help.

L: I ... I ...

S: It's okay, Farilla. We can do it together.

Dr: Well, two people sorted. Now what about you Lorraine?

| | |
|---|---|
| 26. | (seminar) paper |
| 27. | crashed |
| 28. | rough copy |
| 29. | (2000 word) summary |
| 30. | a credit |

---

**Practice Test 4**　　　　　**Section 4**

---

## Questions 31–37

And how did it all start? Many times I have been asked how someone becomes a journalist; and how I myself became a music critic. There is no set path. After doing an MA in music, I worked in a London bookshop for a couple of months, then as **a sub-editor for an educational publication**. After I left that, like many of my colleagues, I wrote **freelance features** for various newspapers and magazines in the music world. My counterparts on other newspapers made their entry to music criticism by totally different routes. Some took courses in journalism; some wrote features which they then sent round newspapers and journals until they were published; while others

took some less orthodox steps. After a couple of years freelancing, rather than moving into the editorial field in journalism, I was given the rare opportunity to become **a music critic on a national newspaper**, on a retainer. For those of you who don't know what it is, a retainer is a fixed yearly sum paid for a certain number of, in my case, concert reviews. Cheap labour with the prestige thrown in by way of compensation!

To many, the work of a music critic is glamorous, and, in some respects, I have to admit, it is. I have the rare chance to meet interesting people, but like any other profession it has its downside. The concert-going public do not seem to be able to take on board the fact that when I am reviewing a concert, I am working. At concerts, people have the habit of descending on me like vultures to talk music; would they appreciate it if I pounced upon them at work to enthuse about accountancy, obscure legal matters? I think not! **And also it can be a very lonely profession**; working on your own for days, weeks sometimes, without human contact except by telephone or computer. **Another drawback is having to write reviews to deadlines on a daily basis.** And despite what many people believe, **the salary is not that good** unless you occupy one of the prestigious posts on a national paper.

Yet, it is not all negative! The travel, I must say, I do enjoy tremendously. On the street near my flat, I was once stopped and asked to help complete a survey. Washing machine, madam? No. Microwave? No. Television? Just. And how many times do you go abroad per year, madam? About once every ten days! I never tire of seeing new places, or indeed of revisiting old friends. The States I visit about three times a year on average; **other countries in Europe about ten to 12 times a year.** With about six of these being the Scandinavian countries. The rest of the trips tend to be one-off special journeys to exciting places like Greenland, Japan, Nova Scotia, Iceland, the Pacific Islands, etc.

| | | | |
|---|---|---|---|
| **31. I** | **32. C** | **33. G** | **34. C** |
| **35. E** | **36. H** | **37. C** | |

## Questions 38–40

And what is the role of the music critic today? Listening has always been a talent: now it is a rare and fragile one. The journalist Michael Ignatieff has recently presented us in the United Kingdom with a provocative television series on the **three-minute culture**. Three minutes, he says, is just about as long as the **average person can concentrate**. There is such a wash of music around us which threatens to become a tidal wave. Audiences coming out of London's Festival Hall and setting out for the journey home, put on their Sony Walkmans with their overcoats; avid festival-goers, likely to be hearing three or four recitals a day, pack their cassette tapes and CDs in their luggage in order not to have to endure silence in their hotel rooms.

The critic's job is to foster the talent of **discriminating listening** against all odds. People have a real inferiority complex when it comes to trusting their own ears. Friends and acquaintances often expect me to tell them what they should think after a concert. But if I don't, then someone else surely will. A critic's responses or pointers can, at least, perhaps act as disinterested **touchstones** amongst the babble of hype and market forces.

| | |
|---|---|
| 38. | 3/three-minute culture/ average person's concentration |
| 39. | discriminating listening |
| 40. | touchstone |

*Note how the level of difficulty as regards the content of the speech increases in this section. Again, remember that you do not have to understand everything to complete the tasks.*

# Reading Exercises

## Key to Exercises 1–22

## Exercise 1

1. **A** Sentence 2 contains the function of the building described.

   **B** Sentence 4 describes the physical structure.

   **C** Sentence 3 contains information on the location of the building.

   **D** Information on the history of the building is in Sentence 1.

2. The reason is that each phrase relates to the information in one sentence only. Each phrase summarises only one sentence, *not* the whole paragraph.

3. The writer wrote the paragraph: *to describe the Mussenden temple.* The answer **A** gives you the purpose for writing the paragraph. **B** only gives you the writer's purpose for writing the last sentence. The text contains no information about whether Frederick Hervey was mad or not. The writer only states that Hervey was enigmatic. Therefore, **C** is not possible as an answer. As for **D**, it only describes the writer's purpose in writing the second sentence. It is clear that only **A** states why the writer wrote the whole paragraph, rather than just the parts of it.

4. *building/folly/library/temple/structure*
   The word *library* is probably the main one. Read the organisation of the second sentence.

5. The synonyms are used to develop the text and reflect different qualities throughout the paragraph. The writer uses the different synonyms to bind the text together and to express the different qualities of the *building* in each sentence: *folly*, an act of madness; *temple* as tribute to Mrs Mussenden; and then the main focus, *library*.

6. It is descriptive. Note that the paragraph is a list of information:

   *The building was completed in 1785*
   *The building was erected by Frederick Hervey*
   *Frederick Hervey was enigmatic*
   *Frederick Hervey was Earl of Bristol*
   *Frederick Hervey was Bishop of Derry*

   and so on. There is no argument, nor opinion in the paragraph. Learning to recognise the different types of paragraphs and texts is another important aspect of learning to read the *meaning* and *organisation* of a text. See **Reading Exercises 5 and 10-13.**

7. The most appropriate title is **C**: *The Mussenden Temple.* The title reflects the purpose of the author in writing the paragraph. (*See* **3** above) and is a summary of all the information in the paragraph. The other titles refer only to parts of the text and cannot, therefore, act as summaries of the whole paragraph.

   In the IELTS exam, exercises where you have to give a title or heading to a paragraph are quite common. It is a type of exercise which many candidates find rather difficult. You can see the title here is the sum of the four sentences i.e. *the function of the building, the physical structure of the library, the location of the building and the history of the building.*

8. The first sentence gives background information against which the writer describes the function of the building in the second.

9. The function of the third sentence is to describe the geographical location. Into this setting fits the physical appearance in the fourth sentence.

10. Between the second and third sentences. See the answers to **8** and **9** above.

11. The first two sentences give non-physical information about the building (i.e. its background history and function). The last two sentences give physical information about the buildings (i.e. its location and appearance). Notice how you can bring the first two sentences into one unit and the latter two again into one unit. You can then add these two together to give you the title of the passage.

12. The information has been put in a different order. The most important information in the original text is: **The library was built in honour of Mrs Mussenden.** The other information given by the writer is subsidiary to this main point. The information contained in the phrases: ... , **completed in 1785, ... by the enigmatic Frederick Hervey, Earl of Bristol and Bishop of Derry, ... , the Earl's cousin** is extra. Note the commas around the phrase, **completed in 1785,** and the comma and full stop around **... , the Earl's cousin.** to mark off this information from the main text. You can understand the first sentence in this explanation without difficulty, but you cannot understand the additional information on its own. It adds to the text, but by the organisation in the sentence the writer shows that it is additional, not central.

   You need, therefore, to understand the hierarchy of information within a sentence and within a text. You need to recognise what information in a text is important and what is really just additional or background information. *See* **Reading Exercises 12 and 13.**

   In the sentence in the exercise, the information was reorganised with the main information being: *was completed in 1785.*

## Exercise 2

a. **Answer: False.** The paragraph talks about drivers and the opinion they have of themselves, not their opinion of other matters or people. The text then goes on to talk about the results of this arrogance. Candidates often read too quickly and do not look carefully enough at the exact meaning of the important words in a text. So be careful!

b. **Answer: False.** The second sentence gives you the focus of the paragraph: the general effect of drivers' having a high opinion of themselves.

c. **Answer: False.** The paragraph contains two examples which illustrate drivers' high opinion of themselves. The last sentence is a comparison of a similar situation outside motoring.

d. **Answer: True.** The second sentence states a general consequence of the first sentence. In this way, it leads the reader from the general statement in the first sentence to the specific examples in sentences 3 to 5 and helps the text to move smoothly from general statement to focus, to example. It is in this sense a transition sentence. See **e** below.

e. **Answer: True.** You could remove the second sentence and put **For example,** at the beginning of sentence 3. The paragraph, however, reads much better with the sentence than without it, as it helps to direct the reader through the text.

f. **Answer: False.** As we have seen the organisation of the paragraph is:

| General statement | Result | example + example + analogous example |
|---|---|---|

   You can look at the text in another way. **Sentence 2** is a general effect of the problem which is mentioned in the first sentence. **Sentences 3, and 4** are specific examples of effects:

| problem/ cause | general effect | specific + effect | specific + effect | analogous example |
|---|---|---|---|---|

You can see that the examples are *examples* of the effects of the problem/ cause in the first sentence. The paragraph is, therefore, basically one of *cause and effect*.

Note that the sentences in the paragraph could be linked together with the word **and**. You could put the information into a list:

*Drivers often have an over-inflated opinion of their own driving abilities and think that most other people on the road fall well below their own high standards and some take it upon themselves to show their fellow road users how to drive and car drivers commonly ...*

You can see that it would be very difficult to extract information from large chunks of text like this. Hence, the need for sentences.

It is in effect, therefore, a **list** or **and** paragraph. Look back at the text in *Exercise 1* and you will see that it is also a list paragraph.

g  **Answer: False.** The text does not need any more text markers. The meaning of the sentences is obvious. Part of the problem that students have when they read a text, is the fact that there are no text-markers. You can write a paragraph as here without obvious or overt markers.

*Read the text again and:*

i) insert the word *then* in the second sentence after *Some*.

ii) insert the phrase *For example*, at the beginning of the third sentence.

iii) insert the phrase *Moreover*, at the beginning of the fourth sentence.

iv) insert the phrase *Similarly* (i.e. a similar situation/ For example,) at the beginning of the fifth sentence.

The organisation of the text is then more obvious: *then* = effect; *example* = example of effect. The academic texts that you need to be able to read for the IELTS will in many cases not have these obvious or overt markers. So you need to learn to read and summarise each sentence instantly. This comes with practice.

h  **Answer: True.** The paragraph, in fact, answers the question: *What is the effect of drivers' high opinion of themselves?* The writer then wrote the paragraph to answer this question!

i  **Answer: True.** It is important to look at the direction of the text up to and away from the focus or topic sentence, when you want to work out the overall meaning of the paragraph. Remember the meaning of the paragraph is the sum of the meaning of the sentences ... and something else. That something else is the direction of the paragraph as in (f) and (h) above. The statement made in the focus sentence is supported by examples of the consequences of drivers' opinion of themselves; hence, the title.

## Exercise 3

a  **Answer: False.** The first sentence is an example of how people relieve their frustrations.

b  **Answer: False.** The purpose of the paragraph is to show the best way to deal with frustrating situations: the last sentence. In the first three sentences, the writer gives examples of how people *relieve* their frustrations. If the statement in the exercise referred to these three

sentences only, it would be **True**. The writer does not think that this is the best way to deal with pent-up anger: the first three sentences are examples of what *not* to do. Against this background, the writer then gives his opinion about how to deal with the situation. Recognising the purpose or reason why a paragraph has been written is important for working out the organisation and then the title of a piece of text.

c  **Answer: True.** The paragraph is one of subjective argument/opinion. The writer has set out to show that the way that people normally get rid of their frustrations is wrong and against this background he proposes his own solution. Note that the first three sentences are, in fact, a concession i.e. *Although we tend to take out our pent-up emotions on other people by (Sentences 1-3), I believe a better way ... .* The writer puts what other people do first. Then, against this background he puts his own opinion. The first three sentences contain specific examples of how people get rid of their frustration. The fourth acts as a summary of the previous examples giving specific examples to support a generalisation. Note that you could put the fourth sentence at the beginning. Then you would be arguing from the general to the specific.

The type of organisation in this paragraph is quite common in written texts. For more on paragraph types see **Reading Exercises 4 –11.**

d  **Answer: True.** The text reads from particular (specific) to general.

e  **Answer: True.** It states what the writer thinks against the previous background. The word **But** shows that the writer is making a contrasting statement about the previous examples of how people deal with frustration. The word **surely** shows that he is making a fairly strong statement.

f  **Answer: False.** Note the difference between the paragraph in this exercise and the previous two texts. The first three sentences could be connected by **and**. Between the first three sentences and the fourth sentence the connection is also **and**. Between the fourth and fifth sentences the connection is **but**. This is, therefore, a **but** paragraph.

Note also that it is impossible to work out the organisation of the paragraph and the title by reading the first and last sentences.

g  **Answer: False.** Only two of the titles are suitable. Title (i) covers only the background information (specific examples) in the first three sentences and the general statement in the fourth. It does not take into account the fifth sentence. Title (ii), **The best way to relieve frustration,** is also unacceptable. The purpose of the paragraph was to show that the best way to deal with frustration is to control it, not relieve it. Title (iii) reflects the purpose and direction of the paragraph (*see* a to e). Note the difference between this title and the previous one: the title reflects the purpose and focus of the paragraph and, thus, it appears to be focusing on one piece of information only. Yet, it is a good title. Title (iv) is suitable, because the word **deal** covers both relieving and controlling.

## Exercise 4

1. **Answer:** (i) **G**, (ii) **L**, (iii) **A**, (iv) **K**, (v) **H**, (vi) **M** , (vii) **E**

The writer gives examples to explain the focus in the first sentence. The focus here is not so clear, perhaps, as the following:

*Let us look at the different types of thinker. Some thinkers, content to ...*

The phrase *different types of thinker* is much clearer, but do not expect the focus sentence of a paragraph, if there is one, to be so obvious, or overt.

2. **Answer: A.** See 3 below.

3. This is an example paragraph. Note the examples are part of an explanation.

4. **Answer: No.** It is a **but** paragraph. First, the writer lists examples, which could all be joined by **and** (Sentences (ii), (iii) and (iv)). The information in this list then forms the background for the more important information, which comes in the text after the word **however**. In Sentence (vi), the writer gives another example and a warning. Then, in the last sentence, he develops the information in Sentence (vi) to make a conclusion and to give you the title.

   Reading is very much like writing: in both, you need to know in which direction you are going. For reading, you have to follow the signs the writer gives you to extract the full meaning. In writing, the burden is upon you to give the signs so that the reader can follow you; and so that you can follow yourself!

   We said above that the text in the exercise is an example paragraph. It is also a paragraph that argues from particular to general. Sentences (ii) – (v) give specific information from which the writer draws a general conclusion.

5. It is similar to the text in **Reading Exercise 2**, but notice the difference! The *Examples* in 2 are also effects. The paragraph here is also similar to the text in **Reading Exercise 3** where the writer lists specific examples and arranges them inside a concession (*see* 3c).

6. The answer is **No**. See **Reading Exercise 2 g**.

7. From the last two sentences. The title comes from the reason why the writer wrote the paragraph: to show which thinkers are the dangerous ones.

## Exercise 5

### Paragraph 1

The following are **false**:

b The paragraph is not descriptive. Look at the text in the first exercise in this section.

c This is not the reason why the author wrote the passage. The statement refers only to the first three sentences. Statement a) gives you the answer.

d The sentence **The repercussions are grave** is the transition sentence in the paragraph. It links the situation described in the first three sentences with the consequences or repercussions in the last sentence.

h The focus is in the fourth sentence.

j The first two are good summaries of the text, as they reflect the writer's purpose in writing the paragraph. The last title covers only the information in the first three sentences.

The following are **true**:

a The first three sentences act as a background for the more important information in the last two sentences. The text is directed towards the conclusion that too much information affects people's ability to work. Note how the last two sentences depend on the first three. Note also the dramatic effect of the fourth sentence. The shortness of the sentence brings you up short and makes you notice it.

e All of the information in the passage can be connected by **and**.

f Compare the organisation of this paragraph with the previous exercises. In Exercise 1, the text is a

*description*, where the writer has woven a list of information into a text. The paragraph in Exercise 2 is one of cause and effect. In Exercise 3, the text is organised around the principle of *concession/contrast* with opinion. Exercise 4 also contains a list of information. As you read, you should look out for different types of paragraphs. Then gradually you can recognise them easily.

g The first three sentences describe the situation and the last sentence describes the implications/repercussions/consequences. The fourth sentence acts as a marker between the problem and the consequences in the last sentence. The sentence summarises the repercussions before they are mentioned; it predicts the text which is coming.

i See the answer for (a) above.

### Paragraph 2

a It is an explanation paragraph. The writer explains how failure and success are linked to each other.

b It is a **but** paragraph. Notice how the word **Instead** marks and divides the text.

c The focus of the paragraph is in the first sentence.

d The paragraph is *similar* in organisation to the text in Exercise 3, but not the same. The information in Exercise 3 is arranged around a concession/contrast, here there is just a contrast.

e The last sentence.

f **Answer: (iii).** When you are trying to work out the title for a paragraph the first thing you should do is ask yourself: why did the writer write the paragraph? You can see that (i) is not suitable because the paragraph shows you how failure and success are linked. As you have seen, the focus of the paragraph is in the first sentence and the rest of the paragraph explains the focus. The last sentence in the paragraph acts as a conclusion. Note that in this case, you can work out the title from reading the first and last sentence. Compare this with the other paragraphs you have read so far. The other two titles are purely distracters.

g **Answer : (iv). This is the only alternative which answers the question in f) above.**

   Title (i) is almost correct, but it talks only about failure and not about its connection with success. Titles (ii) and (iii) are obviously wrong.

## Exercise 6

You can see that each sentence has different layers of meaning.

1. **Answer: C.** Sentence 1 gives the topic of the paragraph and helps you organise your reading. It does this by asking a question, which then obviously has to be answered.

2. **Answer: J.** The second sentence answers the question in the first sentence describing the situation as it is now. It thus provides some background information, however brief. The sentence contrasts the fact that writing and numeracy are taught badly, but thinking is not taught at all. Note how the sentence expresses all of the meanings at the same time.

3. **Answer: E.** This sentence gives more general background information and states a problem as regards education in general, not just thinking. It gives more detail about the

information in the second sentence and explains why the art of thinking is not taught. Note, in particular, that the sentence states a problem.

The sentence can have other meanings, which are not mentioned here. It could also be stating a reason, i.e. why thinking is not taught.

4. **Answer: A.** This sentence is similar to the previous one. The writer is expanding further and explains why thinking is not taught. Note that this sentence is also stating a reason again and making a criticism.

5. **Answer: B.** The writer is now moving back to the central theme of the paragraph: teaching thinking. The sentence is again a criticism and, therefore, an opinion. This sentence is a particularly good example of meaning operating at different levels.

Note how sentences 3 and 4 give background information to the main focus of the paragraph.

6. **Answer: H.** This sentence has many different functions. The writer is making a proposal in the form of a wish. He is making a criticism and a complaint, and he is also being sarcastic. He also believes that his proposal would solve the problem.

You can see, from this sentence and from 5 above, what the implications are if you are not able to read meaning. Look at the following sentence:

*To the author, it is regrettable that thinking skills are not being taught.*

The sentence paraphrases part of the information in sentence 6. Where is the word **regrettable**? So think about the meaning of a text!

7. **Answer: F.** The sentence contains the result or develop-ment of the proposal in the previous sentence! Note that the result is simultaneously hypothetical and certain, that is, providing the proposal is taken up.

8. **Answer: D.** The statement concludes the paragraph.

Note that this is a problem/solution type of paragraph. Look at the following summary of the text:

*Focus/present situation/present situation-general problem/reformulation of problem/ specific problem/ solution/proposal/ result/conclusion*

---

### Exercise 7

The functions listed below are **not** suitable.

1. *stating a disadvantage; stating the focus of the paragraph*
2. stating an advantage; stating the main argument for; making a criticism
3. stating an argument for; making a proposal
4. stating a disadvantage; stating a reservation
5. stating a subjective argument against; giving an opinion; stating a reservation
6. summarising the disadvantages
7. stating an argument for; stating an opinion; stating a tentative result based on a condition

The functions which remain after you remove those in the Key above act as summaries of the sentences they relate to. The sum of the functions gives you the meaning of the paragraph.

The last sentence tells you why the author wrote the paragraph: to support the use of trolley buses and trams.

Look at the title: *A case for trolley buses and trams*. It is easy to make the mistake of reading the first sentence of the paragraph and thinking that the writer is presenting arguments against the introduction of trolley buses and trams. The writer agrees that the arguments *against* are strong (Sentence 6) and uses this as background information to present a statement about the strength of the argument *for*.

The organisation of this paragraph may at first sight appear to be unpredictable and is of a type that can confuse readers. The writer presents the opposite view to his own, only to knock it down. If you look carefully enough you will see he goes from negative to positive, then vice versa. This is quite a common type of organisation.

You can see that the functions are basically the same as other paragraphs you looked at.

You may now have begun to realise that sentences have a limited number of functions, but that each sentence can have different functions. A writer can also put the functions in a different order. The repetition of the same words within a passage is considered bad English. The repetition of exactly the same structure in every paragraph is also bad. So you can see why a writer needs to vary the organisation, even if only slightly. Sometimes, the organisation is varied by keeping the same structure between paragraphs, but giving the sentences in a paragraph extra functions (see **Reading Exercises 4-6**). Note the multi-purpose aspect of Sentence 7 above!

If you bear this in mind as you read, you will learn not to treat each reading passage as something new. You can approach it with an understanding of structure, and with this skill you can bring every passage under your control.

---

### Exercise 8

#### Passage 1

**Sentence 1** is the focus sentence. It is an organising sentence.

**Sentence 2** is describing a suggestion. Note that it is not making a suggestion.

**Sentence 3** is a result, a development, a hypothetical implication. Note that this sentence functions as a concession or an although clause.

**Sentence 4** is stating a probability, a real implication and a contrast.

**Sentence 5** expresses a reason, a result and a hypothetical implication. It is also stating a probability.

**Sentence 6** expresses a reservation.

**Sentence 7** is an objective conclusion.

#### Passage 2

**Sentence 1** is the focus sentence. It is an organising sentence.

**Sentence 2** is making a suggestion; note the writer says **should initiate**. Note that the sentence is making, not describing, a suggestion.

**Sentence 3** is stating a fact. It is also a result and a development. It expresses a reservation. Note that this sentence functions as a concession or an although clause.

**Sentence 4** is a result, a real implication and a contrast.

**Sentence 5** expresses a reason, a result and a real implication. Note that it is not stating a probability: 'will certainly', but a certainty.

**Sentence 6** expresses a reservation.

**Sentence 7** is a subjective conclusion. It is, therefore, expressing an opinion

Note how similar, and yet how different, the paragraphs are. The first paragraph describes a proposal and gives the implications. It is objective. The paragraph is basically one of recommendation and result/implication.

'The second paragraph is different in that it makes a proposal; it does not just describe it, and gives the implications. It is also subjective. The paragraph is basically one of recommendation and result/implication. However, the implications are real this time, and the writer is stating an opinion.

Note Sentence 3 in the second paragraph. It is expressing a reservation. This is not possible in Paragraph 1!

---

### Exercise 9

(i) Cloning's bright future

　　1. C, **2.** B, 3. A, **4.** B, 5. C, **6.** A, **7**. C, **8.** A

(ii) The unacceptable face of cloning

　　1. B, **2.** A, **3.** B, **4.** C, 5. A, **6.** B, **7.** B, **8.** C

(iii) The dangers of cloning

　　1. A, **2.** C, 3. C, **4.** A, 5. B, **6.** C, 7. A, **8.** B

You should repeat this exercise many times. Try to find and read the paragraph for each title and, as you do so, block out the ideas from the other titles. The three paragraphs add up to a short article on cloning. As you have seen in this exercise and the previous one, the similarity of the subject matter in a text can cause problems. If you are aware of this, you can tackle the problem.

> *Note:* You should be able to read the paragraphs by predicting the function of the next sentence. Try title (ii) and think of reasons why cloning is unacceptable. You will then see how easily the other two alternatives do not fit in!

---

### Exercise 10

You can see that the paragraph contains a list of examples to show how life is moving at a faster pace or rate. Sentences 5, 6, 8, 9 and 10 give examples. Note, however, the fact that there are no specific words to state that they are examples. Sentence 7 is a result of Sentence 6. The last two sentences are the conclusion of the paragraph.

Sentence 8 is a general example; the next two sentences give you more specific information.

Microwaves, computers, trains and planes are quite common examples.

---

### Exercise 11

The paragraph is very similar in content to Exercise 7, but you can see that it goes in a totally different direction. If you read the title and then read a few of the phrases in the first sentence, you have an idea of what is coming: rather out-moded forms of transport; mistakenly. As you go through the text, you can see that the writer is using negative language to convince you of his view here:

> Trolley buses and trams, **rather out-moded forms of transport**, are mistakenly being hailed as the answer to the ills afflicting modern transport systems. A vast swathe of South London from Tooting on the Northern Line to Croydon **is being churned up** to build a new tram system. Motorists **obviously don't like it**, because the roads are in the process of **being ripped up** in preparation for the tramlines being laid. When the trams are finally up and running, most people **will be against the idea**, because the system **will lead to** more one-way systems, **thus hindering** their freedom of movement and **most certainly increasing** the congestion that it was designed to get rid of. **Then, when the problems start arising, they will have to start dismantling the whole network again at great inconvenience to the motoring public!**

Much of the detail is the same, but by changing a few elements the direction and purpose of the text changes dramatically.

If you did not predict the content exactly, it does not matter. The main thing is that you got part of the answer and understood the technique. Leave the exercise for a while and try it again and see what happens.

The sequence of functions is:

> *a criticism; background information/*
> *an example; a result/ consequence; a result/*
> *consequence; a result/ a criticism/ a conclusion.*

---

### Exercise 12

1. **Answer: E.** Look at the following plan of the organisation of the meaning of the paragraph. Compare the list in Passage 1 in Exercise 10. When you are able to recognise paragraph types it helps you to read with organisation and hence more efficiently.

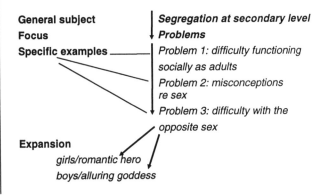

**General subject**
**Focus** → *Segregation at secondary level*
**Specific examples** → *Problems*

*Problem 1: difficulty functioning socially as adults*
*Problem 2: misconceptions re sex*
*Problem 3: difficulty with the opposite sex*

**Expansion**
*girls/romantic hero*
*boys/alluring goddess*

A book for IELTS

You can see from the scheme above that the paragraph is not a description of segregation of boys and girls at secondary level. The paragraph is basically a list or **and** paragraph, which contains examples of problems. The author wrote the paragraph to show that segregation at this level causes a number of problems.

The problems are also consequences, implications or the negative effects of segregation. So you can see here again that there are different levels of meanings when sentences are placed together in a text. Compare the texts in the previous reading exercises in this section. This, obviously, is of great importance, if the IELTS exam is based on testing meaning.

The only heading which summarises all the information we have here adequately is E. Note that the distracters H and L relate only to part of the text i.e. **Problem 2**.

## 2. Answer: K

| | |
|---|---|
| *General subject* | *Segregation at secondary level* |
| *Argument against* | *Unnatural to some* |
| *Explanation* | *Segregation not a realistic environment* |
| *Focus* | *Segregated schools better* |
| *Supporting argument* | *Girls held back by immature boys* |

You can see from the above list that the writer starts with the opposite opinion to her own (see the paragraph in **Reading Exercise 7**). So it is easy to misread the direction of the paragraph. However, the word mistakenly should give you a clue to the direction in which the text is going: *This is the viewpoint of other people; mine is the opposite and I am going to show it to you.*

Note that the information is basically the same as that in the previous paragraph. However, because the writer has decided to use it in a different way, the end result is different. The writer could have put the focus at the beginning and could have arranged the information in a different way. However, remember what we said in the **Key** to **Reading Exercise 7** about the need to avoid repetition of the structure of paragraphs.

Is this an *and* paragraph? The answer is no; it is a basically a *but* paragraph. In the first two sentences, the writer presents an argument which opposes her own. She then knocks this argument down by presenting her own opinion, which is the opposite. This relationship in the text is like that between the general information you have in an introduction with a general statement and focus. The first two sentences provide the background for the focus of the paragraph: the writer's opinion.

Some may be tempted to put **F** as the answer, but nowhere does it mention that the paragraph is **the main argument**, and the writer is **for** segregation.

## 3. Answer: L

As you are reading, always ask yourself why the author wrote the paragraph. The author wrote it to show that segregation at this level is unnatural. The main aspect he deals with is misconceptions about sex:

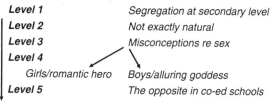

| | |
|---|---|
| *Level 1* | *Segregation at secondary level* |
| *Level 2* | *Not exactly natural* |
| *Level 3* | *Misconceptions re sex* |
| *Level 4* | |
| *Girls/romantic hero* | *Boys/alluring goddess* |
| *Level 5* | *The opposite in co-ed schools* |

You can see from the scheme above the text is dealing with only one aspect of segregation. Compare this with the list of problems in the first paragraph. You can see that one of the problems from the first paragraph has been turned into a separate paragraph.

## 4. Answer: C.

Now let us look at the paragraph in another way.

**Change** causes **problems,** not least because it **upsets people's routine** and makes them feel **uneasy.** A good example is the introduction of technology in the workplace. The Luddite in all of us comes out as we are **faced with adapting to** the onslaught of technological change at work. In the early 19th century, the Luddites revolted against the introduction of what was new technology in their time by breaking machinery which replaced workers. The pace of change today is much faster, and thereby more **unsettling.** Thousands of workers in factories have been replaced by computers and robots; now voice recognition programmes **threaten** to replace secretaries; computerised switchboards receptionists and computer video packages instructors and teachers. **What area of life is safe from the advance of machines?**

You can see that there is a thread which runs through the text. Sometimes, it is difficult in another language to see that thread, because there is a lot of background information which fills in the detail. The text in bold above is the foreground information in the paragraph, which gives you the meaning of the paragraph and hence the title.

If you are able to read a text and just use the foreground information as stepping stones, you can read much faster and more efficiently. Obviously, the more competent you are at doing this in the IELTS exam the higher your grade will be in reading.

Note that **A** is not a suitable title, because it is only a summary of part of the paragraph (the historical example). The same applies to **I**, which is only a summary of the modern day example of the text. Title **D** is unacceptable, because the paragraph is talking about the unsettling effect of the introduction of new technology. Title **D** summarises only part of the text. Note also that title **D** applies only to the Historical example, and the Modern example applies both to factory and office workers. So it does not cover the meaning of the whole paragraph.

## 5. Answer: B. Note again how the diagram below shows you the thread of meaning of the theme of the paragraph.

Technological change
|
Belief it destroys jobs/ unfounded

Historical Example      Modern Day Example
|                   |
Luddites          Computers

No reason to fear technology

As you can see, title **B** summarises the paragraph. As in paragraph 4 above, **A** and **D** are not suitable titles, because they are summaries only of parts of the paragraph. The same again applies to **I**, which is a summary only of the modern day example in the text.

Note again how the same background information can be used to support different foreground information.

## 1. Heading: Hooked on change

The theme is developed by the following:
- *Change*
- *Yet, there are people who seem to thrive on change, enjoying the constant flow of challenges.*
- *a situation in which a certain type of person flourishes.*
- *change is like a drug.*
- *They become addicted*

Now go back to the paragraph and read it, looking for the words and phrases above. You may want to underline the text with a pencil or put a box around them. Can you see that the rest of the text provides background information for the foreground information above? This is a slightly different way of looking at paragraph headings from the previous exercise.

## 2. Heading: Welcome to new technology

The theme is developed by the following:
- *But the belief that it destroys people's jobs and lives is totally unfounded.*
- *It is now clear, however, that, far from destroying work, many more jobs have been created in factories*
- *Witness the development of 'silicon valleys' throughout the world.*
- ***The advances in the field of technology should, therefore, be embraced with open arms rather than feared.***

Now go back to the paragraph and read it, looking for the words and phrases above. You can see how the thread of information is very different from the previous paragraph. Nearly all of the first half of the paragraph is devoted to providing background information to the foreground information above. The writer uses the background information as a setting for the point he wishes to make in the paragraph. He then draws a conclusion in the last sentence (in bold above). For more details as to the difference between the foreground and background information, look at the previous exercise.

## 3. Heading: The North/South driving divide

The theme is developed by the following:
- *standards of driving seem to deteriorate markedly as you travel down the country.*
- *A much more calm and relaxed manner of driving is noticeable to those visitors to Northern cities*
- *in areas like the South-east and London*
- *down the M1 from the North,*
- *the nearer you approach London.*
- *In the two to three hours drive South, the journey changes from a pleasant drive to a mad aggressive rush as the traffic hurtles towards London.*
- *Is this yet another example of the differences between the North and South?*

This paragraph has a very obvious thread running through it right from the beginning. Note here the conclusion in the last sentence, which is drawn from the total of the

information in the first part of the text. Note how the summary or purpose of the paragraph provides the heading. Compare this with the rest of the texts in the exercise.

## 4. Heading: Peace at the wheel

Now, it is hoped that you can see the thread through the paragraph which gives the heading easily:
- *how much more relaxing*
- *A calm and relaxed manner of driving*
- *There does not seem to be the same mad rush and lack of respect for other road users*
- *and feel the traffic gradually slow down,*
- *The tension at the wheel subsides; a car journey changes into a very pleasant drive at a respectable pace.*

Now go back to the paragraph and read it, looking for the words and phrases above.

## 5. Heading: The stupidity of ageism

Look at the theme as it runs through the text below.

*Age discrimination is rife among the business community. **The folly inherent in this process is nothing less than a criminal act.** It does not seem to have dawned on employers that the workplace is changing. The number of people dealing with knowledge compared with manual workers is increasing. **In the near future, we may find companies clamouring over each other to attract old people** as the demographic make-up of the working population changes. **Some companies already have a policy of employing older people** in their stores and they have seen a marked turn around in sales. **Could this possibly have something to do with a thing called experience?***

You can see from the text above how the foreground information stands out against the background detail. The background detail sets off the main or foreground information. It is not advisable to mark your book with a highlighter pen, but you could make a photocopy of the texts in this exercise and mark the foreground information in pencil. This will show you how the information stands out, if you know where to look for it.

Being able to recognise the thread of meaning in a text and to distinguish between background and foreground information is crucial to reading fast and efficiently.

## 6. Heading: The need for legislation to protect older people

Look at the theme as it runs through the text below.

*Age is commonly used as a criterion to prevent people from entering a job and, indeed, to rid an establishment of excess personnel. Young people are seen as being fitter physically and mentally, and as costing less. **The experience of older people is overlooked. A dose of ageism is needed here, but ageism where there is discrimination in favour of old people.** Some companies already have a policy of employing older people in their stores and have seen a marked turn around in sales. **So, perhaps there is a case for legislating in favour of old people in the workplace.***

The foreground information to give you the paragraph heading stands out again.

You should repeat **Reading Exercises 1-13** as often as you can in order to absorb the mechanisms they contain. The information that is contained in them is of much less importance than the skills they aim to teach. And never be afraid of using the **Key** to help you at all times. When you feel comfortable with the exercises, then repeat them without using the **Key**.

---

## Exercise 14

1.  The highlighted words are nouns, verbs, adverbs and adjectives. In other words, all the 'content' words are kept and all the small words are left out. As in speech, the big words carry the stress in the sentence. They act as the stepping stones through the text and allow you to skim the surface of the text.

2.  The gaps between the stepping stones are larger, so you have to run through the text more quickly! You can increase your reading speed by first reading the text as in number 1 above and then, as you become more confident, you can decrease the number of words you read as in number 2.

    You can see that in number 2 you effectively have a summary of the text.

3.  The minimum number of words you need in order to have a summary of the texts are given below.

    (a) *Participation in the Euro, the new European currency, hinged on whether the criteria set out in the Maastricht Treaty were adhered to strictly. Several countries would like to have seen some of the qualifying conditions relaxed, but that did not happen, as the banks were against any slackening of monetary control. What remains to be seen is whether the governments concerned can stick to the stringent monetary goals they have set themselves.*

    (b) *The swingeing cuts introduced by the government have created quite a fracas, but many people believe that they are necessary for the future health of the country. The main target areas appear to be spending on welfare, defence and the road network.*

    (c) *One member of the public, a Gladys C Roach, who took part in the survey, stated that she felt it was dangerous to shop in the department store as it was so full of tempting food. She added that she always had to make sure that she went there to shop only on a full stomach. Otherwise, she would spend a fortune.*

    Read the texts above several times. As you do so, look at the words in bold, but also see the other words. When you are doing a listening exercise, you can hear all the words, but you do not usually listen to all of them. Try to develop this skill with reading.

4.  The answers are as follows:

    | | |
    |---|---|
    | a. cause | implication/ result/ consequence |
    | b. statement | clarification/ expansion/ explanation |
    | c. cause | effect/ implication/ consequence |
    | d. concession | contrast |
    | e. action/cause | implication/ result/ consequence |

This is an even more economical way of reading. You are here reading the meaning of chunks of texts. This is exactly what you have already been doing in **Reading Exercises 1-13**. A good way of developing this technique is now to go back and read the earlier exercises in the section. As you read, summarise the texts, as in the exercise you have just read. You will then be able to read the organisation, meaning and words much more efficiently.

5.  The answers are as follows:

    | | |
    |---|---|
    | a. Problem | firm solution/proposal |
    | b. Problem | tentative solution/proposal |
    | c. Problem | consequence |
    | d. Statement | Reformulation/explanation |

    Notice how the information is similar, yet the meaning relationship is different. It shows you how important it is to be able to read meaning and recognise the information in a text.

6.  The words are in bold below.

    *This shows, say many teachers, that **standards of English** for many secondary school pupils and university students **have declined** over recent years. The answer is, obviously, that **the teaching of grammar should be made compulsory** in secondary school and on relevant teacher training courses.*

    Note how the words in bold summarise the text. More importantly note how much you do **not need to** read to extract the information.

    You can practise these techniques with any text. You could spend ten to fifteen minutes a day reading newspaper articles. Underline the stepping stones in one article, or in another underline only the main words as here. Then go through the same texts and as you read give each sentence a name which shows its relationship with the sentences around it. Over a period of time you will be able to train your eye to do all three at the same time. This is obviously a very efficient way of reading.

---

## Exercise 15

1.  **a** the launch of the anti-smoking campaign will fail miserably.

    **b** (in males) the amount of deep sleep declines with age, thus leading to a reduction in the body's rejuvenation process.

    **c** Scumbling, is a simple, but subtle technique.

2.a

| New | New |
|---|---|
| A car | was driving slowly along a road. |
| **Old** | **New** |
| It | turned into the drive of a large white house. |
| **Old** | **New** |
| The car | stopped just short of the front door, |
| **Old** | **New** |
| but the driver | did not get out. |

**b**

| New | New |
|---|---|
| *Her first acting break in a major film* | *was doing a voice-over in a spy film.* |
| *Old* | *New* |
| *This* | *led to a string of similar jobs doing work on adverts.* |

**c**

| New | New |
|---|---|
| *Mr Maguire* | *made a number of predictions for the future of further education in the UK.* |
| *Old* | *New* |
| *His forecasts* | *are seriously flawed.* |
| *Old* | *New* |
| *They* | *are much too optimistic to be credible.* |

**d**

| New | New |
|---|---|
| *A woman with a manic grin* | *entered a building.* |
| *Old* | *New* |
| *The building* | *collapsed. When the dust settled,* |
| *Old* | *New* |
| *she* | *walked into another building.* |
| *New* | *New* |
| *Her grin* | *was now even more hideous.* |

**e**

| New | New |
|---|---|
| *The government's version of events* | *was not believed by anyone.* |
| *Old* | *New* |
| *It* | *was seen by most people as a cover-up.* |
| *Old* | *New* |
| *The whole affair* | *serves to illustrate the fears people have of politicians' inclination to abuse power.* |

3. **Answer:** Statistics show that the threat of violence drives young people away from home.

   *Block 1: According to the statistics available on homelessness,*

   *Block 2: what drives young people away from home is*

   *Block 3: the threat of violence from those within the household.*

   Note how the answer makes the information in the three blocks above more accessible.

4. **(a) Answer:** Mavis.

   **(b) Answer:** Brother and sister.

5. **Answer:** The rules were laid down by Mrs Cartlebury.

   Notice how easy it is to extract the information from the text. A good way to train yourself is to filter the information and discard what is not useful for your answer. Here all the other names but Cartlebury are irrelevant. Reading is also about learning about how not to look at every piece of information as equal.

---

## Exercise 16

1. comfortably.
2. connecting/connection.
3. modernise the company.
4. the rubbish pit.
5. soon run into trouble
6. foolproof
7. the Italian Renaissance.
8. rise in crime
9. most pressing aspects.
10. sides of an argument.

*The words in the original texts have not been given so you will not be tempted to concentrate on them!*

---

## Exercise 17

1. Sentences a and b do not mean the same. The first sentence only says that the man bit into the dog's ear. It does not say he bit it off. Notice also ear/ears!

2. A common confusion among students. Sentence a means that Joseph was smoking and he stopped. Sentence b means that Joseph was doing something and he stopped in order to smoke. Note that the infinitive is connected with the future (I want to go home; I would like to help you) and the -ing form here with past experience. The sentences do not have the same meaning.

3. The sentences do not have the same meaning.

4. The sentences do not have the same meaning. The word *should* indicates that the sentence is a suggestion, proposal etc; in Sentence b the phrase *It is necessary* does not convey the same meaning.

5. This is an interesting one. The sentences have the same meaning and paraphrase each other. However, the phrase *A variety of* has two meanings, namely: (i) various and (ii) a group/type of. If, in a text, the phrase *A variety of* in Sentence b had only meaning (ii), there is a strong possibility that it might not paraphrase sentence a! Meaning and words are not the same!

6. The sentences have the same meaning.

7. Although *Sentence b* is a paraphrase of *Sentence a*, *Sentence a* does not paraphrase *Sentence b*! Note that there are two pieces of information in *Sentence a* **going to rain** and **soon**. *Sentence b* only focuses on the first piece of information; **not both!** This is identical to the first example in the exercise. Remember, in the reading tests, to read primarily *from the sentence in the exercise to the text. Remember that the sentence in the exercise may be testing a discrete point in a text, not a large chunk.* In this pair of sentences, you can see clearly how narrow this point can be.

8. This pair of sentences is rather interesting, as it illustrates clearly the problem candidates have with IELTS. *Sentence a* has the same meaning generally as *Sentence b*. *Sentence a* summarises *Sentence b* and is a good example of a paraphrase as a summary. However, *Sentence b* does not summarise *Sentence a*. This obviously confuses students, because they expect the meaning to be exact in both directions!

A book for IELTS

Remember some sentences in the test exercises may have exactly the same meaning as the information in the text, as in 6 above.

9.  The sentences do not have the same meaning as each other. *A final contract* and *What was approved in the end* do not mean the same thing.

10. Note the difference between the sentences: secondary/primary. So the meaning is not the same.

11. They are the same. Note how different the words are!

12. The sentences have the same meaning and they also paraphrase each other. This one is difficult. The first sentence means that, roughly speaking, there is, say, a 5% chance that the accused did not commit the murder and, say, a 95% chance that he did. The second sentence means that there is, say, a 95% chance that he did commit the murder and, say, a 5% chance that he didn't.

13. The sentences don't have the same meaning. The phrase, *Everyone is aware* is the opposite of the phrase, *It is not widely appreciated.* Moreover, the phrase *got better* does not tell you the extent of the improvement. So you cannot say whether it is significant or not.

14. The two sentences have the same meaning and also paraphrase each other. Note, however, that Sentence b can mean either that he may be more than 65 years of age or less than 65 years old.

15. The two sentences have the same meaning and paraphrase each other. Note the word *priceless*. Students often confuse the meaning of words like this, e.g. valueless, limitless, powerless and so on. Check their meaning in a dictionary.

*Note: You can see the difficulty that meaning can cause. Basically, an exercise sentence may have the same meaning as a sentence in a reading passage. However, the sentences in the test exercises may also paraphrase or summarise discrete points of information in the text. In this instance, the summary does not need to contain all of the information as in some of the examples above. So, remember that your analysis does not work both ways. This causes a lot of confusion for students, because a paraphrase is often explained as just a word or phrase with the same meaning.*

A **paraphrase** has basically two main forms:
 — it is a phrase, sentence or expression with the same meaning, which you can use to replace another phrase etc.
 — a summary of the meaning of a piece of text.

A **summary** states a larger text in a shorter form.

In both cases, the substitute sentence etc. in the exercise uses different words, expressions, or the same words in another way, but carries the same meaning as particular points of information in the original text.

## Exercise 18

Eight of the sentences have matching texts with the same meaning.

1. **Answer: m.** Note that **j** is not suitable because it talks about the future Project not the future of the Project. Also the time scale is different.

2. **Answer: f.** It was the speed of the change that surprised the government, not the reversal of their fortunes. So **c** is not correct. At a first glance, many students think that 2

and **c** have the same meaning, because superficially they deal with the same idea. Note that sentence 2 can refer to either good or bad fortune, but **c** to only bad fortune. In the exam, you need to be careful about jumping to conclusions too quickly.

3. **Answer: g.** Note **e** is not correct, because it says that it is *completely unknown.* Sentence 3, however, says that it is *not completely obvious.* Note that **l** is also not correct. It has the opposite idea of Sentence 4: compare previous/second.

5. **Answer: n.** Note the distracter **d.**

8. **Answer: o.** The distracter **h** is the opposite of Sentence 8.

9. **Answer: k.** Compare 12, which, at first glance, has the same meaning as both. Sentence 12, however, expresses an opinion about what happened: it criticises the government (should have acted). The other two sentences describe the fact that the government was criticised!

10. **Answer: b.** Note the distracter **p.**

14. **Answer: a.**

## Exercise 19

1. **j small** (healthy)
   **p big loss** (healthy profit)
   [not **h**: publishing does not turn the statement into a contradiction.]

2. **l crawled slowly by** (sped past).
   [not **i**: slightly covered, because this has the same meaning flecked.]

3. **t old** (new).
   [not **m**: hampered and hindered mean the same thing.]

4. **g deplorable** (commendable).

5. **a duplicity** (honesty)
   **c atypical** (typical)

6. **e (not sanguine enough)** too optimistic
   **r pessimistic** (optimistic).

7. **o true** (apocryphal).

8. **f As he lay dying** (In the very middle of his life)

9. There are no contradictions for this sentence.

## Exercise 20

1. **Answer: J.** Because Sentence G is a question many students may be tempted to put it as an answer. However, this question does not have the same meaning as the original text. The question in the text indicates that there is a difference: What ... ? The question in G asks whether there is a difference.

2. **Answer: L.** Notice how Sentence A talks about information *not knowledge.*

3. **Answer: P.** The distracter here is Sentence M.

4. **Answer: H.** Sentence D is obviously wrong.

5. **Answer: I.** Sentence K covers the information in Sentences 5 and 6.

6. **Answer: C.** Sentence K covers the information in Sentences 5 and 6

7. **Answer: N.**

8. **Answer: E.**

9. **Answer: Q.** The distracter here is sentence F. It is wrong, because limited is the opposite of endless.

   Note that B is not a sentence and cannot replace sentence 1. It is a title for the whole passage! Note also that O is not suitable as a paraphrase of any of the sentences as it summarises Sentences 1- 5.

---

## Exercise 21

1. **a** **Not Given.** To find something rewarding means to find something satisfying. So the statement does not give any information about how much money lecturers are paid.

   **b** **No.** Notice the original sentence says *Many* not *All* lecturers.

   **c** **Not Given.** The sentence does not tell you whether the majority of lecturers get satisfaction from their work. It does not say what proportion of the total **Many** represents.

2. **a** **Not Given.** The sentence states that computers are expensive (despite the cost), but does not say whether they are becoming more expensive, becoming cheaper or whether the cost is static.

   **b** **Yes.** See *despite their cost*.

   **c** **No.** If computers are gaining in popularity, then they must have been less popular in the past than they are now.

3. **a** **Not Given.** The sentence only tells you that the number is increasing, but does not tell you what proportion of the total this represents.

   **b** **Yes.** People are becoming more affluent.

   **c** **Not Given.** The sentence does not mention anything about the cost of cars.

4. **a** **Yes.** Schools have been getting better.

   **b** **No.** The sentence contradicts the original text.

   **c** **Not Given.** This sentence means that educational standards were unsatisfactory before and now they have improved. The sentence also implies that they were unsatisfactory before and are still unsatisfactory. The original sentence does not tell you about the 'satisfactory/unsatisfactory' state of the educational standards before.

5. **a** **Yes.** Unemployment does affect the male/female roles and hence the way families operate.

   **b** **Not Given.** The original sentence says nothing about the relationship between family members where the woman has a job, and men and women usually having traditional roles.

   **c** **No.** Unemployment does affect the role of a man in the family.

6. **a** **Not Given.** There is no mention of the government's desire either way.

   **b** **No.** If the hazards are well publicised it means that they are well known. If you had the word *widely* rather than *well* in the original, you would not know if the publicity had been successful or not.

   Note that if the original sentence had said *publicised well*, you would not know whether the publicity had reached many people. You would only know that the publicity material was good, or that it had been well handled.

   **c** **Yes.**

7. **a** **Yes.**

   **b** **Not Given.**

   **c** **Not Given.**

8. **a** **Not Given.** There is no mention of people writing to politicians about animals becoming extinct. Note address here means to tackle/deal with.

   **b** **Yes.**

   **c** **No.** It is only recently that they have been looking at the problem; they have definitely not been fighting against it.

9. **a** **Not Given.** Most people would be amazed, (if they realised ...) clearly means that people are not amazed. Also the text does not mention gardeners; nor does it tell you whether they are amazed or surprised.

   **b** **Not Given.** You can perhaps guess that it is impossible to count the different types of insect life in a garden, but the text does not tell you that this is the case!

   **c** **Yes.** This one is obvious.

10. **a** **Not Given.** We do not know from the text whether all houses were heated in the past. All we can say is that an unspecified number were not heated adequately.

    **b** **Not Given.** The text does not say whether our lives are better now compared with the past.

    **c** **Yes.** Two things today are better than they used to be: to name but two.

---

## Exercise 22

1. **a** **Yes.** Notice how the sentence summarises the information in the last two sentences.

   **b** **Not Given.** The text doesn't mention anything about this at all.

   **c** **Not Given.** The text does not quantify the number of people.

2. **a** **Not Given.** The text does not tell you anything about part-time students.

   **b** **Not Given.** The author thinks that financial support from parents is a possibility for some students, not all students. However, note the text does not say whether the parental financial support is easily available. The information in the statement is therefore not given.

   **c** **Yes.** See the first two sentences.

3. **a** **Not Given.** The text says that the young and fit throw themselves with enthusiasm into ... . However, it does not say whether the activities mentioned should be attempted only by young people. In other words it does not tell you what the author thinks.

   **b** **Yes.** ... *the physical challenges many such activities involve.*

   **c** **No.** Look at the opening sentence.

4. **a** **Not Given.** There is no mention of high-rise flats in the text.

   **b** **Not Given.** There is no mention of the information in this statement in the text.

   **c** **Not Given.** The text does not tell you how people died.

5. **a** **Yes.** See the end of the text.

   **b** **No.** The text says: that all students encounter throughout their academic career.

   **c** **No.** The text says many theories.

# Reading Tests

# KEY

---

| Test 1 | Passage 1 |

---

QUESTIONS 1-6

1. **Answer: distinct races.** It is better to have both words, but it would also be possible to have the word **races** on its own.

2. **Answer: albas.** The clue is in the example, *Alba x semiplena*, For **Questions 2, 3 & 4**, you need to be careful. The temptation is to put the names of the roses in the order that they occur in the second paragraph, i.e. gallicas, albas and damasks. Doing that would not test whether you can find your way round the text! In fact, you need to use the other information given at 5 and 6 to help you work out the names in **Questions 2-4**.

3. **Answer: damasks.** The clue lies in the phrase **Origin obscure**.

4. **Answer: gallicas.** The marker here is **13th Century**.

5. **Answer: (highly) scented petals.** You can have two words here and leave out the words in the brackets.

6. **Answer: recorded.**

This exercise is a summary of the second paragraph. It is basically checking whether you understand the organisation of the paragraph, i.e. it is a classification paragraph with information about different types of roses. The technique you need to use here is one of basic skimming and scanning. As you are reading the paragraph, you should scan or look out for organisational features: the writer organises the paragraph around the phrases: **diversity and antiquity** and **three distinct races:**

> Before examining the cultural advantages of shrub roses, mention should be made of their **diversity and antiquity**. There are **three distinct races** of rose, which can be traced back to the Middle Ages, the **gallicas**, the **albas**, and the **damasks**. **Gallica roses** were first recorded in the 13th century, and probably the most famous of all, *Gallica officinalis*, is among the flowers depicted on the famous Ghent Altarpiece, painted by the Flemish artist Jan Van Eyck in the 14th century. Another gallica, *Rosa mundi*, with its characteristic red and white petals has been cultivated for at least six centuries. **Albas** too have a long history. *Alba semiplena* is the world's oldest 'working' rose and is still grown in the Kazanluk region of Bulgaria for its highly scented petals, which are harvested each June to make the perfume, attar of roses. **Damasks**, as the name implies, were thought to have come from Damascus. Their origin is more obscure, but they are certainly related to wild roses still growing in parts of the Middle East and Iran. There are in cultivation more recently introduced varieties of roses too, such as Bourbons, hybrid musks, and hybrid perpetuals as well as rugosas, which originate in the Far East.

You can see how the words in bold type help you to read. The writer wanted to present the information in a way that makes the detail easily accessible. The phrase **diversity and antiquity** is the first stage of the process of organisation; the phrase is the focus of the paragraph, not **cultural advantages**. The phrase **three distinct races** then gives the writer a peg on which to hang the next layer of details: **gallicas, albas and damasks**. At the next stage, under each of the three headings, he organises detail about the antiquity and diversity of each type of rose. The words in bold, therefore, summarise the paragraph for you. So, if you are able to train yourself to read the organisation of a text, you can scan more efficiently and learn to look from the top down onto the organisation of the text rather than from the bottom up. Most people, and not just students, are so caught up in the detail, that they read a text as if they were drowning. So, to prevent a text from drowning you, learn to skim the surface information and dip into the detail when you need to. This applies to all reading and is a strategy you should train yourself to develop.

Another strategy to help you read this text is to learn to read the organisation of the question. If you look at the diagram for **Questions 1-6**, you can see that the structure of question number 1 gives you a clue to the organisation of the exercise: **There are..., namely:** The question is asking you to classify the central information in the paragraph, or reduce it to a list. It is checking whether you understand the organisation or skeleton of this type of text.

Note that the second paragraph is a digression from the main focus of the text: **cultural advantages** as mentioned in paragraph 1. See also the first sentence of paragraph 2 and again the first sentence of paragraph 3.

Note how the organising words: **diversity and antiquity, three distinct races, gallicas, albas and damasks** do not stand out in the second paragraph. They are hidden by the detail until you are able to recognise their importance as organising words within the paragraph. Once you highlight them, the organisation jumps out at you, as above. Now go back to the original passage in the exercise and skim the surface of the text to see if you can pick out the organising words. You may have to do it several times to feel comfortable with it. Then try it on other parts of this text and other passages. (See also **Reading Exercises 10-12**.)

---

*Question type.* The questions in this section test:

- whether you are able to scan a text for specific information.
- whether you are able to skim a text to recognise the organisation.
- whether you are able to skim a text to recognise a specific type of organisation i.e. classification.
- whether you can analyse a text from the top down without being dragged down by detail which is irrelevant to the question.
- whether you can summarise a text.

## QUESTIONS 7–13

7. **Answer: benefit.** You need a noun here; **beneficial** (adjective) does not work. The word advantage does not work here either. The word **advantage** appears in the original text, but you cannot use it. If the text read '...and soils, features which are an advantage to...', it would be acceptable.

8. **Answer: area available.** You need to be careful here. The answer is a paraphrase of the word **space** in the original text. **Spacing** is to do with the arranging of the layout of the plants.

9. **Answer: Most.** This is a translation of **the majority of** in the passage, but the word **majority** alone does not fit here. If you use the word **majority,** the text should read: **The majority of.**

10. **Answer: blossom.** The word is a paraphrase of the word **flower** in the text. A difficult one. If you read the sentence, you can see that a verb is needed here for the text to make sense. This sentence is a paraphrase of the first part of the second sentence in the fourth paragraph. The word **spread** fits grammatically in the sentence itself, but the sentence is not then a paraphrase of the original text: the passage does not say that the roses spread. The word **spread** in the passage refers to the extent, diameter, circumference of the rose bush, as it grows.

11. **Answer: in the end.** This phrase paraphrases the word **eventually** in the original text. The word **also** does not work here. The sentence does not give additional information (also). The sentence states a fact (In fact) about what happens when shrub roses are not cut back regularly. It is, therefore, also a development of the phrase **without having to be cut back.** Compare the original text.

12. **Answer: across.** The phrase **up to three metres across** paraphrases **with a spread of two to three metres.** The word **circumference** would not work here as you would need to say 'in circumference'. The same would apply to the word 'diameter', if it were in the list.

13. **Answer: dictates.** This sentence summarises the penultimate paragraph.

Note that this exercise tests your understanding of a section of text. It checks whether you are able to understand a paraphrase of the text and again tests if you can dip into the organisation for detail. The exercise is basically organised around the cultural advantages first mentioned in the first paragraph.

Note that in the exam you may have a summary, as in **7–13,** where there is no **Wordlist.** Then you will have to take the words from the text. See **Practice Test 2, Reading Passage 2** and **Practice Test 3, Reading Passage 1.**

*Question type.* The questions in this section test:

- whether you can summarise a text.
- whether you are able to scan a text for specific information.
- whether you can recognise a paraphrase of words and ideas.

## QUESTIONS 14 and 15

14. **Answer: B.** If you look at the penultimate paragraph, you can see that the writer is talking about shrub roses. It is not clear whether the phrase **of all** in **probably the most intensely fragrant rose of all** refers to shrub roses or all roses. The writer of the article didn't know when he was asked!

15. **Answer: D.** The first reaction for many students is to give **A** as the answer. The sentence then would mean that 'all shrub roses have a short but spectacular flowering season'. The word **many** in the text shows you that there are other flowering seasons. Like **A,** alternatives **B** and **C,** each only covers one group of shrub roses.

*Question type.* The questions in this section test:

- whether you are able to scan a text for specific information.
- whether you can recognise a paraphrase of words and ideas.
- whether you are able to understand specific points in the text.

## Summary of questions

Notice that you had two summarising sections and a section looking at specific points. Why? The reason is because the texts lend themselves to this type of question. Therefore, as you read the other passages in this book, and elsewhere, you can try to predict what type of questions would test the way the passage is written. Of course, the questions in this reading passage could be replaced by others, but they might not have been able to test your understanding of the text quite so well. Could you replace **Questions 1–6** with **Yes, No, Not Given** questions?

---

| Test 1 | Passage 2 |
|---|---|

## QUESTIONS 16 and 17

16. **Answer: 80**. The answer is at the end of the fourth paragraph. You simply need to scan the text for the words **Lex Report** and also for a percentage.

17. **Answer: 90**. The answer is at the beginning of the fifth paragraph. Again like number 16, you simply need to scan the text for the words **RAC Survey** and also for a percentage.

These two questions are particularly easy as you just have to scan the text for references to particular items. The questions do not ask you to analyse any particular part of the text.

*Question type.* The questions in this section test:

– whether you are able to scan for specific information.

## QUESTIONS 18–23

18. **Answer: Yes**. The answer to this question is in the seventh paragraph:

> The 1991 Road Traffic Act takes a very dim view indeed of dangerous and careless driving and, as with assaults, provides stiff custodial sentences for those guilty of such crimes. *To date, however, there is no such offence in the statute books known as 'Road Rage'.* There can be assaults or criminal damage followed or preceded by dangerous driving, but *no offence that incorporates both* – a change in the law which the public are crying out for in the face of increasing anarchy on the roads.

The statement in the exercise is basically a paraphrase of the text in italics. When you are scanning, you need to look out for references to **Road Rage** and information about whether it breaks the law, violates the law, or is a violation of the law. To do the first is not easy, because the phrase 'Road Rage' occurs many times in the passage. To scan for the latter is even more difficult, because you are searching for an idea that appears in another form. It is like seeing a person whom you do not know very well out of context or wearing different clothes. It is sometimes difficult to recognise them.

Scanning a text for ideas in the form of a paraphrase rather than specific words or phrases requires an advanced level of vocabulary and flexibility in English. If you are aware of the need to develop this skill, it will help you in doing not just this type of exercise, but many of the other exercises you have to deal with in the IELTS exam.

19. **Answer: Yes**. The answer to this question is in the second paragraph:

> *A psychologist*, employed by the Royal Automobile Club (RAC) defines 'Road Rage', thus: 'unchecked behaviour designed to cause harm to another road user; behaviour which is not normally in the behavioural repertoire of the person. *'Road Rage'* is an altering of an individual's personality *whilst driving caused by a process of dehumanisation. This dehumanisation is caused by road use frustrations and an artificial sense of insulation, protection and empowerment provided by the car*. This leads the person to behave in a way designed to cause harm or endanger other road users.'

Note that again you have to scan the text to find information relating to the psychologist and then the idea of cars making drivers feel artificially safe.

---

A book for **IELTS**

Note that the statement in the exercise does not check whether the text mentions the idea of **empowerment**. It is checking only the discreet point about **an artificial sense of insulation, protection**. Some students may want to put **No** as the answer here, because the statement in the exercise does not cover the idea of **empowerment**. The statement is, however, a paraphrase of only part of the statement in the text.

20. **Answer: Not Given.** The writer mentions that he is a motorcycle instructor, (The end of paragraph 3), but nowhere in the passage does he say that he thinks motorcycling is exciting or safe.

21. **Answer: Not Given.** The answer is in the fourth paragraph:

> *The report* states that a survey carried out by **Lex** confirms that up to 80% of motorists have been the victims of road rage and that *driver confrontation is on the increase*.

The statement in the exercise is almost a paraphrase of the text. The words **is rising** mean the same as **is on the increase**. This statement is different from the **Not Given** in number 20 above. In number 20, there was no reference as to whether motorcycling is exciting or safe.

Here the text mentions **driver confrontation** (conflicts between drivers); **is on the increase** (the incidence...is rising). The sentence in the exercise, however, qualifies the increase by saying it is rising **rapidly**. The text itself does not give you any information about the quality, e.g. rate/size, of the increase. It is important to note here that the exercise asks you to decide if there is any information about the **statement** in the original text. You, therefore, have to look at the statement as a whole.

Students often ask how they can change a statement to make the answer **Yes** or **No**. To make the statement in the exercise into **No** you would have to make the statement contradict or disagree with the original text. You could do this by finding an opposite word for one of the words in the sentence. The most obvious one is **rise**. If you remove the word **rapidly** from the sentence and change **rising** to diminishing or decreasing, then the answer would be **No**:

> The Lex Report states that the incidence of conflicts between drivers is decreasing.

To make the answer **Yes**, then all you have to do is remove the word **rapidly** from the exercise sentence:

> The Lex Report states that the incidence of conflicts between drivers is rising.

You would also have a **No** answer if you had a word in the original text which contradicted **rapidly**, e.g. slowly.

22 **Answer: Not Given.** See the first sentence of paragraph 5. The writer mentions that the RAC has much to say about it ('Road Rage'), i.e. it talks about the quantity of the survey, but the writer does not talk about the quality i.e. whether the survey is thorough, or otherwise.

23. **Answer: No.** The answer is at the end of the first paragraph:

> *To many people the term 'Road Rage'* describes a relatively modern concept of drivers 'getting worked up due to some incident whilst on the road and resorting to physical violence or damage to property'. Most people would say that this has only really become a problem in the last five years or so. It has certainly become of great media interest in recent times, *but it has, in fact, been part of motoring for quite some time now.*

The latter part of the text in bold states what the writer thinks, while the first sentence states what **many people think,** not the writer.

Note that the questions are not in the sequence that the information appears in the text. Do not always expect the questions to be in order.

For help with this type of question, see **Reading Exercises 18–22**.

*Question type.* The questions in this section test:
  – whether you are able to scan for specific information.
  – whether you can recognise an idea which is expressed in another way.
  – whether you can recognise a paraphrase.
  – whether you are able to analyse a small part of a text and not allow the information around it to interfere with your analysis.
  – whether you are able to juggle several pieces of information at the same time.

## QUESTIONS 24–27

24. **Answer: uphill struggle.** You need to scan the text for the word **professionals**. See the fourth paragraph from the end.

25. **Answer: Stiffer penalties/Stiffer sentencing.** The first answer is in the third paragraph from the end. The sentence is a simple paraphrase and again you scan the text for the word **courts**. For **Stiffer sentencing** see the last sentence of the text.

26. **Answer: male preserve.** The answer is in paragraph 9. The sentence is a paraphrase of the words in bold below:

> Most of us probably imagine *violence on the road to be an entirely male preserve*, as men are naturally more competitive and aggressive, especially when it comes to driving.

It is a little bit more difficult to scan the text for the information here, as it is an idea that you are looking for rather than a specific marker like a word or phrase as in 24 or 25.

27. **Answer: interest and reporting.** The answer is in paragraph 8. To find the answer, you scan the text for the words **Association of Chief Police Officers**. The phrase **causing unnecessary anxiety** does not fit in here, because to fit the phrase into the blank space you would have to make the word **media** into a noun and put an article in front of it: **the media**. In the exercise sentence, **media** is an adjective and is the clue to the answer. The text says:

> There have been suggestions from the Association that *media interest and reporting are, in fact, creating the problem* by causing unnecessary anxiety in the minds of the motoring public in a direct analogy with fear of crime.

The sentence in the exercise is a paraphrase of the text in italics. The phrase **causing unnecessary anxiety** tells you how the **problem is created,** whereas **media interest and reporting** tells you what the Association think are responsible for creating driver confrontation.

Note that as in the previous section the questions are not in the order that the information appears in the text.

*Question type.* The questions in this section test:
- whether you are able to scan for specific information.
- whether you can recognise information or an idea which is expressed in another way.
- whether you can recognise a paraphrase.
- whether you are able to analyse a small part of a text and not allow the information around it to interfere with your analysis.

## QUESTIONS 28 and 29

28. **Answer: C.** The answer to this question is in paragraph 9. The alternative is a paraphrase of the text:

> Women can be more aggressive in cars than they ever would be when they're walking along the street.

Alternative **A** is not correct, because the text does not say that cars make all women stronger. It says:

> It makes some women feel stronger than they really are.

As for **B**, 'can' contains the idea of 'sometimes', not 'frequently'. Answer **D** is wrong, because the opposite is possibly true:

> ...you could even argue that smaller or weaker people, who might be victims when they are out of their cars, often feel they can even things up a bit when they are behind the wheel.

Remember the text is talking about women here.

29. Answer: **B.** The answer is in the last paragraph. The inclination for many students is to give **D** as the answer. This is a value judgement, as it implies that you have a standard against which to measure the writer's statement in the last paragraph. If you choose **too pessimistic**, you are judging the statement against your own opinion. The question asks you to summarise the writer's view; you are not expected to give your own opinion unless you are asked to do so.

**C** is wrong because the text does not indicate whether the author is depressed about the situation or not.

**A** is obviously wrong.

*Question type.* The questions in this section test:
- whether you are able to scan for specific information.
- whether you can recognise information or an idea which is expressed in another way.
- whether you can recognise a paraphrase.
- whether you are able to analyse a small part of a text and not allow the information around it to interfere with your analysis.

A book for IELTS

| Test 1 | Passage 3 |
|---|---|

## QUESTIONS 30–33

30. **Answer: x**. The answer to this question is in paragraph **D**. The marker in the text to look for is **the effigy of Queen Elizabeth 1**. There are two distracters here. Number **vi** is not correct, because the text says the effigy **was dismissed (considered) as a poor copy (replica)**, not that it was a poor copy. Distracter **ii** is wrong, because the effigy was not completely restored.

31. **Answer: iv**. The answer to this question is in paragraph **C**. The marker in the text to look for is the name of the church. Note that **iv** summarises the idea of how suitable the replacement for St Peter's was as argued in the first three sentences of the paragraph. The distracter here is **i**; the text says that it was **not regarded then as an act of vandalism.**

32. **Answer: vii**. The answer to this question is in paragraph **E**. You need to look in the text for a reference to a comprehensive assessment of the past or the same idea expressed in another way. The complete sentence is a summary of the last paragraph. The distracter here is **viii**; note that it is not the validity of the works, but **the restoration work...the physical reality of the works exhibited** that is being compared.

33. **Answer: v**. The answer to this question is in paragraph **B**. The marker in the text to look for is the word **restoration** and references to its meaning, which occurs at the beginning of paragraphs **B** and **C**. The clues here are in the words 'modern' and 'narrow; paragraph **B** gives **the modern meaning** and paragraph **C** gives you the 'wider' meaning.

The difficulty in this exercise is that the first part of all the sentences ends in a verb, with three ending in **was** and one with **is**. This means that you cannot just try to fit the two parts together by looking at the grammar. You have to understand the meaning of the text that they summarise.

*Question type.* The questions in this section test:
— whether you are able to scan a text for specific information.
— whether you can recognise information or an idea which is expressed in another way.
— whether you can recognise a paraphrase.
— whether you are able to analyse a small part of a text and not allow the information around it to interfere with your analysis.
— whether you are able to summarise a text.

## QUESTIONS 34–36

34. **Answer: A**. The answer to this question is in paragraph **B**:

> ...with the campaign of comprehensive repair.... This programme of work, covering the entire building both inside and out...

The distracters **C** and **D** are obviously wrong, which leaves **B**. The word **conscientiously** does not mean the same as **self-consciously**.

35. **Answer: C**. The answer to this question is in the second sentence of paragraph **A**. Notice the word **but** in the sentence, which shows you that a contrast is about to be made with the transformation and change just mentioned.

36. **Answer: B** The answer to this question is in paragraph **D**, the last sentence. This question also relates to number 33. It shows you that the writer supports the idea of the wider meaning of restoration.

*Question type:* The questions in this section test:
— whether you are able to scan a text for specific information.
— whether you can recognise information or an idea which is expressed in another way.
— whether you can recognise a paraphrase.
— whether you are able to analyse a small part of a text and not allow the information around it to interfere with your analysis.

**QUESTIONS 37–40**

37. **Answer: iv.** You need to read each paragraph to extract the central meaning. In other words, you need to work out why the author wrote the paragraph (See **Reading Exercises 11 and 12**) and to find the direction of the paragraph (See **Reading Exercises 6–10**). If we look at the organisation, we can see, the first two sentences deal with the change the Abbey has experienced over the past 900 years: **transformed/change and change**. The second sentence also mentions a permanent aspect of the building during the period: the fact that the Abbey has not lost its identity. These first two sentences provide the background information to the focus of the paragraph in the third sentence. Here the theme of change is taken up again: **this process of change deserves chronicling**. This sentence is in effect the foreground information or most important information in the paragraph (See **Reading Exercises 10–12**). It is as if all the other details in the paragraph dance around this point. The fourth and fifth sentences describe elements of change. The last sentence concludes the paragraph by repeating the theme in the third sentence, i.e. the foreground information of the paragraph.

The main purpose of the paragraph is to show that the changes that have taken place in the Abbey are worth telling or deserve chronicling:

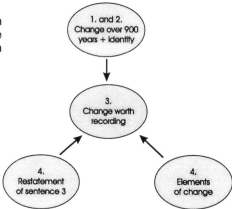

1. and 2.
Change over 900 years + identity

3.
Change worth recording

4.
Restatement of sentence 3

4.
Elements of change

You see you need to read meaning not just words!

38. **Answer: v.** Again, you need to ask yourself why the author wrote the paragraph. He wrote it to explain what restoration means by giving the example of the Abbey's repair scheme (campaign of...repair) at the end of the seventeenth century, which was all-embracing (comprehensive) and unusual (exceptional) for its time. The title neatly summarises the paragraph. Notice how the information is built up: the phrase **campaign of comprehensive repair** in the first sentence. Then the point is taken up again in the second sentence and expanded.

When you first look at this reading passage, you see that the paragraphs have letters at the beginning. This indicates that there is likely to be a question on paragraph headings. As you are reading a passage for the first time write down a brief heading of your own. Then when you do the exercise you can compare what you have written with the exercise.

39. **Answer: vi.** The focus of the paragraph is in the phrase **but respecting the meaning and ethos of the building,** which occurs at the end of the first sentence. The next sentence gives a good example of this, i.e. St Peter's in Rome. The last sentence then states how the Abbey was restored, but its meaning was kept. So the heading reflects why the author wrote the paragraph.

40. **Answer: ii.** This is an easy one. The word example occurs in the first sentence, giving the focus of the whole paragraph. Many students attempt all questions in the order they occur on the question paper. This means that they waste a lot of time on the questions that they cannot do. You could give a title to this question easily and then attempt the more difficult ones.

Remember it is not enough to just to read the first and last sentence of a paragraph to work out a heading.

*Question type.* The questions in this section test:

– whether you are able to scan a text and knit together the information.

– whether you can summarise information or an idea.

– whether you can recognise a paraphrase.

– whether you are able to analyse a small part of a text and not allow the information around it to interfere with your analysis.

**A book for IELTS**

---

**Test 2**        **Passage 1**

---

## Questions 1–3

1. **Answer: substituting (some) words.** The answer is in the third sentence of the first paragraph. The sentence in the exercise checks whether you understand what the writer means by translating, i.e. that it is not just a matter of replacing words in one language for words in another language. It is more than that: it is about translating **sense**.

   Note that in the text, it says **substituting one set of words for another**. In the exercise, you can use only a maximum of three words, so the word **words** summarises **one set of words**.

   Note that you cannot say 'substitution of words' here, because you would need to have the definite article, the. You would then have four words.

2. **Answer: a purpose.** The answer is in the first sentence of the second paragraph. The sentence here is a summary or paraphrase of the paragraph. In that sense, it is like a paragraph heading. The phrase **whether ... or instructive** covers the different types of text, the purpose of which the translator must consider.

   Note you cannot have 'its purpose' because of the latter half of the sentence: **that the translator** . . . Nor can you have 'the purpose'.

3. **Answer: (very) sparse.** The answer is in the first sentence of the fourth paragraph. Two types of reader are covered in the fourth paragraph: readers with good knowledge and sparse knowledge. If you remove the word **only** from the statement in the exercise, you could have both **good** and **(very) sparse**. With **only**, you can have only the latter.

   *Question type.* The questions in this section test:
   - whether you are able to scan for specific information.
   - whether you can recognise information or an idea which is expressed in another way.
   - whether you can recognise a paraphrase.
   - whether you are able to analyse a small part of a text and not allow the information around it to interfere with your analysis.

## Questions 4–6

4. **Answer: B.** This is a paraphrase of the information in the second sentence of the fourth paragraph:

   It has been said that everything is translatable 'on condition that the two languages belong to cultures that have reached a comparable degree of development'.

   **A** is not correct, because the text talks about the development of cultures, not of languages. **C** is not correct, because the reference in the text is to the reader being **up-to-date with the requisite technical knowledge**. The reader being up-to-date in this way is incidental to the cultures being of the same level of development. The question posed by the writer here is an afterthought to the main part of the sentence. **D** is not correct, because the text mentions that the translator has to balance the writer's and the reader's expectations; it does not talk about the translator's.

5. **Answer: A.** The answer is in the third sentence of the fifth paragraph:

   However, this is not to ignore the fact that there might well be instances in which a text – awkwardly written in the original – could be made more accessible by the translator.

   Answer **A** gives you a paraphrase of the text. **B** is not correct, because the writer says it would be **wrong to over-simplify an erudite piece of prose**. So, making something overly simple is not advised. **C** and **D** are not correct, because the writer advises against making an amusing text ponderous.

6. **Answer: A.** The answer is in the first sentence of the sixth paragraph. Notice the writer's paraphrase of the word **style: how she says it**. Compare this with the paraphrase of the word **style** in the multiple choice i.e. **the way in which a writer says something**. Alternatives **B, C and D** are not correct, because they are not aspects which are stated as being important when translating. Allusions and subliminal messages (**B** and **C**) are examples of what makes up style. They provide information which is subordinate to **A**. Alternative **D** is wrong, because the text compares the translator's job to doing a jigsaw puzzle, because she has to **solve appropriately** the problems a text represents. The text does not say that it is important.

---

*Question type.* The questions in this section test:
- whether you are able to scan a text for specific information.
- whether you can recognise a paraphrase of words and ideas.
- whether you are able to understand and analyse specific points in the text.

## Questions 7–10

7–10. **Answer: A/C/D/F** (in any order).

**A** is mentioned in paragraph 2, the first sentence of the paragraph: **considers the purpose of the said text**. **C** is mentioned in paragraph 5. A translation should **. . . mirror that of the original**, but the translator also has to make a judgement about making a text clearer, or more accessible . . . **It is a question of judgement'**. (See number 5 above and 13 below). **D** is mentioned in the first sentence of paragraph 3: . . . **needs to consider who the readers of the translated text will be**. **F** is mentioned in paragraph 4 in the last sentence.

If you look at the last few words in the first paragraph you can see how the writer organised the text: ' **and asked herself a number of questions'**. The judgements that the translator has to make as she answers the questions help organise the text. **A** is like a summary of paragraph 2; **C** summarises paragraph 5; **D** summarises paragraphs 3 and 4; and **F** relates again to paragraph 4. The judgements are, therefore, like headings that summarise the main body of the text.

As regards the distracter **B**, 'a poem' is mentioned in the first sentence of paragraph 6, but nothing is said about whether a translator has to decide if poetry is important or not. As for **E**, it is incorrect, because the translator does not have to make a judgement about this. In paragraph 7, it says: **The target language, for the best results, should be her mother-tongue . . .**, meaning that translating is best done 'into' the mother tongue. Moreover, the writer is not putting this forward as a point on which a decision needs to be made. It is important to read the options carefully to make sure that they contain exactly the same information as the text.

**G** is not mentioned in the text and **H** is wrong. See paragraph 5: **it would be wrong to oversimplify**. The decision, in any case, would be whether to simplify rather than 'oversimplify'.

*Question type.* The questions in this section test:
- whether you are able to scan a text for specific information.
- whether you can recognise a paraphrase of words and ideas.
- whether you are able to understand and analyse specific points in the text.
- whether you can recognise the function of points in a text.
- whether you are able to summarise a text.

## Questions 11–14

11. **Answer: culture and truth**. The answer is in the fourth sentence in paragraph 1.
12. **Answer: certain characteristics/the same expectations**. The answer is in paragraph 3. Note that both answers are possible.
13. **Answer: style and register**. The answer is in paragraph 5. This question asks you about the focus of the fifth paragraph. Compare **C** in questions 7–10 above. Notice how questions 5, 7–10 and 13 examine different aspects of the information in paragraph 5.
14. **Answer: the whole text**. This question takes you back to paragraph 1, the last sentence.

In short answer questions such as these, the important thing to remember is to scan the text and look for the clues you have been given in the question: words or phrases that often appear in the same or similar form in the text.

*Question type.* The questions in this section test:
- whether you are able to scan a text for specific information.
- whether you can recognise a paraphrase of words and ideas.
- whether you are able to understand and analyse specific points in the text.
- whether you can recognise the function of points in a text.

---

**Test 2**                                                            **Passage 2**

---

## Questions 15–20

15. **Answer: offshoot.** The answer here is in paragraph **D**, in the first sentence. The word **offshoot** is a paraphrase of the word **branch** in the text. The distracter here is the word **offspring,** which does not mean the same as **branch**.

16. **Answer: in vogue.** The answer here is in paragraph **A: For the past few years one of the buzz terms . . ..** The rest of the paragraph then shows how fashionable/common combinatorial chemistry is.

17. **Answer: appearing.** The information for this part of the summary is again in paragraph **A**. There is no particular word there which the word **appearing** paraphrases.

18. **Answer: follow religiously.** The answer here is in paragraph **B: These reviews all have the same format.** And then the paragraph describes the repeated formula of the paragraph. Note that the word **religiously** means faithfully/exactly here. The distracter **usually follow** does not paraphrase exactly the meaning of the phrase quoted above.

19. **Answer: Once.** The answer here is in paragraph **E: After the development of solid phase peptide synthesis . . . .** The word **Once** is a paraphrase of the word **After**.

20. Answer: **limitless.** The answer here is in paragraph **E**, in the last sentence: **The numbers of possible sequences are truly innumerable!**

*Question type.* The questions in this section test:
  — -whether you are able to scan a text for specific information.
  — whether you are able to scan a text to recognise the organisation.
  — whether you can analyse a text from the top down without being dragged down by detail which is irrelevant to the question.
  — whether you can summarise a text.

## Questions 21–25

All the answers to complete the flow chart are found in paragraphs **I** and **J**. This summary covers a much smaller part of the text than the previous exercise and is more precise.

21. **Answer: (polypropylene) mesh sacs.**

22. **Answer: thermal sealing/being thermally sealed.** Note that you have to change the words here slightly to fit the wording of the chart. The diagram already mentions the fact that the sacs are **closed**, and you are being asked to say here how that happens.

23. **Answer: resin beads.** Note that here you are being asked to state what the **solid supports** are, or are made of.

24. **Answer: pot to pot.** Note that you cannot use the word **reagent** here; you are only allowed to use three words. Note also that the word **pot** on its own is not enough.

25. **Answer: characterised and purified.**

   Note that this section tests the same skills as **Questions 15–20**.

*Question type.* The questions in this section test:
  — whether you are able to scan a text for specific information.
  — whether you are able to scan a text to recognise the organisation.
  — whether you can analyse a text from the top down without being dragged down by detail which is irrelevant to the question.
  — whether you can summarise a text.

## Questions 26–28

The answers to this section are found in paragraph **B**. Note that the sections are not in the order in which the information appears in the passage.

26. **Answer: F.** Description **B** is not possible, because the first director mentioned in the original text is not directly involved in research: **a person who has not worked at the bench for years . . . .**

---

A book for **IELTS**                                                                   

27. **Answer: E**. The distracter here is **A**. The text does not say that the second contributor is typically **a director of a technology business park** , but a director whose company is situated **in a new business park.**

28. **Answer: C**. The distracter for this one is **D**. The original text does not say whether the third category of contributor is an amateur or not. The text also says that the chemist **can probably synthesise a few thousand compounds per week**; not that they do.

    Note that the details in the exercise and the text are very similar. This means that you have to jump back and forth between the two as you juggle the information.

    *Question type.* The questions in this section test:
    - whether you are able to scan a text for specific information.
    - whether you are able to scan a text to recognise the organisation.
    - whether you can analyse a text from the top down without being dragged down by detail which is irrelevant to the question.
    - whether you can summarise a text.
    - whether you able to juggle bits of information between the text and the exercise at the same time.

## Questions 29

29. **Answer: A**. The answer to this question is in paragraph **C**. It is important to read the multiple choice answers here very carefully, as you are juggling lots of small pieces of information within a short area of text. If you then answer the question too quickly, you can easily match the wrong bits of information.

    *Question type:* The question in this section tests:
    - whether you are able to scan a text for specific information.
    - whether you can recognise a paraphrase of words and ideas.
    - whether you are able to understand specific points in the text.

---

| Test 2 | Passage 3 |
|---|---|

---

## Questions 30

30. **Answer: C**. The answer is in paragraph six. **A** is not correct, because **four-wheel- drive vehicles** are listed among **essential travelling companions** (the last paragraph). The text does not say that they connect towns. **B** is not correct, because the writer was referring to the earliest travellers to Iceland (also in the last paragraph). **D** is not correct, because the text does not say that the entire island is connected or served by a fleet of coaches.

    Note that the question refers to the end of the text.

    *Question type:* The question in this section tests:
    - whether you are able to scan a text for specific information.
    - whether you can recognise a paraphrase of words and ideas.
    - whether you are able to understand specific points in the text.

## Questions 31–36

31. **Answer: Yes**. The answer is in paragraph 2 in the third sentence. The statement is a paraphrase of the phrase: **. . . landscape is constantly being carved . . .**

32. **Answer: No**. The answer is in paragraph 3. At the end of paragraph 2, the writer mentions that Iceland was a Danish colony. Then in the next paragraph it states that the island gained full independence in 1944. So Iceland is no longer a colony of Denmark.

33. **Answer: No**. The answer is in paragraph 2. There is a double negative in the statement; **not dissimilar** = the same, but the text says that Iceland and Scandinavian countries are not similar, so the statement contradicts the information given in the text. It is very important to check negative statements carefully, especially when there are double negatives such as this.

---

34. **Answer: Yes**. The answer is in the last sentence of paragraph 1:·

    . . . those who recoil in horror at the bleak lava fields which surround its airport may never return.

35. **Answer: Not Given**. The answer is in paragraph 1. In the text, it talks about **those once intoxicated by it . . .**, but we do not know if **those** are the majority or not; the text does not say how many people.

36. **Answer: Not Given**. The text nowhere states whether the author of the article is intoxicated by Iceland or not. The writer is talking about the reactions of other people. She starts with a quote from the poet W.H. Auden and goes on to describe the reactions of other people to Iceland, but we do not know what the writer thinks about Iceland.

    Note how the questions in this section jump around the text.

    *Question type.* The questions in this section test:
    - whether you are able to scan for specific information.
    - whether you can recognise an idea which is expressed in another way or a paraphrase.
    - whether you are able to analyse a small part of a text and not allow the information around it to interfere with your analysis.

## Questions 37–39

37. **Answer**: flourishing and (internationally) respected. The answer is in the first sentence of the fourth paragraph. You need to scan the text for the words **movie business/film industry**.

38. **Answer: (the) geysers**. The answer is in the second sentence of the third paragraph. In this case, it is not possible to give any more information about the geysers without exceeding the word limit given.

39. **Answer: (a) sense of danger**. The answer is in the second sentence of the fourth paragraph. As soon as you find **Icelandic art** by scanning the text, it is easy to find the answer required.

    Note the exercise asks for a maximum of **FOUR** words. In the exam, always read the instructions in each exercise. Do not assume that they are the same as the books you read as you were preparing for the exam.

    Note that, in this section, you have to jump around the text to find the answer to the questions.

    *Question type.* The questions in this section test:
    - whether you are able to scan for specific information.
    - whether you can recognise information or an idea which is expressed in another way.
    - whether you can recognise a paraphrase.
    - whether you are able to analyse a small part of a text and not allow the information around it to interfere with your analysis.

## Questions 40 & 41

40. **Answer: limit damage**. The answer is in the last sentence of the fourth paragraph. Be careful about the grammar in this type of gapfill. It is not possible to write **damage limitation**, as a noun does not fit the grammar of the sentence. A verb is needed here. Remember that the exact words you need do not always appear in the text; particularly where filling gaps in a text is concerned, you may have to change the form of some words.

41. **Answer: protecting and developing**. The answer is in the second sentence of the fifth paragraph. Note the change in the form of the verbs. Note you cannot use nouns here, as you would have to write: **the protection and development of**.

    Question type. The questions in this section test:
    - whether you are able to scan for specific information.
    - whether you can recognise information or an idea which is expressed in another way.
    - whether you can recognise a paraphrase.
    - whether you are able to analyse a small part of a text and not allow the information around it to interfere with your analysis.

The answers to questions in some of the reading texts in the IELTS exam may be like those above; not always one after the other.

| Test 3 | Passage 1 |
|---|---|

## Questions 1–5

1. **Answer: xii.** Remember to ask yourself why the writer wrote this paragraph. The paragraph explains what the Alexander technique is about. The key words here are: **It is a technique for the elimination of ... habits of 'misuse'**, which are described as having negative effects.

2. **Answer: x.** Again, why did the author write the paragraph? She wrote it to show how the Alexander Technique teaches people how to **'use' themselves better**. This applies to everyone (all), both able-bodied and disabled people alike.

3. **Answer: iv.** The author wrote the paragraph to show how the Alexander Technique is adapted to suit different disabilities. The text gives two examples of how the approach varies according to the particular problem:

   The approach and what results can be expected **vary greatly depending on the** directly on eliminating tension habits that have developed to compensate for the loss of **disability. For the stroke patient**, especially if lessons are commenced early after the stroke, the Alexander Technique can play an important role in rehabilitation and mobility retraining. **With a blind person**, the work is likely to focus instead more sight, e.g. insecurity leading to stiff and overcautious walking, balancing difficulties and poor head poise.

4. **Answer: ii.** The author wrote this paragraph to show the connection between tension and **everyday activities** (daily routine):

   Working with the disabled pupil, the Alexander teacher can offer help with **everyday activities**, things that the average person takes for granted, such as the ability to brush one's teeth, shave, tie one's shoelaces or cut a slice of bread. By looking at **compensatory tension** patterns, the teacher can, in many instances, help the disabled person find a new means whereby they can perform these everyday tasks.

5. **Answer: viii.** The paragraph is about helping carers to help the people they are looking after:

   In this respect, the lessons may extend to include the disabled person's carer ... .

   The rest of the paragraph then deals with this point.

   *Question type.* The questions in this section test:
   - whether you are able to scan a text and knit together the information.
   - whether you can summarise information or an idea.
   - whether you can recognise a paraphrase.
   - whether you are able to analyse a small part of a text and not allow the
   - information around it to interfere with your analysis.

   For more details about this type of exercise look at **Questions 37–40** in **Reading Test 1**. Compare the differences in the paragraphs in this text and the exercise in **Test 1**. Can you see any difference in the type of paragraph? Look at **Reading Exercises 10–13**.

## Questions 6–14

In this type of exercise, you should always check that the form of the words fit the sentence structure of the summary.

6. **Answer: re-educated.** This is the only word which fits the blank space here. The word **re-education** occurs in the first sentence of the text, but to fit the grammar you need to change the form of the word.

7. **Answer: reflex mechanisms/ reflexes.** The words occur in the first sentence of paragraph **B**. The first answer given is the better of the two.

8. **Answer: in harmony/harmoniously.** The answer is in the second paragraph, the third sentence. The adjective **harmonious** (paragraph **A**) does not work here, because you need an adverb (**harmoniously**) or an adverbial phrase.

9. **Answer: eliminated.** The word **elimination** occurs in paragraph **A** and **eliminating** in paragraph **D**. You need to change the form of the word here to fit the grammar of the summary.

10. **Answer: use.** The Alexander technique is about better **'use'** of ourselves. See paragraph **B**.

11. **Answer: the disabled.** See the title of the article and throughout the text.

12. **Answer: requirements/disability.** For the answer, you need to jump to the latter part of paragraph **G**. Again you need to change the form of the word here to fit the grammar of the text. The verb **require** needs to be changed to make it into a noun. You may put **disability** here as well, but it is repetitive.

13. **Answer: factors**. The text mentions the word **factors** in paragraph **G,** the first sentence. The word **effects** is not suitable, because it would not summarise the text in paragraph G.

14. **Answer: a challenge/challenging**. The answer is in the last sentence of paragraph **G**. Note that this exercise tests your understanding of the whole text. It checks whether you are able to understand a paraphrase and again tests if you can dip into the organisation for detail. The exercise is basically organised around the main points covered by the writer.

In **Reading Passage 1 Practice Test 1**, you had a similar summary with a **Word List**. In the exam, you may have either. It is better, therefore, to practise both types of exercise.

*Question type.* The questions in this section test:
- whether you can summarise a text.
- whether you are able to scan a text for specific information.
- whether you can recognise a paraphrase of words and ideas.
- whether you are able to scan a text to recognise the organisation.

## Question 15

15. **Answer: Not Given**. In paragraph **D**, it says:

For the stroke patient, especially if lessons are commenced early after the stroke, the Alexander Technique can play an important role in rehabilitation and mobility retraining.

The text tells you the Technique **can play an important role**, but it does not give information about the success rate of the Technique with stroke patients.

*Question type.* The question in this section tests:
- whether you are able to scan for specific information.
- whether you can recognise an idea which is expressed in another way or a paraphrase.
- whether you are able to analyse a small part of a text and not allow the information around it to interfere with your analysis.

| Test 3 | Passage 2 |
|---|---|

## Questions 16–19

In these short answer questions, the answers do not need to be full sentences. All you have to do is find the necessary information, usually a short phrase, in the text.

16. **Answer: science and technology**. The answer is in the first sentence of the second paragraph:

History may well dub the 1900s *The Century of Change* – **the era when science and technology forged a permanent partnership** and unleashed the first products of their unique alliance on a largely illiterate, earthbound civilisation.

17. **Answer: measurement**. The answer is in the second sentence of the third paragraph.

Even if you do not know the word **elusive**, all you have to do is scan the text for the phrase **speed of change and the volume of knowledge**. What the two things have in common is the fact that they could <u>not</u> be measured, i.e. measurement was elusive: **they defied measurement**.

18. **Answer: rampant stress**. The answer is in the penultimate sentence of the third paragraph.

Note that **inexorable change** and **cut-throat competition** are not the main contributory factors here. They cause the stress which management consultants are then called in to address. Hence, the growth in their business.

19. **Answer: benefit**. The answer is in the third sentence of the fourth paragraph. The text reads: **Progress implies change with benefit**. This means that change does not have benefit. Note that you do not have to write **change with benefit** as the word **change** is already in the question.

*Question type.* The questions in this section test:
- whether you are able to scan for specific information.
- whether you can recognise an idea which is expressed in another way or recognise a paraphrase.

- whether you are able to analyse a small part of a text and not allow the information around it to interfere with your analysis.

## Questions 20–23

20. **Answer: B**. The answer is in paragraph 4, the fourth sentence:

*It reflects action taken only after management has considered relevant past experiences, current priorities and future objectives.*

**A** and **C** are too limited in their reference to only one time. **D** is not specific enough, as it does not include **current priorities**.

21. **Answer: B**. The answer is in paragraph 4, the fifth sentence:

*Change for change's sake may reflect the response of a novice manager*

The phrase **Change for change's sake** shows that the novice manager carries out change without having any particular reason for doing so. **A** is not the right answer, as **change for change's sake** does not mean **always changing**. There is no reference in the text to how often changes are made. **C** is not correct, as the text says that change without benefit leads to low staff morale, not that the latter is something that managers want to increase. **D** is not the right answer, because **an advisory committee** are not colleagues, i.e. people you work with.

22. **Answer: A**. The answer is in paragraph 5, the third sentence:

*Many in the worldwide audience viewed and listened from the comfort of their homes.*

**B** is not correct, because it is the other way round! **C** is not correct, because it was the astronauts that joked, not people in general. **D** is not correct, because the text does not compare science fiction and Christmas in the sense that one became like the other. The text means that they had similar characteristics.

23. **Answer: C**. The answer is in paragraph 6:

*that such accidents, although unfortunate, were also inevitable.*

**A** is not correct, because the text says that it was the second moon expedition that showed that nothing is exciting anymore, not the space shuttle explosion. **B** is not correct, because there is no reference in the text to TV. **D** is not correct, because the text says that the astronauts knew the risks, but this does not mean that they were to blame.

*Question type.* The questions in this section test:
- whether you are able to scan a text for specific information.
- whether you can recognise a paraphrase of words and ideas.
- whether you are able to understand specific points in the text.

## Questions 24–28

These questions are a variation on the **Yes/ No/ Not Given** format. In the exam, it is very important that you read the instructions carefully and that you write the appropriate letter on your answer sheet.

24. **Answer: C**. The answer is in paragraph 7:

*. . . computer-based programmes are replacing textbooks, blackboards and tutors.*

Note that the exercise is only asking about teachers (tutors); it is not asking about textbooks and blackboards as well.

25. **Answer: F**. The answer is in paragraph 8:

*. . . will open the door to a future filled with a kaleidoscope of scientific and technical wizardry.*

The vocabulary here may be a problem, but the tense is clear.

26. **Answer: NG**. The answer is in paragraph 7:

*Factors such as the need for skilled and costly support services are rarely discussed.*

In the text, there is no time reference regarding this development, even when it is discussed.

27. **Answer: C**. The answer is in paragraph 7:

*The principles of learning are established: the way they may be best used in different settings and the results evaluated will vary with client needs.*

The answer here is tricky. The **will** here is not the **will** of the future, but has basically the same meaning as the Present Simple i.e. every time it happens.

**A book for IELTS**

28. **Answer: C**. The answer is in paragraph 9: The time has come to . . . (i.e. now).

*Question type.* The questions in this section test:
- whether you are able to scan for specific information.
- whether you can recognise an idea which is expressed in another way or a paraphrase.
- whether you are able to analyse a small part of a text and not allow the information around it to interfere with your analysis.

| Test 3 | Passage 3 |
|---|---|

## Questions 29–32

When matching opinions, statements or topics to people it is important to scan the text to find the name of the person. The answer you are looking for will then be easy to locate.

29. **Answer: C**. The answer is in paragraph **D**. The sentence in the exercise is a paraphrase of the information in the last two sentences of the paragraph:

*However, one point that is well understood is that a national minimum wage could cause a run of differential–maintaining pay claims. The fact that the beneficiaries of a minimum wage usually lack bargaining power (Lucas 1995) and that they are unlikely to be a 'reference group' for any sector of organised labour, takes the edge off this argument.*

30. **Answer: D**. The answer is in paragraph **B**. The sentence is a paraphrase of the findings of Card & Krueger in the third sentence:

*A review of such studies by Card and Krueger (1995) concluded that minimum wages had no effect on employment.*

31. **Answer: B**. The answer is in paragraph **C**. The sentence in the exercise is a paraphrase of the information in the last sentence of the paragraph:

*Certain types of service industry, for example, can show positive employment effects (Alpert 1986).*

32. **Answer: A**. The answer is in paragraph **B**. Note the sentence in the exercise uses a negative to paraphrase the information in the text. Remember here that you are scanning for an idea rather than just specific words: you are not scanning for the words **does not have a positive effect as regards teenagers**, but the idea that the minimum wage has a negative effect as regards teenagers. So be careful about just scanning for specific words.

*Question type.* The questions in this section test:
- whether you are able to scan a text for specific information.
- whether you can recognise a paraphrase of words and ideas.

## Questions 33–39

33. **Answer: low paid workers.** The answer is in paragraph **D**. You can scan the text here for the words **save/ saving** and **benefits**.

34. **Answer: 'bad' employers.** The answer is in paragraph **D**. You can scan the text here for the word **subsidise/ subsidy**.

35. **Answer: certain/ some service industries.** The answer is in paragraph **C** Note how this answer is connected with 31 above. In 31, your ability to find the source of the information was being checked. Here it is your ability to see how this information fits into the summary that is being tested.

36. **Answer: development of training.** The answer is in paragraph **D**. Note you have to change the form of the words: **develop** to **development** and add the preposition **of**. Note that you cannot use the phrases **better market functioning/ more competitive conditions** (in the same paragraph), as they do not fit the grammar of the text; you would have to leave out the word **the** in the diagram. Note also the word **even** in the diagram and where it occurs in the text.

Note the division here in the organisation of the information. In 33 to 36 above, the information relates basically to the positive aspects of a minimum wage. The details that you are looking for in 37 to 39 are about the negative effects.

37. **Answer: differentials.** The answer is in paragraph **D**.

38. **Answer: out of business.** The answer is in paragraph **C**.

39. **Answer: teenagers.** The answer is in paragraph **B**. Note how this particular question is testing different details re teenagers to that tested in number 32 above.

The specific references within each paragraph have been omitted on purpose. This will give you extra practice in scanning a text for information.

When completing diagrams it is important first to look carefully at the diagram so that you understand what kind of information is missing in each case. It is also important to look carefully at the diagram itself, particularly the directions of arrows and other connections between the various parts or boxes. As in questions 29 to 32 you will need to scan the text to find the information given in the diagram, and then look around this to locate the answer required.

Remember also to pay attention to the word limit set.

**Question type.** The questions in this section test:
- whether you can summarise a text.
- whether you are able to scan a text for specific information.
- whether you can recognise a paraphrase of words and ideas.
- whether you are able to scan a text to recognise the organisation.

## Questions 40–42

40. **Answer: B.** The answer is in paragraph **D**:

    *Critics of the minimum wage would, of course, argue that it only benefits people who have a job.*

    **A** is not correct, because the cost of services is not referred to directly, although service industries are (paragraph **C**):

    *. . . but, more importantly, showing the strategic processes which managers use* **to cope with an imposed rise in the price of labour.**

    **C** and **D** are not mentioned as being effects of the minimum wage.

41. **Answer: D.** The answer is in paragraph **E**: . . . **they are best executed through local rather than national government.** (fiscal counterbalance = adjustments in taxation). **A** is obviously then not correct. **B** and **C** are not correct, because the type of taxation is not specified in the text.

42. **Answer: C.** The answer is again in paragraph **C**:

    *the dearth of studies based on local labour markets and on those of specific industries.*

    Even if you do not know the meaning of the word **dearth,** you can work out that it has a negative meaning by the reference to **a criticism. A, B** and **D** are all obviously incorrect.

*Question type.* The questions in this section test:
- whether you are able to scan a text for specific information.
- whether you can recognise a paraphrase of words and ideas.
- whether you are able to understand specific points in the text.

| Test 4 | Passage 1 |

## Questions 1–7

The answers to the questions in this section relate only to paragraph 2.

1. **Answer: protostars.**
2. **Answer: plasma.**
3. **Answer: nuclear fusion.**
4. **Answer: helium.**
5. **Answer: a red giant.**
6. **Answer: maintain (mechanical) equilibrium.**
7. **Answer: the Main Sequence.**

Be careful about the numbers here!

*Question type.* The questions in this section test:
- whether you can summarise a text.
- whether you are able to scan a text for specific information.
- whether you can recognise a paraphrase of words and ideas.
- whether you are able to scan a text to recognise the organisation.

## Questions 8–11

8. **Answer: C.** The answer to this question is in paragraph 3:

   *. . . , so that they are squashed into closer proximity with each other, until a limit is reached where they resist any further compression. This phenomenon is called degeneracy, and is a manifestation of the Pauli Exclusion Principle.*

   So **A** is incorrect. **B** is wrong, because:

   *The temperature is so great that degeneracy cannot then be maintained . . .*

   (See the end of the third paragraph). **D** is wrong, because degeneracy happens to all stars.

9. **Answer: C.** The answer is in the first sentence of paragraph 3: *The Pauli Exclusion Principle states that no two identical particles can occupy the same quantum state.* **A** is obviously a distracter; the Principle does not say anything about stars being the same or different. Alternative **B** is not true. The author uses the example of low mass stars to illustrate the Principle and the phenomenon of degeneracy (See the third sentence in the third paragraph and the subsequent text). **D** is wrong, because:

   *. . . this pressure . . . remains constant while the temperature continues to increase.*

10. **Answer: B.** The answer is in the first sentence of the penultimate paragraph. Alternative **A** is not correct, because the statement applies to all stars. **C** is not correct, as it again happens to all stars. As regards **D**, only smaller stars undergo a helium flash (See the first sentence of paragraph 4).

11. **Answer: C.** The answer is in the first paragraph: *Their journey along the evolutionary path, and ultimate fate at stellar death, is determined by their initial mass, . . . So it is **their mass when they are first formed** (their initial mass), which affects their development throughout their lives.*

    Note the answers to the questions are not in the same order as the information occurs in the passage.

    *Question type.* The questions in this section test:
    - whether you are able to scan a text for specific information.
    - whether you can recognise a paraphrase of words and ideas.
    - whether you are able to understand and analyse specific points in the text.

## Questions 12–14

You can answer the questions in this section simply by scanning the text to find the references to the different solar masses.

12. **Answer: white dwarfs.** See the beginning of the fifth paragraph.

13. **Answer: neutron stars**. See paragraph 6.

14. **Answer: Black Holes**. See the penultimate paragraph.

**Question type.** The questions in this section test:
- whether you are able to scan a text for specific information.
- whether you can recognise a paraphrase of words and ideas.
- whether you are able to understand and analyse specific points in the text.

| Test 4 | Passage 2 |
|---|---|

As you read the passage for the first time, you should try to write down beside the paragraph a quick heading of your own. You should try, however, not to spend a lot of time doing this. If you cannot think of a title immediately, you should continue reading. When you come to do the exercise, you will also find that some paragraphs are easier to do than others, so do them first.

For each of the paragraphs, ask yourself the same question: why did the writer write the paragraph? See also **Reading Passage 3, Practice Test 1** and **Reading Passage 1, Practice Test 3**. Please also see **Reading Exercises 10 –13**.

If there is an example, cross it from the list before you do the exercise. You then reduce the number of alternatives you have to look at.

15. **Answer: iv**. The writer wrote this paragraph as an introduction. The purpose of the paragraph is to show what envy means. Note that **xiii** is not acceptable, because it refers to only part of the paragraph i.e. the second sentence, and not the whole paragraph.

    Always remember that the title is a brief summary of the whole paragraph and reference to part of the paragraph is not acceptable. If you have problems with this look at **Reading Exercises 10–13**.

16. **Answer: vii**. The paragraph talks about (a) the Swahili in Coastal East Africa, (b) their views about envy and (c) how the Swahili deal with envy: they try to convince people that there is no reason to envy someone else's success. Note that (a) and (b) lead up to the focus of the paragraph.

    This title is also a paraphrase of the title of the whole article. The distracter here is **(x)**.

17. **Answer: xiv**. Note that the paragraph is about the Evil Eye and the fact that it is a universal or global phenomenon. The paragraph mentions some parts of the world where pendants depicting the Evil Eye are worn to protect the wearer against Envy. It does not say that the wearing of the pendant is a global remedy. It says that the Evil Eye is universal, but the text only refers to parts of Europe where the wearing of a pendant is a way of repelling envy. So **iii** is not acceptable. Note also how **v** refers to only part of the text.

18. **Answer: ii**. This is an easy one as the paragraph is devoted to a particular example of envy. The first few sentences are only by way of introduction.

19. **Answer: ix**. Note that the paragraph is not limited to poor societies. The example given at the end of the paragraph could happen in rich as well as poor societies.

    The writer is saying that the idea of limited good holds true for both poor and rich societies. It does not matter that the main part of the paragraph talks about poor societies. If you, therefore, choose **xv** as your answer, you are only summarising part of the paragraph, i.e. poor societies.

    It is a common mistake for students to choose a title which covers part of a paragraph - you need to be able to hold all the parts of the paragraph together to arrive at the correct title. Compare number 15 above.

20. **Answer: xii**. It is tempting to put **i** as the answer, but again it is only a summary of part of the text, sentences 2 and 3. The paragraph also talks about what envy is and in this sense it is similar to paragraph **A**. However, the paragraph talks about something more than what envy is **iv**; it talks about envy as opposed to other feelings, namely: jealousy, love, and gratitude and ambition.

*Question type.* The questions in this section test:
- whether you are able to scan a text and knit together the information.
- whether you can summarise information or an idea.
- whether you can recognise a paraphrase.
- whether you are able to analyse a small part of a text and not allow the information around it to interfere with your analysis.

## Questions 21–24

You can answer the questions in this section in two ways. You can look for the **Concepts**, or you can look for the names. In fact, when you look through the questions before you read through the passage for the first time, you should automatically notice that you are going to have to match names with theories and give titles to paragraphs. As you read, therefore, you should mark the names in some way. Our advice is to put a light box in pencil around each name as you read. Then it will be easy to identify the names and match them with the concepts.

Note that one of the people mentioned in the passage does not occur in the exercise.

21. **Answer: v**. The answer is in paragraph **C**. You just have to scan the text for the name and then check the paraphrases against the concepts in the exercise. You can also scan the text for the idea, but this is more difficult, as you are trying to match an idea that is expressed in a different way, even if just slightly. Note how the previous exercise can help you with this particular answer. The heading for paragraph **C** tells you what is in that paragraph. It shows you the value of being able to summarise a chunk of text and see the organisation. You then know where to find it quickly.

    As in all tests, if you can find the principles which govern the testing, then you have a greater chance of succeeding in that test.

22. **Answer: i**. The answer is in paragraph **F**. The same methods apply here as for 21 above. Notice again how the previous exercise helps you around the text. Read the paragraph heading, then the first sentence of the paragraph and then the name attached to the **Concept**. Did you do this exercise without reference to the information you gathered as you did the previous exercise?

23. **Answer: vii**. The answer is in paragraph **G**. Note here how the information you gathered in the previous exercise is still able to help you. While you were looking for a heading for paragraph **G**, did you consider the heading (i) as a possibility? If you looked at it, you then might have remembered it, when you came to do this exercise.

    This exercise gives you a clear example of how information is organised in an extended piece of text. You should, as you read generally, always look for markers that help you organise your reading of a text: here it is themes, which are more difficult, as they require you to collect together larger chunks of information (See **Reading Exercises 10–13**); and names which act like pegs to hang information on. Look at the other passages in this book and read them for the organisation. Do you remember **Reading Exercises 1–5**? Also look back at the Key to **Questions 1- 6** in **Practice Test 1 Reading Passage 1**.

24. **Answer: ii**. The answer is in paragraph **D**. Notice the inter-relationship between the spread of envy and illness.

    *Question type.* The questions in this section test:
    - whether you are able to scan a text for specific information.
    - whether you can recognise a paraphrase of words and ideas.

## Questions 25–28

25. **Answer: More fortunate/ Successful/ Powerful/ Prosperous**. For the first answer see the dictionary definition in paragraph **A**. Compare this with the distracter heading for this paragraph in the first set of questions for this text. For the second, see the last sentence of paragraph **B**. For the word **Powerful** see the last sentence of paragraph **E**. For **Prosperous** see the word prosper Paragraph **A**.

26. **Answer: source of harm**. See the second sentence of paragraph **C**.

27. **Answer: dangerous pastime**. The answer is at the beginning of paragraph **B**.

28. **Answer: minimise personal success**. The answer is again at the beginning of paragraph **B**.

    *Question type.* The questions in this section test:
    - whether you are able to scan a text for specific information.
    - whether you can recognise information or an idea which is expressed in another way.
    - whether you are able to analyse a small part of a text and not allow the information around it to interfere with your analysis.

---

| Test 4 | Passage 3 |
|---|---|

## Questions 29–33

29. **Answer: C**. The answer is in paragraph 5. The condition that needs to be met is in the first sentence and the result or implication is in the last sentence of the paragraph:

> *If you, or a colleague, have a problem with some aspect of work share it with everyone in the tea-room.* One of your colleagues will, doubtless, have had similar difficulties in the past and will have found a ridiculously simple solution. To your surprise, you will discover he is more than happy to share his experience and answers with you over a cup of tea. *Both of you will then go back to your desks with added commitment and make a positive contribution to the work of the group.*

Note how the sentence in the exercise summarises the two parts of the text, and the paragraph. Notice the clues: **Provided. . . / If . . .** both give you a condition, which is followed by a result/implication: . . . will work harder . . . / . . . will then go back . . . .

30. **Answer: F**. The answer is in paragraph 7.

> *Who will be trained? Keen, eager, people: the raw recruits. Released from the inhibitions of the office environment in the relaxed atmosphere of a tea-room, they have the confidence to ask dumb questions. This is, in fact, the best place to find solutions to problems; and conduct training. In the tearoom, old hands, freed temporarily from the modern technologies* they often do not fully understand, *will invariably offer advice.*

Note again how the exercise sentence summarises the text. The sentence paraphrases the information to show you the underlying meaning/ organisation of the text in bold: a **condition** followed by an **implication**.

31. **Answer: G**. The answer is in paragraph 4.

> *What will the Boss say, however? If he has any sense, he will also come and join you.* Perhaps, he supports another team? You can discuss the merits of the players and show him how competently you can present a case. *He will realise that the tearoom is an ideal place for informal meetings with his staff, where any number of day-to-day problems can be sorted out over a cup of tea,* and where anyone who needs a tender warning about something can be quietly given it without the march to 'The Office'. ....

Again the meaning is made clearer/ summarised by the sentence in the exercise.

32. **Answer: A**. The answer is in the last paragraph.

> *But let us say we allow staff to enjoy staggered breaks.* The morning coffee is between 10.00 and 11.00. Lunch is sometime between 12.00 and 2.00. Afternoon tea is between 3.00 and 4.00. *The tea-room can then be used by time-conscious executives to have their meetings. And since the room is required for refreshment, these meetings must never overrun, unless they are scheduled after afternoon tea...* Who wants to work late anyway?

Note the phrase **let us say we allow staff to enjoy = If we allow** . Note also the implication in the text is expressed by: . . . can then be used by . . . ; . . . must never over-run . . .

33. **Answer: D**. The answer is in paragraph 4:

> . . . can be quietly given it without the march to 'The Office'. *If, as a consequence, the communication process improves, the boss may even dispense with a layer of middle management 'twixt you and himself.* He will then no longer need to have expensive 'Off Site Meetings' where his middle managers experience 'Free Expression'. He can spend some of the savings on light refreshments for his staff to enjoy!

Note how the **conditions** and **implications** summarise the main points in the text. The writer is trying to convince the reader of the merits of having a **tea-room**. He sets out to show that, if certain **conditions** are met, there will be a number of **implications** for the workplace.

Note that the **conditions** are in a different order to what they are in the text.

Note how the text lends itself to this kind of summary rather than a gap-fill exercise.

*Question type.* The questions in this section test:
- whether you can summarise a text.
- whether you are able to scan a text for specific information.

---

A book for IELTS

- whether you can recognise a paraphrase of words and ideas.
- whether you are able to scan a text to recognise the organisation.

## Questions 34–38

34. **Answer: Not Given**. The text says at the end of paragraph 4:

    *He can spend some of the savings on light refreshments for his staff to enjoy!*

    However, nowhere in the text does the writer say that **a variety of snacks should be provided in tea-rooms.** The statement in the exercise is stating an opinion about all tea-rooms, whereas the text is giving an implication, *if* the boss gets rid of a layer of management. They are not talking about the same thing, even though the ideas are similar!

35. **Answer: Yes**. The answer is in paragraph 1:

    *but how do they manage to make one packet of chocolate digestives last one whole week?*

36. **Answer: Yes**. The answer is in paragraph 3, in the first sentence.

37. **Answer: No**. The answer is in paragraph 6 in the second sentence:

    *They are normal people in their everyday lives, but there are*

38. **Answer: Yes**. The answer is in paragraph 7:

    *in the relaxed atmosphere of a tea-room, they have the confidence to ask dumb questions.*

    Look at **Reading Exercises 17–22** and the Key to **Practice Test 1 Reading Passage 2**.

    *Question type.* The questions in this section test:
    - whether you are able to scan for specific information and ideas.
    - whether you can recognise an idea which is expressed in another way.
    - whether you can recognise a paraphrase.

## Questions 39–42

39. **Answer: damned few**. The answer is in paragraph 2
40. **Answer: light refreshments**. The answer is in paragraph 4 in the last sentence. See number 34 above.
41. **Answer: cringe**. The answer is in the penultimate sentence of paragraph 8.
42. **Answer: modern technologies**. The answer is in paragraph 7.

    *Question type.* The questions in this section test:
    - whether you are able to scan for specific information.
    - whether you can recognise information or an idea which is expressed in another way.
    - whether you can recognise a paraphrase.
    - whether you are able to analyse a small part of a text and not allow the information around it to interfere with your analysis.

# Key to
# Section on Writing

# Section on Writing – Graphs and Diagrams for Task 1

### Exercise 1

1. The data in the chart can be divided into three categories just like the example at the beginning of the exercise. The three main groups are physical, mental, and 'other' i.e. the activity does not fit exactly into either of the other two categories. The physical group can be further sub-divided into two types: light exercise i.e. 'Walking', 'Playing with children' and heavy exercise: 'DIY', 'Visiting a sports centre', 'Gardening'. The 'other' group includes 'Evening classes' and 'Voluntary work'. Note that 'Playing with children' and 'Gardening' could come into either the heavy or light work category.

2. You can see that the information on the chart is presented in a different way from Figure 1, but the activities are the same. So they can be divided into the same categories. Now that you can see the data in categories, it is easy to compare across the charts. For example, you can compare Gardening in both charts under physical activity and, say, Walking and see the differences.

3. You can group the information in this chart in several ways: team sports and individual sports; sports that can be played anywhere and sports that require special conditions e.g. hang-gliding; and cost: expensive sports like sub-aqua and cheap sports like football. You can also describe the data across the three categories just mentioned!

4. At first sight, the data in the graph is difficult to analyse. In the previous bar charts, the information is neatly packaged in blocks and because of the number of items, they are easy to classify. The appearance of the line graphs is more complex. They go through one another and it is difficult to see patterns, but the patterns and organisation are there, nonetheless.

    The first obvious pattern is that the value of two of the companies goes up and the third down. Grouping the former two together, you can see that the trend for the Berk Corporation is steadily upwards, while that for F&B Enterprises is more irregular. The pattern for the former can be divided into two parts: a sharp rise in share price within the first year and a half followed by a period of relative stability. Each of these two periods can then be subdivided. For example, the price for the first period increases slightly and then it rockets. Can you divide the line for the Berk Corporation? Look for gradual and sharp rises.

    Note also how the price appreciation for SPQF LTD in the first year partly mirrors that for the Berk Corporation and how the rise and fall are repeated with the decline in the third year dividing into two sections: a dramatic plunge followed by a more gradual decline.

    You can see that the same principle of patterns applies between the graphs and within sections of the graphs.

5. You can divide the items into two groups: beef versus the other three, i.e. fall and relative rise. Within the larger group there is a difference in the consumption between poultry and the other two.

    There is another pattern. The total amount of protein consumed over the period declines steadily. Add the totals at the beginning and at several points in the middle and then at the end.

    You may be able to see more patterns than are mentioned here. If you can, then that is very good. Hopefully, you can see that once you find a framework within which to work, it is easier to write about the information.

### Exercise 2

A    4, 6, 8, 12

Note the different words to describe the 'fall': collapse, plummet, fall steeply and plunge. The verb 'fall' by itself does not describe completely enough the drama of the graph.

B 3,7,17;        C 1,11,16;        D 9,15;        E 14;        F 2;        G 10,18;        H 5,13

*See also* Exercise 8.

**Exercise 3:** The correct chart is D.

### Exercise 4

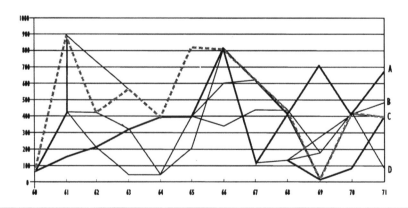

---

## Exercise 5

Compare your answer with the line graph below.

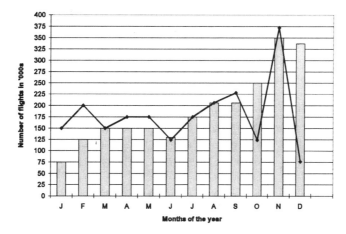

Months of the year

Now you can try to describe the line graph above and check your answer with the model in the exercise!

## Exercise 6

1.  relationship between coal and natural gas. This is called an inverse relationship.

2.  other main features are:

    The rise in natural gas, which first overtakes coal in mid 1992 and then petroleum for part of 1995.

    The minor peaks in coal at the end of/beginning of 1993/1994 with corresponding dips in the consumption of nuclear and hydro-electricity.

    The relative stability of the consumption of petroleum over the period.

    The slight increase in the use of Nuclear and hydro-electricity.

    The amount of energy consumed at the beginning of the period is not much different from that at the end. So over the period the amount of energy consumed is relatively constant.

    Rises in one energy source are mirrored by falls in another, e.g. coal/gas, coal/nuclear and hydro-electricity.

3.  You can divide the energy sources into two types, fossil: petroleum, coal, natural gas and non-fossil: nuclear and hydro-electricity.

4.  Look for a pattern. Nuclear and hydro-electricity is below the line, coal above, and so on.

5.  No, not unless you are asked to do so.

6.  The Present Simple and the Simple Past. You use the Present Simple when you are describing the graph as you are looking at it. Remember that the information on the graph remains the same. It doesn't change. It is like a fact: Water boils at 100 degrees Centigrade. See the answer to number 2 above. You can use the Simple Past by way of contrast to talk about the dates. In the middle of 1992, coal was overtaken by natural gas and then in 1995 natural gas outstripped petroleum to become the main source of energy.

7.  Consumption can be divided into two parts: the relative stability of 1992/93 and the more erratic behaviour in the subsequent years.

8.  Consumption: use, usage; the amount consumed

    Fall: decline, drop. (Not: fall down).

    Rise: increase, climb, go up (Not: rise up).

## Exercise 7

Look at the corrected text below. The changes are in bold.

1.  The graph shows the energy consumption **in the UK** in million tonnes of oil/coal equivalent from 1992 to l995.

2.  A striking feature of the graph is the rise in the use of natural gas. Gas consumption was steadily upwards, **overtaking** coal towards the end of 1992 and finally **outstripping** petroleum in 1995 to become, for a period, the second most **common** energy source.

3.  This increase **coincided** with a drop in the use of coal during the period 1992 to 1995. At the beginning of 1992, coal **consumption** stood at **approximately** 65 million tonnes. In the first **quarter** of 1992, there was a **brief**, steady climb and,

from then until the beginning of the third quarter in 1995, the trend was markedly down. The **fall, at first**, was quite steep. From the end of 1993, consumption was steady with two **minor peaks** at the end of 1993 and 1994, which **corresponded** with two **dips** in the use of nuclear and hydro-electricity. Then from the beginning of 1995 coal consumption resumed its **decline**.

4.     **As can be seen**, petroleum was the main source of energy throughout the period with little or no **change** in the **amount consumed**. The use of non-fossil sources of energy, i.e. nuclear and hydro-electricity, over the period **increased** gradually with no dramatic rises or falls.

5.     Despite the variations, the overall amount of energy consumed during the period shown on the graph was **little changed** at the end of 1995.

       **Note:**

       Some of you will be surprised to learn the text above is too long. It contains 245 words, when the exam only requires at least 150. You could remove about 60 or 70 words quite easily.

       The changes in the text above include avoidance of repetition. Look at paragraph 2 and check for synonyms of words like rise and fall. For example the last word in paragraph 3 has been changed to **decline** to avoid the repetition of the word fall.

       The above text is not the only answer. You could divide the four energy sources into two groups: fossil i.e. petroleum, natural gas and coal; and non-fossil, nuclear and hydro-electricity.

       The text does not contain all of the information contained in the graph. Look at the comprehension questions in Exercise 6.

       Note the complex sentence in paragraph 2:
       Gas consumption was steadily upwards, overtaking coal towards the end of 1992 and finally outstripping petroleum in 1995 to become, for a period, the second most common energy source.

       Note the change from popular to common in paragraph 2.

## Exercise 8

1.     Answer:     F and C

2.     Answer:     M and L

3.     Answer:     K and N

4.     Answer:     E and D

5.     Answer:     B and K

6.     Answer:     K and C/M/P

7.     Answer:     H and O

8.     Answer:     G and I

9.     Answer:     J and I

10.    Answer:     C/M/P and F

## Exercise 9

In each case below, where there are two possibilities the first answer is the better one.

| | | | | | | |
|---|---|---|---|---|---|---|
| 1. | m | as can be seen from the chart | 9. | h | declined further | |
| | e | in the chart | | x | went down | |
| 2. | r | double the estimate for the period | 10. | j | November saw a noticeable turnaround | |
| | o | which is twice as much as the estimated figures | | a | in November the number of shoppers increased again | |
| 3. | s | before picking up | | | | |
| | k | before they went up | 11. | y | during which time they did better than the figures predicted | |
| 4. | f | outstripping projections by a wide margin | | g | outperforming the figures predicted | |
| | z | doing better than expected | 12. | u | hitting a peak | |
| 5. | t | proved | 13. | q | reveal a marked shift | |
| | v | were | | w | show that there was a change | |
| 6. | i | being | 14. | d | experienced a hefty fall | |
| 7. | c | those | | b | fell by a large amount | |
| | p | they were | | | | |
| 8. | l | forecast for the period | | | *Note the difference between 4 and 11.* | |
| | n | which were predicted for the period | | | | |

### Exercise 10

Read the version below.

*The prediction is that European Internet music sales will go up a lot over the period which the graph covers. They will rise erratically at first and will then leap in two stages to reach a high of $3900 million in 2012, before going up to a new peak of $8000 million at the end of 2014. Album sales, on the other hand, which will climb at first until the end of 2006, are then set to drop steadily throughout the next five years, before they bottom out and end the period a lot below $1000 million.*

*With European cinema attendances, there are two diverging forecasts. The first estimate is for numbers to rise steadily between the year 2003 and 2008, and increase from just below 900 million visitors to 1200 and the biggest jump in cinema people is projected to be in the year 2008. But, the second forecast is different. The projection for the first three years of the period shows a rise, but after that cinema attendances will fall to below 400 million people.*

You can see that the above version is not as good as the original. Most students at a high grade will write a text somewhere between the two versions! Read the two texts several times so that you can see the difference clearly.

### Exercise 11

7. A **comparison** of the borrowings for 1996 and 1997 shows that they **(9) fall into three categories. (12) On the one hand**, those for fiction and the other category fell, **(13) the former** by 50% from 30% of borrowings to 15% and **(8) the latter** again by 50% from ten per cent to five per cent.

6. **By contrast,** borrowings of children's books, romance and sci-fi all rose **(14) by varying degrees**. Children's increased by several percentage points, **(4) whereas** books taken out from the romance section rose by 50% between the two years. The number of books borrowed by those reading science-fiction **(10) ,however,** went up threefold.

3. **In the third category come** non-fiction and crime, neither of which saw any rise.

The contents of the library are **(1) in no way** reflected by the books that are taken out in either of the years. **(2) For example,** sci-fi books make up five per cent of the books in the library, while in both years borrowings exceed this amount, by three times as we have seen in 1997. Take non-fiction **(5) as another example**. Lendings in both years stand at five per cent, **(11) whereas** 20 per cent of the books fall into this category.

### Exercise 12

| | | | | | |
|---|---|---|---|---|---|
| 1. Blank | 2. d | 3. j | 4. f | 5. Blank | 6. Blank |
| 7. g | 8. **h** | 9. a | 10. e | 11. c | 12. Blank |
| 13. Blank | 14. i | 15. b | | | |

### Exercise 13

The sentences below contain the corrections. Can you find them?

1. There was a sharp decrease in the number of people attending the theatre over the period.

2. The increase in the incidence of petty crime has continued in spite of the measures introduced.

3. The charts indicate that the price of the various types of cars fell considerably.

4. It was predicted that industrial production in Western countries will/would  level out, while that in the so-called Tiger economies will/would rise in the early '90s.

5. The price of computers has been dramatically reduced over the period.

6. As regards noise pollution, a fairly big rise in the number of complaints was recorded for 1997.

7. As can be seen, the rate of increase slowed over the last five years of the period.

8. In 1974, its output began to stage a gradual recovery.

9. Between February and May, the income was fairly erratic.

10. It is estimated that the number of cars on the road will plunge when road pricing is introduced.

11. Sales hit a peak in late summer and then fell back in the subsequent months.

12. There were, according to the graph, no significant changes in sales from 1973 to 1976.

13. The rate of inflation dropped slowly, but surely, in the early '80s.

14. The main characteristic of the bar chart is the large drop in male students applying.

15. The birth rate rose quite slowly over the period.

### Exercise 14

| | | | | |
|---|---|---|---|---|
| 1. b | 5. a, e, h, n, o | 6. e, h n | 8. i | 9. e, h, j, n, o; not q |
| 12. e, h, n, p | 13. e, n | 14. d | 17. f, m | 18. f, m |

**Exercise 15**

1.      fall down. Students often user this instead of fall. A person or a house, for example, falls down.

2.      Has declined; has dropped; has been reduced; has been dropped; has gone down; has decreased. These simple verbs cause a lot of confusion. You can divide the verbs in the list into three types: (i) decline, go down, fall, subside, deteriorate. All of these verbs are intransitive i.e. they do not take an object, and so you cannot use them in the passive. (ii) reduce. This verb needs an object when it is active i.e. it is transitive. Therefore, you can use it in the passive. (iii) drop, decrease and slow down. These verbs are both transitive and intransitive. You can, therefore, use them in the active and passive: they dropped the price; the price has dropped and the price has been dropped. You cannot use the verb reduce in the same way!

3.      The second one is the correct answer. Dip and dramatically do not go together.

4.      a) you need to use falling instead of dropping.
        b) cost of living
        c) plummet is the wrong word here; you cannot use the word plummet as a noun. You need to use a noun like fall.
        d) deterioration is the wrong word. The word deterioration usually relates to quality rather than number s , e.g. the situation deteriorated; the value of the dollar deteriorated against the euro. You would have to use fall, decrease etc.
        e) diminution is the wrong word; should be a word like decrease, fall etc.
        f) You should use trend rather than tendency.

5.      Whereas/Whilst

6.      To be erratic; to go up and down; to be volatile; to be unstable; to go through a period of instability; to go through an erratic period; to experience a period of instability/volatility.

7.      There was no change in the birth rate over the period. Note the change from verb to noun. Try to vary your writing like this. It makes it less repetitive. You can express stability as follows: to remain stable, to be stable, experience/go through a period of stability, not to fluctuate,

8.      Deteriorate and decline. For deteriorate see 4d above; note that value etc can plunge etc, but the word deteriorate cannot interchange with the other words in all situations. As for decline, it is neutral in that it does not really indicate the quality of the fall; the other words relate to a sharp fall.

9.      You could use the following phrases as synonyms: the teenage crime rate; crime rate among teenagers; teenage crime rates; the number of crimes committed by teenagers; the number of crimes committed by young people in their teens.

10.     Regarding; With regard to; Concerning; As for; Where _____is concerned; when it comes to _____; Turning to; In the case of; To turn to. These words and phrases are important, because they help connect information. They are especially helpful, when you describe charts or when you are referring to items in a list, e.g. in an essay title because they point to the items.

11.     Illustrates; plots.

**Exercise 16**

1.      Possible answers are as follows:

        After that, the information is collated and sent out electronically to other agents.
        At the next stage, the information is collated and sent out electronically to other agents.
        The next step/stage is to collate the information and send it out electronically to other agents.
        Subsequently, the information is collated and sent out electronically to other agents.
        The information is then collated and sent out electronically to other agents.
        Following that, the information is collated and sent out electronically to other agents.

2.      characteristic, feature, aspect. Note that the word aspect is not always a synonym for the first two words.

3.      The number of companies who registered approval of the new currency rose with an increase of more than 35%.
        Or  rose by 35%

4.      ... in the first three months followed by a steady decline ...

5.      Both are correct. At first sight, the second sentence appears incorrect, but it is possible for the management of the cinema to have increased attendance. The agent is not mentioned.

6.      You would normally say 'rise(s) or fall(s)'.

7.      The word prophesy does not fit in here.

8.      It is forecast that the number of people on waiting lists will rise steadily in the coming years.

9.      No. It sounds odd, because you have   projected  and  in the coming years, both referring to the future. It is probably better to leave out the word projected.

10.     The word interesting makes the statement subjective. The word significant is more neutral.

11.     The fall in investment in science is almost the same as that for training.
        The fall in investment in science is not that different from that for training.
        The fall in investment in science almost exactly mirrors that for training.
        The fall in investment in science is mirrored by that for training.

12.    All of the sentences depend on the emphasis you wish to put on the particular parts of the information Sentence a is probably the simplest of the alternatives given.

13.    ... is not as big/large/great as that for science.

## Exercise 17

Reconstructed text.

The data in the table relating to passenger death rates by mode of land transport in Great Britain between 1981 and 1993 can be divided into three categories.

The first group, consisting of cars, vans and bicycles experienced a significant reduction in the rate of road death over the period under study. For example, death among the car and van users declined by more than half, falling from 6.1 per billion passenger kilometres to 3.0 and 3.8 to 1.7, respectively. Cycling, however, despite a significant decrease from 56.9 per billion to 41.3, remained the second most dangerous type of land transport.

In the second category, comprising motorcycles and rail, the rate dropped slightly between 1981 and 1993. Motorcycling was the most dangerous type of transport, averaging more than twice as many fatalities as cycling, and more than twenty times as high as cars.

Regarding the third group, buses and coaches, the road death rate almost trebled over the period under review. Nevertheless, buses and coaches were still the second safest type of vehicular transport.

## Exercise 18

As **(17) can be seen** from the maps, the area of Barton Bingham **(6) changed** significantly between 1937 and 1995. The road bisecting the area **(16) was straightened** and on both sides various developments **(7) took place**. On the north side, the manor house **(8) was converted** into a health farm and part of the surrounding scrubland and adjacent woodland **(1) became** a golf course. The area immediately adjacent to the road **(3) gave way** to housing along its entire length.

On the south side of the road, a railway station **(5) was constructed** in 1990, which **(15) was connected** by a minor road to the main thoroughfare. In 1991, the disused railway line **(10) was reopened**, with a bridge **(4) being built** across the road. In the scrubland to the east of the lake, a leisure complex **(11) was completed and opened** in 1993. In addition, the area of agricultural land which **(2) existed** in 1937 **(13) was halved** to make way for the construction of a new hospital and a car park both also with road access to the main highway. A farmhouse **(14) was built** on the remaining agricultural land. Next to the agricultural land, the marshes that **(12) were** there in 1937, **(9) were turned over** to a wildfowl sanctuary.

### Notes

Note the different words which are used to avoid repeating the word change: convert, become, turn over to, give way to.

Note that you cannot replace 3 with 9. This is not just because 9 is in the plural. The expression 'give way to' has the idea that the land was surrendered to something bad or negative. The expression turn over to is suitable in both cases.

Now try to write a description of the changes in the maps without looking at the text in the exercise.

## Exercise 19

The sequence of texts is:       l, d, o, a, j, k, c, i, b, g

Sentences e, f, h, m, n, are distracters.

Note that the language in the diagram is in the present simple. This is like looking at a graph and describing the graph as a picture. You are concerned here with the sequence of the events not the time.

When you write the description and add the dates the tense has to be the simple past, because the text is describing a specific sequence of events in the past. For practice, you could try to write a description of how a documentary is made rather than how a specific documentary was made. Compare the language here with the language in the next 5 exercises.

## Exercise 20 : The suggested answer is:

*To create a daily newspaper the necessary material is taken from two sources, timber and recycled paper, and then passed through a series of machines.*

*Trees are cut down to provide timber. In the first machine, the bark is removed and then the timber is chopped up into small pieces. These chippings are put into a mechanical refiner, and subsequently a hydrapulper where they are mixed with water and made into a pulp. At the next stage, the pulp is put into a blend chest where it is mixed with pulp from recycled paper. This mixture is then refined, cleaned and screened, before going into a large piece of machinery where it is made into rolls of paper.*

*Once the newspaper has been printed, it is distributed. After the reader has finished with the paper, it is recycled. The recycling process first involves the paper being put into a hydrapulper to turn it into a pulp. A de-inking cell then extracts the ink. After that, the solution is put into the blend chest: and the whole process is repeated.*

Note that the tense is used is mainly the present simple and most of the verbs are in the passive. Compare the tenses in Ex. 19.

# Section on Writing – Essay Writing for Task 2

**Exercise 21**

    1. B;    2. F;    3. C;    4. K;    5. O;    6. P;    7. H    8. J    9. N    10. R

**Exercise: 22**

    1. A;    2. B, C, D, H;    3. E;    4. None. You could adapt A;    5. None. Again you could adapt A;

    6. D;    7. B, C;    8. G;    9. B, C, D, H;    10. F

**Exercise 23**

1. **Answer: D/N**. The question in the focus means: what is your opinion? Note that the general subject in the essay title is presented in such a way that it gives you two sides of an issue. If you think about it, it is difficult to give an opinion about something unless it has an element of controversy and at least two sides to it. Would you ever have a question like: *Water boils at 100°C at sea level. Where do you stand on this matter?/ To what extent do you agree? etc.*

2. **Answer: D/N**. See number 1 above.

3. **Answer: G**. Some people make the mistake of writing about the disadvantages and the advantages. A danger can be a disadvantage, but a disadvantage may not be a danger! Moreover, you are usually asked to write about advantages and disadvantages, not disadvantages and . . Note also that the question has two elements to the focus: *dangers and advantages*. Note how the explanation gives you synonyms for these words.

4. **Answer: H**. Be careful when you are reading the essay title. It is easy to miss the word *not* here. The focus has one element and note the synonym for disadvantage.

5. **Answer: F**. Note the focus has two elements: *problems and opinion.*

6. **Answer: L**. You are being asked a question here, which requires you to give a Yes/No answer: your opinion.

7. **Answer: B**. There are two elements to the focus here: *dangers and your opinion*. Note the synonym for dangers.

8. **Answer: M**. Note the question two elements in the focus: *opinion and reservations.*

9. **Answer: J**. There are three elements to the focus: *arguments for, against and opinion.*

10. **Answer: C**. You are being asked a question which requires you to answer yes or no, hence your opinion. The word *should* here also indicates that your opinion is required. Note how the two questions mirror both sides of the issue as presented in the general subject. When you give your opinion it is possible to give your views 100% on one side; 60% on one side, 40% on the other; and so on. There are different ways of asking you for your opinion as we have seen here: What is your opinion? Where do you stand? Do you feel ? Should ? Or should ? To what extent do you agree? How far do you agree? They are basically all the same, but the last two just point out to you that there is a range of opinion i.e. you can give your opinion 100%, 60%/40% and so on. The question is helping you! Note also the exam cannot always ask: . What is your opinion!

**Exercise 24**

**Version B** is obviously the better of the two. **Version A** is too short; it contains only 167 words. **Version B** contains 299 words.

The text in bold is the text which has been omitted in **Version A.**

1. In many countries, a charge is levied for entrance to museums and art galleries, but, in some instances, entrance is free.

2. **Where a charge is, in fact, levied, the argument is that** the up-keep of such institutions is not cheap and **while the tax-payer might be expected to provide some funds,** it is only fair that some contribution should come by way of an entrance fee or, at least, a voluntary contribution. An exception is usually made for certain categories of people, **like the unemployed, the elderly, the disabled, school children and students, on the grounds of financial hardship.**

3. **Personally, however, I believe that**, if people are made to pay to visit museums and art galleries, then this is effectively a tax on education. People should be encouraged to visit such institutions, **as they contain a wealth of material relating not only to the history and culture of their own countries, but also of other civilisations. They can, of course, obtain information from books films etc, but this is nothing to seeing the real objects.**

4. Moreover, children who have visited a museum or a gallery with their school may not be able to go again with their parents, **if there is an entrance fee. So** a fee, **in my opinion**, would act as a deterrent to people wanting to visit a museum.

5. Often people want to spend maybe only half an hour in a museum rather than spending a long time to justify paying a fee. **This would deter many people, myself included, from visiting museums. Having said this, however, I am not against voluntary charges or people being encouraged to make donations.**

6. **So, all in all, my personal view is that** people should not have pay to visit museums and art galleries.

    **Paragraph 2.**

        You can see that **Version A** has 3 extra pieces of text: the first two phrases frame the argument in a much better way and the third piece of text gives examples.

A book for IELTS

**Paragraph 3**.
There are two extra pieces of text here. The first one clearly highlights that this is the writer's opinion.
The second text provides further evidence for the writer's opinion/ argument.

**Paragraph 4.**
The additional text provides further evidence and highlights the writer's opinon.

**Paragraph 5.**
Again, the additional text provides further evidence.

If you go back and read **Version A** again, you will now see that it is superficial and lacks evidence.
Moreover it does not frame the writer's opinions well.

# Section on Writing – Writing Tests

## TEST 1

### Writing Task 1

Model answer: 163 words

It is estimated that UK yearly private car sales will increase over the period covered by the chart, rising in two stages to reach a high of almost three and a half million by the year 2014, from a starting point of 1.5 million in 2003. The sale of company cars, by contrast, will barely change over the period, climbing from just under 250,000 cars in 2003 to just under 500,000 in the year 2014. The only year where sales are expected to exceed the 500,000 mark is 2010.

As regards motorcycle sales in the UK, the predicted trend is steadily upwards with yearly sales rising from just over 150,000 in 2003 to approximately 400,000 units in 2014. Between 2003 and 2005 the increase in sales is expected to be fairly steep, followed by a moderate rise over the next five years. Then, after 2011 sales are set to accelerate at much the same pace the first two years of the period.

### Writing Task 2

Model answer: 319 words

The use of prisons as a means to combat crime has always been a matter of debate and is becoming more so as prison populations increase, and crimes become more violent.

Some people believe that prisons are merely a breeding ground for criminals, and are, therefore, not doing the job they are supposed to do. They point to the incidence of re-offending among former prison in-mates and the rise in the seriousness of crimes committed by re-offenders as evidence for their case. They maintain that young people enter prison for minor offences and come out equipped with the skills to commit more serious crimes. For this group the prison process is not working.

Others are of the opinion that prisons are not harsh enough. They argue that prisoners lead a life of luxury inside at the expense of the taxpayer, quoting estimates of the high cost of keeping people inside compared with staying in luxury hotels. Another argument put forward is that, for many criminals, prisons are a soft option, as they are often released after serving only a small portion of their sentence to ease the over-crowding in jails. Prisons are, therefore, not seen as a deterrent.

I am personally inclined to agree with the latter viewpoint. I feel that, to make penal institutions more effective, the regime needs to be much harsher than at present, with no sentence remission. It is unrealistic to think that this would be a panacea for all the ills of prisons. However, at the same time, this increased harshness should be coupled with an attack on the causes behind crime. Poverty is often quoted as a factor behind criminal activity as is a lack of education, but there are rich criminals as well as well-educated ones. By generally improving the standard of living and the quality of life for everyone, and at the same time making prisons very harsh regimes, such institutions will become effective.

## TEST 2

### Writing Task 1

Model answer: 198 words

The charts show the answers to two questions as part of a public survey on mobile phones. The first bar chart reveals that the disapproval rating for mobile phones is higher among females than males by quite a large margin, 70 per cent for the former as against 45 for males. Compared to the public as a whole, women object more to mobile phones. As far as the 'Yes' responses are concerned, men outstrip women by more than 50 per cent. The difference is smaller when it comes to the 'Don't know' replies, but with males again being higher in this category.

In answer to the second question in the survey, a large percentage of both men and women feel that mobile phones could damage the health of their children, roughly 45% and 55% respectively. As in answer to the first question, women's attitude to mobile phones is more negative than the general public in the All category. For both men and women, the 'No' replies make up just under 30% in answer to this question with men exceeding women. As for the 'Don't know' responses, for women it is approximately 20%, while for men the figure is higher, at about 27%.

### Writing Task 2

Model answer: 319 words

*Mercy killing is a highly contentious issue, giving rise to strong emotions on both sides of the debate.*

*Some people believe that ending the suffering of fellow human beings is an act of mercy and as such should be enshrined in law. Admittedly, there are instances where people are experiencing appalling suffering and the only way out seems to be to end that suffering. However, are we as human beings able to decide when the life of another person should be ended? Surely not! That would be presumptuous in the extreme. And who is to guarantee that people will not be murdered in the name of euthanasia so that someone can have access to their personal wealth.*

*Whilst I am prepared to admit that the arguments put forward by advocates of euthanasia are forceful, I personally feel that it is totally unacceptable to take another person's life. Doctors are bound by oath to preserve the life of their fellow human beings and as such should not be forced into a situation where they are legally bound to terminate a life.*

*And what about the possibility of a mistake being made and the wrong person being killed? The advocates of euthanasia will no doubt say that there will be safeguards to guarantee that this will not happen. But there is a whole catalogue of human error that flies in the face of this argument: babies have been switched, people given the wrong doses of medicine, wrong limbs removed. The list is endless. There is also the possibility that a cure could become available just as, or just after, a person has been killed.*

*Once we have embarked upon the slippery slope of euthanasia, who knows where it might lead. There are some things in life that are best left well alone and, in my opinion, this is one of them. Once we start who knows where it might lead to.*

# TEST 3

### Writing Task 1

Model Answer: 164 words

*As can be seen from the maps, the area of Laguna Beach witnessed considerable change over the 40-year period from 1950 to 1990.*

*In 1950, there were only a few beach huts at the back of the beach between the sand dunes and the woodland, but, by 1970, these had been replaced by villas. By 1990, the villas themselves, in turn, had given way to a hotel with an adjacent swimming-pool. The dunes, which occupied the area on the western side of the beach, remained until 1970. Then between 1970 and 1990, they were replaced with landscaped gardens.*

*To the east of the beach, the track which originally led to the beach huts became a main road. The woodland, which in 1950 covered the area south of the track, had been cleared by 1970 to make way for a caravan park. This, in turn, had been converted into a car park by 1990, and, in addition, a surfing school appeared on the beach itself.*

### Writing Task 2

Model answer: 345 words

*Stress and stress-related illnesses seem to be an unavoidable consequence of the life most of us now lead. There are, of course, many forces at play here.*

*The main contributing factor is the growing complexity of the modern world, which is compounded by the undoubted speed of change that pervades all aspects of our lives. Not very long ago people were guaranteed a job for life, but this is now no longer the case. In fact, people may be obliged to change career more than once in their life-times. The root cause here is the pace at which technology is developing. Furthermore, the use of computers now means that we have to work faster and are at the same time expected to be more accurate. The speed of development also means that we are constantly living in a state of change, having to update more and more frequently.*

*Another cause is population growth, which puts more pressure on our immediate environment. For example, the roads and public transport are becoming more crowded and there are ever longer queues for hospitals and other services. As resources become more scarce, they also become more expensive, which adds to the pressure. The easy availability of goods puts enormous pressure on everyone, but especially families with children. Of course, the media only serves to compound the problem with the constant barrage of advertising directed at the public.*

*Although there are many factors behind the stress in our lives, and they are continuing to grow, there are several courses of action open to everyone. The most important of these is education. Health services could, for example, embark upon a massive stress-awareness campaign to make individuals and families aware of some of the contributing factors. This would increase people's threshold of coping with and managing stress. Employers could also be involved by running relaxation classes and making work less stressful for their employees, and themselves.*

*The problem is there and is growing, but solutions are available and as in all previous situations, human beings have the capacity to adapt and survive.*

# Speaking
# Section
# KEY

---

## Exercise 1

Key for Cue Card A

    (a) 4       (b) 5       (c) 8       (d) 9       (e) 3

Key for Cue Card B

    (a) 4       (b) 6       (c) 9       (d) 15       (e) 18       (f) 23

Key for Cue Card C

    (1) J, S       (2) M, P       (3) C, L, O       (4) A, I, K       (5) Q

Key for Cue Card D

    (A) v, ix       (B) vi, viii       (C) vii       (D) iv, xi       (E) ii, x       (F) i, iiiI

---

## Exercise 2

Below are the original words. There may be others, for example D and E.

    (A)  Would you like       (B)  What is there       (C) What's the

    (D) I'd like       (E) I'd like       (G) tell me something

    (H) Is there any       (I) Do I have       (J) Can you suggest

---

## Exercise 3

    A. 6       B. 7       C. 10       D. 8       E. 3       F. 9

    G. 5       H. 2       I. 1       J. 4

You can see that the oral exam is unpredictable. As was mentioned in the Introduction to the Speaking Section, students often prepare for the exam by learning mini-speeches by heart. Then, when they are asked a question which they are not prepared for, they cannot handle the situation.

So to prepare for the Oral, it is better just to speak with friends or in class.

---

## Exercise 4

    A. v       B. v       C. i       D. v       E. i       F. i       G. ii

    H. i       I. iii       J. i       K. vi       L. iii       M. vii

---

---

**Exercise 5:** Put meaning into your future

---

1. All the alternatives are correct     2. (a) and (c)     3. (a) and (c)
4. (a), (b) and (c)               5. (a) and (c)     6. (b) and (d)
7. (a)                  8. (d)     9. (b), (c) and (d)     10. (a), (b) and (d)

## Appendix: Seeing the future

**Example 1.**

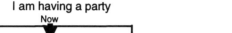

I am having a party

The tense is the Present Continuous. Why? Because (i) the writer/speaker has made an arrangement before **Now**; (ii) the arrangement is true at the time of writing/speaking; and (iii) the event will take place at a fixed time in the future (near or distant)

**Example 2**

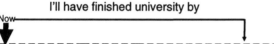

I'll have finished university by

The tense is the Future Perfect Simple. This is a combination of the Simple Future and the Present Perfect and therefore combines the two elements of these two tenses. You can use the tense to show that something will have happened before a particular point of time in the future.

**Example 3**

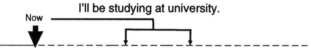

I'll be studying at university.

The tense is the Future Continuous. Like II above this is a combined tense. It combines the future and the idea of continuous action. You use it for an activity which will be in progress around a certain point of time in the future.

**Example 4**

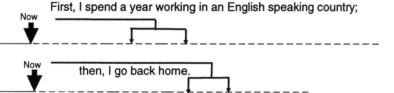

First, I spend a year working in an English speaking country;

then, I go back home.

This is the Present Simple. It is used when you want to show that the events in the future are fixed like part of a time-table.

**Example 5**

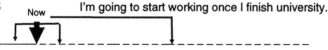

I'm going to start working once I finish university.

The going to Future. You use this future when you want to show that you intend to do something which is based on present information. For example, your nose may be ticklish and you feel you are going to sneeze. You might say: I'm going to sneeze. In the end, however, you may not sneeze. You could not say here: I'm sneezing.

**Example 6**

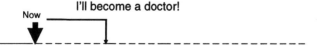

I'll become a doctor!

This is the Simple Future. You use this tense to show that you are making a simple prediction. When you use the Simple Future, you show that you are not planning your action. Your decision is spontaneous.

---

Another example is the following exchange:

    A: I've got a headache.
    B: Oh, I'll get you an aspirin.

B does not really have time to think when making the response. It is spontaneous.

There are of course other ways of expressing the Future in English, but these are the most common forms that you are likely to use as you are speaking in the final section of the oral exam.

Other forms you may want to look up:    It's likely that
    It's probable that
    I'll probably be
    I may
    I might
    I might just
    I may well
    There's a chance I will/ might
    If all goes well,